THE UNCROWNED KING OF CAMBODIA

The Life of Lt Col E D (Moke) Murray

DAVID CHANDLER & ANTHONY BARNETT

KERR

Melbourne, Victoria

First published 2024
Kerr Publishing Pty Ltd
Melbourne, Victoria
ABN 64 124 219 638

© 2024 David Chandler & Anthony Barnett

This book is copyright. Apart from fair dealing for the purpose of private study, research, criticism or review, or under the Copyright Agency Ltd rules of recording, no part may be reproduced by any means. The moral right of the author has been asserted.

ISBN 978-1-875703-59-3 (print on demand)
ISBN 978-1-875703-60-9 (eBook)

BIC Category: BG Biography general
BISAC Category 1: BIO00800 BIOGRAPHY & AUTOBIOGRAPHY / Military
BISAC Category 2: HIS048000 History/Asia/S E Asia
BISAC Category 3: HIS062000 History/Asia/South/India
BISAC Category 4: POLITICAL SCIENCE/World/ Asian

Cover photograph: Surrender ceremony, Phnom Penh, October 1945

Cover and book design: Paul Taylder of Xigrafix Media and Design
Typeset in Caslon Pro 12/16pt

Print-on-Demand services: Lightning Source

National Library of Australia PrePublication Data Service:

 A catalogue record for this book is available from the National Library of Australia

*For Colin Murray, the late Bernice Murray,
and their descendants*

Contents

	Considering Moke: An Introduction, Anthony Barnett	1
ONE	Family Background	19
TWO	Moke's Boyhood and Early Military Career	35
THREE	Moke's First Marriage	57
FOUR	On the Fringes of Empire, 1937–1942	73
FIVE	Moke's War	89
SIX	Southern Vietnam and Cambodia in World War II	115
SEVEN	Gracey in Saigon	139
EIGHT	Moke in Saigon	159
NINE	Becoming Cambodia's Uncrowned King	175
TEN	Cambodia: Closing Phases	191
ELEVEN	Back with the Gurkhas	211
TWELVE	Queen Elizabeth's Coronation, Anthony Barnett	227
THIRTEEN	Flotsam of Empire, 1954–2002	253
APPENDIX	Murray's Promotion	269
	Bibliography	273
	Acknowledgments	287

Considering Moke: An Introduction, Anthony Barnett

EDWARD MURRAY NEARLY DISAPPEARED WITHOUT TRACE. HAD it not been for David Chandler taking an interest in an unpublished interview I did with him, mentions of him in official records would not have been put together. Separately, each would suggest that he was otherwise insignificant. Something that anyone witnessing his funeral cortège would also have concluded, as it consisted of just three people, the couple with whom he boarded and a representative of the Gurkhas whom they had contacted.

Yet he was far from being a nonentity. As David's account sets out, Moke (as he was always called) was an outstanding officer in the Indian Army and became a Gurkha commander in Malaya. In 1939 he fired the crucial shot that dispersed a strike that threatened the Raj. He became an outstanding fighter against the Japanese in Assam and Burma. He suppressed the Viet Minh in Saigon in 1945, in what can be seen as the start of the Vietnam War. He was Allied Land Commander in Cambodia and supervised the surrender of the Japanese there. In 1953, he was cheered by millions along the eight-kilometre route of

Elizabeth II's coronation parade as he marched at the head of the hugely popular Gurkha contingent. But when he died not a single obituary of him appeared, apart from a short notice in the Gurkha gazette.

How we remember the immediate past, and—just as important—how we forget it, is never just neutral or accidental. We inherit the world that our proximate ancestors created and, initially at least, we have to live through the way they framed, perceived and supressed their failures and accomplishments.

Why people are remembered is in large part because of what they did. Why people are forgotten despite what they did, can only be explained by addressing the context. It is not due to them that they are ignored, it is due to something else. We therefore have to situate Moke in the larger history of his country if we are to understand how his striking career could be completely vaporised from the collective memory, despite the thick nostalgia and historical sentimentality that clogs many British minds.

The first half of Moke's life, his military career up to 1950 and its exceptional achievements, is vividly recovered in David's careful account. It is harder to discover the details of what happened in the equally long period of Moke's subsequent irrelevance, which was apparently accompanied by inordinate quantities of alcohol. Nonetheless, David shows us the overall realities and together this study of Moke's life is a revealing account of Britain's imperial officer class and its fate.

In this introduction I'd like to do four things:
1. Explain how I came to interview him in 1981 when he was, so to speak, at the apex of his obscurity.
2. Say how I contributed to "the forgetting", which I now feel is an important part of Moke's significance for us.
3. Describe the peculiar, shapeshifting character of the British nationalism that led to Moke being ignored.

4. Allow Moke's own voice to emerge from the interview, so that readers can experience what he was like.

A popular image of British imperialism is of an old-fashioned, stuffy, racist system headed by Queen Victoria. In fact, the Empire's greatest extent in terms of territory and subject peoples ruled from London was between 1918 and 1939. Along with its ranks and traditions, which were indeed nineteenth-century, it was a modern machine of domination. It had pioneered the development of concentration camps in the Boer War and tanks at the Somme and Cambrai. Now it competed in the development of airpower. So, when Moke joined the imperial army in 1932 and set out for India, he was recruited into an industrial network of military authority that ensured British domination over a quarter of the world's population and one-fifth of its landmass and influenced even more. Far from being archaic, it sought efficiency and enjoyed its privileges in a contemporary fashion. Moke's enthusiastic embrace of photography is an expression of this—David and I developed rolls of film that he took while serving in the Indian Raj and were later found in his belongings. A selection of them is included here. They show us glimpses of the experience and expertise of being in the Indian Army as seen through Moke's eyes in the 1930s, as Fascism grew in Europe: the armoured vehicles, the trained "native" soldiers, the latest portable gramophone on an informal picnic, social gatherings with white women wearing the latest fashions.

Just as we have printed the negatives he left behind, we have tried to bring into the public realm the energy, the role and the fading away of Moke. I say "we", but David Chandler researched and wrote this book. The demanding effort of authorship is his alone. My main contribution was to provide the starting point: the transcript of the 1981 interview.

I found meeting and interviewing Moke fascinating but also

traumatic. It made me a terrible collaborator, at once very enthusiastic and supporting of David's efforts and recalcitrant in failing to deliver my agreed contributions. The source of my distress was the need to understand Moke—and all proper understanding demands empathy—but also to repudiate him and what he did. I still recall the agony I felt when he related how relieved he was at witnessing a massacre of Vietnamese insurgents. For it was my support for their cause that had led to our meeting.

Six years before, in April 1975, I had celebrated the victory of the Vietnamese revolution, when they completed their independence and expelled the US-backed regime from Saigon. I decided to study why and how they were able to win, when every other progressive cause was a shambles. Initially I aimed to focus on Vietnam alone, and not the whole of what had been colonial French Indochina, which included Laos and Cambodia. It did not take me long to understand that the key to the success of Ho Chi Minh's communists was the way they came genuinely to represent Vietnamese nationalism after their 1945 August Revolution.

A consequence of the Vietnamese victory, however, was the Communist takeover of Cambodia led by Pol Pot, who was supported by China. His Khmer Rouge immediately emptied the country's capital Phnom Penh of its inhabitants. In 1977, fighting broke out along the border between Cambodia and Vietnam. I felt I had to understand what had gone wrong.

In March 1980 I made my first trip to Vietnam, a year after China had launched a brief and disastrous invasion to punish Vietnam for liberating Cambodia. I then went into Cambodia itself, where I was among the first Western journalists to witness what had happened, and wrote about it in the *New Statesman*. Later that year I began a short stint as a fellow at Cornell's Southeast Asia program. There I checked out a report, published in the name of Lord Mountbatten, who was Supreme Allied

Commander for South-East Asia in World War II, on the Allied victory in that theatre. One of the concluding paragraphs states that Lieutenant Colonel E.D. Murray was sent to oversee the Japanese surrender in Cambodia in 1945. I knew about the British Army taking control of Saigon, in the south of Vietnam, before handing it over to French colonialists. I had never seen any reference to a British role in Cambodia.

So, I wrote to the British Ministry of Defence to ask if E.D. Murray was still alive. A reply in January 1981 informed me that they had identified him and would forward a letter to him. Moke replied, thanking me. I sent him a list of questions about Cambodia. In August I joined a small, three-day conference in Thailand on what had happened under Pol Pot, where I met Professor David Chandler. It was perhaps the first gathering of scholars who had spent the preceding years studying the ghastly trajectory of the Pol Pot regime, the horrors of which exacerbated the obsessive quality no specialist can be without. Perhaps because we shared the advantage of previous lives that gave us a certain distance, David and I got on. At any rate, he decided that I was honest and the seed of our much later collaboration was sown.

I then made a second trip into Cambodia. After my return to England, I arranged to visit Moke. He lived in Worthing, a seaside town on England's south coast, and he arranged for us to meet in the bar of the Beach Hotel (which is now demolished). We then went round the corner to his two-room apartment, which was well furnished and where he clearly lived alone, to record the interview over a couple of hours. It came to fifty pages of well-spaced transcript.

We corresponded and he sent me various photocopies. His first reply to my thankyou for the interview was typed and signed with a great flourish. He wrote, "Your letter-heading does not ascribe you as a professor; but I so address you, especially after the moment of meeting you, even without a straggling beard and pince-nez. Immediately, on your entrance to the Beach Hotel, I felt a rapport—I felt, with relief, 'Here is someone who will laugh.' I will always remember a P.R.O. [public relations officer] in Malaya who said 'You look more like a bishop every day, Sir.' Collapse of portly colonel."

I quote this as it shows quite a lot about Moke. He trained himself to make fast, advanced judgements on people's character. He covered himself in a camouflage of jokes and humour that was the opposite of being pompous and taking oneself too seriously. But underneath, the portly colonel had not collapsed at all.

He was tall and bespectacled. For all his bonhomie he remained aware of possible political implications of what he said during the interview. His last words before I turned off the recorder were, "I'm getting rather good at avoiding your questions, aren't I?"

My main purpose was to get an account of what happened in Cambodia. In October 1945 Moke became Allied Land Force Commander there for three months, to ensure order and oversee the surrender of more than a thousand Japanese, who were to be sent back to Japan. The country was peaceful, nominally headed by the 23-year-old King Sihanouk. Moke described his role as "political"; to ensure nothing happened. The dramatic highpoint, which David describes, was when he arranged for the French General Leclerc to arrest Cambodia's pro-independence prime minister, Sơn Ngọc Thành. Moke felt it was done shamefully but that it had to be done.

His role during the shorter time he spent in Vietnam was military and he saw pitched battles. As David recounts, Moke was summoned from Burma to Saigon in mid-September 1945 by Britain's General Douglas Gracey, who had been appointed to organise the surrender of the Japanese from the whole of southern Indochina and to hand over control to the French. This is how Moke told me he got his orders from Gracey on the morning he arrived. "'Now Moke you're taking over Saigon … Clear the area. I want the whole of Saigon cleared.' I said, 'What of?' Or words to that effect. And he said, 'You'll find out.' Which I did. Being a good soldier."

To his surprise, Moke, who had just come from fighting the Japanese, was given command of two Japanese battalions. Ensuring order meant using them to prevent the Annamites—the French colonial term for the Vietnamese—from being "a bloody nuisance", as they sought to prevent the full-scale return of the French. Moke described the French as "useless". He justified his and Gracey's role as being to disarm and evacuate the Japanese back to Japan. But unlike Cambodia, Vietnam was alive with insurrection.

"If you are on the ground", he told me, you just get on with it. I hit it straight away … I was sitting in my headquarters when Sato, the Japanese [commander], came in … he said, "I have information that a thousand Annamites are going to cross the bridge at 4.00 o'clock in the morning and attack Saigon", or words to that effect. I said, "What are you going to do about it?" There was more breathing. I said, "Look, I've been fighting you for the last so many years, I know how good you are. I'll leave it to you." That was all I could do. In the morning I went down to the bridge and there wasn't a sign of anybody, nobody. From the bridge I could see a lot of Annamite chaps massing. I thought, my God we really have had it. They all started to cross the bridge and halfway across, every window and doorway on this side opened up with Japanese. They caught them right on the bridge in an ambush. They were killed. That incidentally saved Saigon I reckon from a bloody massacre."

At this point my inner voice said to me, Oh my God, he

started the Vietnam War! As Moke expressed his satisfaction I was thinking, these were my people. I was there in spirit on the other side of that bridge, waving an out-of-date French musket, shouting against a new colonial takeover.

After some questions about where the bridge was, which I asked mainly to recover, I said rather lamely, "It sounds remarkable, I've never seen an account of it." To which Moke replied, "No, of course, I hadn't got the time to report it. Everybody thinks that everything is written down as you go along!" He continued, "It was just after that there was a hell of a battle at the bridge beside the zoo … that was when I asked for air [support; he didn't get it]. They really were being troublesome. Also about a thousand, well-armed and determined. I used a battalion of Punjabi who were bloody good and the French marines with their machine guns, they were very good indeed. I can see them now. And it was very unpleasant."

A few days later, he was ordered to take command in Cambodia. He was accompanied to Phnom Penh by 40 Gurkhas and a turbaned Pakistani intelligence officer. This brought us to the main purpose of the interview.

Much of it consisted of Moke telling me how he enjoyed himself, his status, and some royal occasions. He requisitioned a DeSoto and described, with a great laugh, that he had the Japanese make a small Union Jack, which he flew from the car. It was now pinned on his wall in Worthing, losing its colour. In December 1945 he was driven to Angkor Wat, and the king sent the Royal Dance Troupe to perform, "For my own special edification. At night, with flaming torches. Wonderful." He was given L'Ordre Royal du Cambodge. "He was a little tiny chap, the king, and I'm six foot one. When he presented my medal he tried to kiss me! I stood strictly to attention, he kept on jumping."

Along with some documents and letters the interview

provided a new primary account, brilliant if not wholly reliable, of the founding moment of the contemporary history of Cambodia and Vietnam. I circulated the typescript to Cambodian specialists and began to explore how to publish it. Then the Falklands War led me to write a book about my own country and I turned away from Southeast Asia. Years later, David asked if he could publish the interview with an introduction by himself. I was happy to agree, relieved that the foremost historian of Cambodia could see that there was a story to be told.

David's energy and thoroughness went much further. He researched Moke's record in Burma, which had led Gracey to select Moke as capable of "getting on with the job", then his early life and the study expanded into a biography—and therefore a story about the British class system after World War I.

An Anglophile American living in Australia, David delights in and mocks my country's class differences and is dispassionate about the historic atrocities of the British state. He investigated Moke as a historical anthropologist. But I am a native. I abhor the legacy of imperial power, the class system makes me grate my teeth and, because the nature of being British is unresolved, working with David triggered an even deeper ambivalence in me than Moke's role in Vietnam. It provoked an explosive combination of fascination and repulsion as it ignited a challenge to my identity. On the one hand I reject everything Moke stands for; on the other, I cannot deny that Moke defines my country more than I do, and the bravery of him and his fellow officers has been crucial for its survival.

Their legacy has left us English trapped in a Britishness that is out of kilter with the wider world and prevents us from expressing ourselves as 'The English'. How this happened explains in large part why Moke and those like him have disappeared from the establishment record. He lived through the time when

Anglo-British imperial ambitions were transformed by World War II. It defined Moke personally and shaped my childhood. We belong together yet we are also on different sides of that watershed. My side, of the late twentieth century, sought to forget about him. Two broad processes of collective repression "othered" the Empire. One always accompanied it, the other is "postwar". The first Moke shared, the second made him its victim.

The first process is the arms-length experience of empire—with the important exception of Ireland. When Britain—and it was Britain not England—began self-consciously to rule overseas territories, Edward Gibbon, who sat on the backbenches of parliament but never spoke in its debates, wrote *The Decline and Fall of the Roman Empire*. The first of its six volumes, published in 1776, was a bestseller. With immense hard work and a staggering command of scholarly detail, it established a learned fatalism. Its message was that barbarian energy would inevitably overthrow imperial achievement weakened by Christian idolatry. If Rome itself declined and fell, then Britain's own growing empire could hardly avoid a similar fate. For nearly two centuries after Gibbon, imperial wealth and privilege were pursued to the hilt. But within the British spirit of conquest, genocide and triumph resided the seed of "decline and fall". Even as it became geographically the greatest empire the world would ever know, a worm of wisdom was shared by most of the British Empire's practical soldiers and administrators—the knowledge that it could not last.

It was a perspective Moke shared, if reluctantly. Comparing his role in India as a "good coloniser" to the French who were determined to return to rule Indochina, he told me, "I think that we British knew that independence was coming for a long, long time and we prepared for it, that's why it came smoothly. We admitted that it was going to be. Not everybody, not the cranks, but even I thought it was going to happen. I thought it was a pity, but I knew it was coming. Everybody knew it. Some were very much against it, like the blimps, and some were very sad about it, I was very sad."

This mentality—it is more than just an attitude—required a separation between "being British" and the British Empire, which was always "overseas". In 1939, it was the British Empire that declared war on Nazi Germany. Its huge resources ensured an initial British confidence in victory over the upstart dictator. That self-assurance collapsed in May 1940 with the sudden, shocking surrender of France, when, overnight, Germany became the supreme continental power. The defining attitude switched from confidence to belligerent defensiveness, personified by Churchill but widely shared. It was captured in what became a famous David Low cartoon of a solitary soldier facing Europe across stormy seas and the words "Very well, alone". With its empire of 800 million, Britain was never alone. But now the separation from it allowed the sense of "who we are" as a people to shift, under the immense pressures of war, into a lasting mental distance between the home country and the Empire.

It was violent too. In December 1941, the Imperial Japanese military demonstrated their mastery of air power by sinking HMS *Prince of Wales* and HMS *Repulse*. The confrontation destroyed the British Empire's naval might in the Pacific. It terminated the United Kingdom's global reach. Then, in February 1942, Japanese forces overran Singapore, taking 80,000 prisoners in the course of a week.

But it was also two months after the Japanese assault on the American naval base at Pearl Harbor, which ensured US entry into the war on the British side and thus overall Allied superiority. This initiated the second process that 'othered' the Empire. In addition to being at arm's length, the Empire in its colonial form, with all its powerful symbols, was to become old-fashioned and otiose compared to America's power. This happened without, and this is crucial, the convulsive psychic reckoning that was necessary for England really to change. Instead, the global influence bestowed by the US alliance preserved the psyche of being Great British.

The British Isles were not invaded and the British state survived the war. The completeness of the domestic mobilisation it oversaw and the pride in its survival ensured the emergence of a genuinely modernising, domestic 'British nation'. But, thanks to its alliance with the triumphant United States, the London political class also remained attached to the exercise of global influence and prided itself on being one of the 'Big Three' nuclear powers at the time, along with the Soviet Union and the United States.

In 1951 when, on a smaller popular vote than Labour, the Conservative Party took over and made Winston Churchill prime minister again (we can be sure with Moke's support), Churchill said, "We have to … stand erect once more and take our place among the great powers of the world." Three years later, Sir Oliver Franks returning from being ambassador to Washington, told the nation in a BBC Reith lecture that the reason for the all-party consensus on the need for its NATO alliance with the United States and the Commonwealth "can be stated very simply. Britain is going to continue to be what she has been, a Great Power." Otherwise, "What is the small island with its 50,000,000 inhabitants if it has to go it alone?"

But the path to acceptability in the United States, and legitimacy in the rhetoric of the United Nations, demanded the abandonment of colonialism and its trappings. Now, when independence movements were crushed, as they continued to be up to the 1960s, it was not in the name of the Empire but of anti-communism.

Moke was a casualty of this transition, which went much

deeper than a mere shift in grand strategy, as it demanded a complete cultural reorientation. A neat illustration of this is captured in the 1946 Michael Powell and Emeric Pressburger film *A Matter of Life and Death* (released in the United States as *Stairway to Heaven*). Its hero is an English airman who is killed when he falls from his plane but is 'missed' by the heavenly forces and finds himself still alive on earth. He and a young American woman fall in love and this inspires him to defy the agent of the afterlife who comes to collect him. A trial before all of Heaven, with its audience drawn from every age in history, is then conducted into whether their love is genuine and if he deserves to live or die. The prosecution is led by an anti-British figure from the US War of Independence, the defence by a friend of the hero. The initial jury consists of a French soldier, a Boer, a Russian from the Crimean war, a Chinese who was in 'Peking' when the British destroyed it, an Indian from the Punjab, and an Irishman. "Choose a jury from anywhere, they will always be prejudiced against your country," the prosecutor taunts. But he is upstaged when the defence demands a new jury of his own countrymen "selected from every walk of American life". Along with speeches about freedom and justice the lovers are rewarded with a long life on earth. England would no longer be held accountable for the crimes of its Empire in the eyes of the world. Instead, it was to be celebrated for its embrace of the American way of life.

This was the postwar world in which I grew up. There was an emancipating enjoyment of consumerism, central heating, American music, and putting the starch of Empire behind us. Everything was changing. Except the political system. Headed by Elizabeth II, this wrapped itself in the American alliance in order to preserve its greatness while colonialism became old-fashioned. When there was an attempt to revive it, in 1956, when the British invaded Egypt with the French in an attempt to regain control of the Suez Canal, Washington promptly brought the kingdom to order and forced it to withdraw.

It meant that for us Anglo-British, the history Moke personified, of granular colonial domination, had to be furled along with the regiments he served. Yet his role could not be attacked, after all it had made us what we were. But nor could it be celebrated, for we were not like that anymore. So it was best forgotten.

One episode from 1945, which occupied part of our interview, exposed these tensions. The 28-year-old Peter Dewey was parachuted into Vietnam as the head of an OSS team, in early September. The OSS was the US Office of Strategic Services, the forerunner of the CIA. He was the son of a Congressman and distant relative of Governor of New York Thomas E. Dewey, who had also been the Republican presidential candidate erroneously proclaimed as having beaten Harry S. Truman in the election of 1948 by the *Chicago Sun-Times*. Peter Dewey had been educated in Switzerland, spoke fluent French, and had already been active behind enemy lines in France. Now he witnessed the French, who had been armed by General Gracey, attack the Vietnamese. He cabled Washington, "Cochinchina is burning. The French and British are finished here and we ought to clear out of Southeast Asia."

When I read this to Moke he replied, with a laugh, "I didn't know they were there." Somewhat of an irony given that the United States had been 'there' for quite some time alongside their British and French imperial counterparts through their colonial possessions—both formal and informal—in the Pacific, namely Hawaii, Guam, and the Philippines.

Gracey declared Dewey persona non grata and on 26 September, as he was scheduled to fly out, Dewey was shot, by a Vietnamese insurgent who thought he was French. His body was never recovered. That at any rate is the apparently

Considering Moke: An Introduction, Anthony Barnett

well-documented account. One that Moke flatly contradicted in our interview.

The young Dewey later took on a martyr's significance among Americans who opposed the war and studied its origins. He was the first US citizen to be killed in Vietnam. Had his advice been followed there would have been no subsequent war. Moke spoke about Dewey with contempt and told me he went to his death because, he, Dewey, refused to take Moke's advice. Towards the end of our discussion of this I quoted from a cable from a British official to the Foreign Office in London saying, "At present American imperialism is in the forefront in the conduct of affairs in the Far East and it is trying to elbow us out." Then I asked Moke, "Did you feel involved as one part of an imperial power in competition with the Americans?" He replied, "I'd have fought the Americans if they got in my bloody way." It was an answer that was out of the question in 1945 and beyond the pale in 1981. Moke never made the transition projected by *A Matter of Life or Death*.

Instead, in terms of British politics, he seems closest to Enoch Powell, a Tory politician who had served in India. Powell confronted the reality of the end of empire but repudiated the dominant complacencies of the American alliance. Instead, he called for a new rallying identity of a white English nationalism. He denied the notion that he was a bigoted racist. On the contrary, he continued to laud Indian civilisation and accomplishments, for Indians *over there*. But in a famous speech in 1968 he declared that if the "black man" were given the "whip hand" *over here*, he foresaw violence.

This poses the question of whether Moke himself was racist. He was emotionally attached to the Gurkhas and enraged by anyone who patronised or belittled them. He was especially proud of the way he organised the surrender of 800 Japanese in

Cambodia. He said, "They surrendered to a Gurkha officer. I was determined that should happen. They all handed their swords to a Gurkha."

"Why were you determined on that?" I asked.

"Because the Gurkhas had beat them. I sat at a table, which the Union Jack was on as we hadn't a flag pole. I sat behind it. They came and stooped and bowed to me and handed their swords to my Gurkha officer, that's who the Japanese surrendered to, in Cambodia. The French were looking on."

In the prevailing culture of the day, it is fair to say that Moke was egalitarian when it came to skin colour. At the same time, the nature and culture of empire were intrinsically racist and he had a built-in nostalgia for it and therefore also for its belittling contempt for competing imperialisms, especially French and American and Japanese. He despised the French.

I loathed these familiar prejudices. I found his self-depreciation, "My life's been bloody funny", a well-practised ploy and his anti-Europeanism part of a widely shared parochialism that stunted England's potential to be successful as a normal country.

So there was Moke, the personification of this stubborn culture, sitting opposite me. Brave, good humoured, unpretentious, proud that he was competent, recounting how he'd been dubbed "The Uncrowned King of Cambodia" when few if any in Worthing would have the slightest idea what this meant, and revealing his responsibility for a ghastly episode in the bloody birth of Vietnam's struggle. His jolly, matter-of-fact manner was everything I opposed about my country: its ruthless militarism cloaked in fair play, its colonialism excused by a genuine admiration of the natives, its obsession with its exceptionalism that refused to embrace its European realities, its use of mockery in place of ideology.

I hadn't the stomach to go back and see him. But I also felt bad about this because, while Moke retained his dignity and pride and was comfortable, he was a victim of a particular kind. He was living on his own, with no network, family or institutional support that I was aware of. He had no recognition. He had played a historic role of a special kind yet none gave him the time of day or thought of recording his life. He had been discarded, to become a piece of flotsam of an empire that had disappeared beneath the waves.

Did I want to rehabilitate him? No. I had no desire whatsoever to celebrate him or his role. On the other hand, I despised the injustice of the indifference with which he was treated, and felt this ought to be rectified. That's why when David asked me to help him on a book about Moke I was delighted—until my contradictory impulses returned.

David's research confirmed what I'd instinctively feared. From an Edwardian family, brought up by servants and doubtless unhugged, Moke went straight from school into the army. It didn't prepare him for civilian life after twenty-five years of military service. Instead, it produced a man who when it was his duty to do the dirty work or to risk his life, did his duty and showed no remorse.

A sad aspect of the Moke story that David's research, and my use of Facebook, revealed is that his son Colin, whose education Moke paid for, was alive and living with his now late wife Bernice. We went to see them. Bernice had ensured a determined effort at personal recovery and they lived in a homely, modern estate quite close to where Moke himself had spent his childhood, as well as his final years. Talking with them we learnt that Colin had joined the army at seventeen. He had refused a commission. Instead, he'd joined the Tank Regiment and took part in the abortive Suez campaign in 1956, a year before he returned to civilian life. His father was still in the army, approaching retirement. They never met.

I sought a way to unlock my reluctance to write about Moke and approached what I thought might be an ideal agent to see if he would get the book published. The idea of a biography of a man who was not famous struck him as quite uncommercial. I copied his curt rejection to David, who replied that he didn't mind at all, he just wanted it to be completed for Colin, the memory of Bernice, and their two children, Alyson and Stuart.

David's message ended my ambivalence. I have witnessed how the personal and family consequences of war are lasting but can be overcome. Recuperation, and the creation of a happier normality, are hard work but possible, indeed essential. To make sense of Moke for his grandchildren, and perhaps for some of the many like them whose recent ancestors are lost in the turmoil, humiliations and holocausts of the twentieth century, is a work of the present not the past. David tells Moke's story without condemnation or apology so that we can live better, different lives than his. The purpose is neither to rehabilitate or condemn, but to celebrate our own recovery, as truthfully as possible, which means without denial, cover-up or evasion of the good and bad side of our predecessors and what they did.

ONE

Family Background

EDWARD DYMOKE MURRAY, DSO, OBE (1910–2002) WAS BORN in Beare Green, Surrey, into a prosperous, well-connected English family. His middle name was later shortened to Moke by his Gurkha Regiment and in adult life he was always known by that name. His parents and grandparents were comfortably upper middle class, above what George Orwell memorably called England's lower upper middle class. Orwell was referring to a cohort of non-aristocratic people, including his own parents, whose male members were trained initially in the famous fee-paying preparatory and public schools. Later, after a university education or without one, these men, like Orwell's father, filled the ranks of the professions, the Anglican clergy, the officer corps of the army and navy, and the imperial civil service. This segment of British society is important in what follows because when "Moke" Murray joined the Indian Army as a subaltern or second lieutenant in February 1932, he became a member of it.

From one angle, Moke's eventful life can be seen as a fairly smooth progression from an easy-going, affluent upper middle-class childhood and adolescence through a prestigious, hierarchical but less class-conscious military career. As a soldier,

Moke fought what were then called the King's Enemies in Waziristan, Assam, Burma, and Malaya. He retired from the army as a colonel in 1957, soon after he had married a wealthy woman. The marriage, the second for Moke and the third for his much younger wife, was soon plagued by alcoholism on both sides and broke down eleven years later. From then on Moke—who was inept at handling money and unready for civilian life—drifted downwards into what Orwell, that masterful but inconsistent labeller, has called the impoverished officer class.[1] By then he was also, in John Darwin's evocative phrase, an orphan of empire. His downward social mobility, coinciding with the collapse of the British Empire, must have been painful for him, and we know that in his final years he was very unhappy.[2]

In June 1953, long before his life went dark, "Moke" Murray, then a decorated, 43-year-old lieutenant colonel, took a 100-man contingent of Gurkhas from Malaya to London to parade at Queen Elizabeth II's coronation. Many in the contingent, like Moke, had been decorated for bravery in World War II and Malaya. After the ceremony, he and the rest of the contingent received coronation medals from the young Queen. The coronation and Moke's participation in it are discussed in detail in Chapter 10 below.

---

1 George Orwell, *Coming up for Air* (London: Victor Gollancz, 1939), chapter 14 describes the cluttered cottage of the narrator's father-in-law, a retired colonel in the Indian Army: "For generations past her family had been soldiers, sailors, clergymen, Anglo-Indian officials, that kind of thing. They never had any money, but on the other hand none of them had ever done anything that I should recognize as work." For a room-by-room description of this kind of house, in the militarised zone of Surrey just before the Great War, see Anthony Powell, *The Kindly Ones* (London: Heinemann, 1962), 61–62.

2 See John Darwin, "Orphans of Empire", in *Settlers and Expatriates: Britons over the Seas*, ed. Robert A. Bickers, *The Oxford History of the British Empire* Companion Series (Oxford: Oxford University Press, 2010), 329–46. I'm grateful to Jim Hammerton for this reference. Given the grim lonesomeness of Murray's final years the phrase "flotsam of Empire" seems appropriate.

It's tempting to treat this occasion as the high point of Moke's career, but in his hard-pressed, old age he rarely mentioned it, preferring to dwell on the times that he had spent in combat in Burma, as his neighbour Liam Fox recalls.[3]

Moke's background and upbringing reflected the choices that his parents made for him as their only son, and his own decision, when he entered St Paul's School as a day student in 1924, and opted for a military-oriented curriculum.

Coming from a family that included three strong-minded women—his mother and two sisters—Moke spent the rest of his life in a series of all-male, often misogynistic institutions: preparatory school, public school, and the Indian Army. His two failed marriages and his prolonged estrangement from his daughter Louise (1962–2014) suggest that his relations with women could be maladroit. His neighbour Monica Millest, who cared for Moke in his closing years and was fond of him, told me that, in general, Moke found women "stupid". He made an exception, as we shall see, for Ursula Betts, who had been a colleague of his in Burma in World War II.[4]

To a large extent, Moke was a prisoner of his upbringing, his education, and his imperially-oriented military career. In retirement especially, he did not question or regret the way his career had developed, but the men and women who knew him never accused him of assuming that his background, or class, made him superior to other people. At the same time, the automatic respect

---

[3] See E.D. Murray (ed.), *Brigade of Gurkhas at the Coronation of Her Majesty Queen Elizabeth II* (London: Gale & Polden, 1954). Murray prepared this pleasantly written, well-illustrated volume in 1954 when he was posted to London.

[4] Author's interview with Monica Millest and Liam Fox, Worthing, 10 September 2018. Both authors separately had interviewed the couple in the previous month. They were Moke's neighbours and landlords for the last eight years of his life. Liam told Barnett that Murray was "happy enough in his own company" and that his "real fixation" was with his time in Burma.

that he gained after twenty-nine years of active service and retirement with the rank of colonel evaporated when he re-entered the unwelcoming landscape of civilian life. His neighbours Liam and Monica agreed that in his closing years Moke still felt entitled to greater appreciation.

Moke's parents and grandparents were well-connected members of the English upper middle class, located below the people with titles and the members of the so-called landed gentry whose inherited wealth derived principally from owning substantial rural acreage. His antecedents were kept out of the aristocracy or upper class, probably because they were insufficiently entitled at birth in terms of their ancestry and land ownership. In addition, both of Moke's grandfathers and several of their forebears worked in offices for a living, and members of the British aristocracy by and large did not.[5]

When Moke joined the Indian Army, he didn't enhance the social position he had inherited, though he became a de jure gentleman via his commission.[6] At the same time, however, the privileged status and upper middle-class point of view that he inherited from his parents and imbibed at his relatively unpretentious public school gave him an ongoing self-confidence and *savoir vivre* that were helpful in negotiating his military career. They also helped Moke to overcome the diplomatic obstacles that he encountered as Supreme Commander of Allied Forces in Cambodia in October and November 1945, when, as he remarked jocularly to Anthony Barnett in 1981, he was, very briefly, "Cambodia's uncrowned King". Finally, he could call

---

5   Had his grandfather Charles been awarded a baronetcy or a higher ranking title he would have moved upwards in the class "system". For a persuasive overview of issues like this, see David Cannadine, *Class in Britain* (New Haven: Yale University Press, 1998).
6   See Lionel Caplan, *Warrior Gentlemen: "Gurkhas" in the Western Imagination* (Providence: Berghahn Books, 1995), 57 ff.

on these ingrained resources, with varying success, to see him through the crises (some of them self-inflicted) that he encountered in civilian life after his retirement.

On the paternal side, several of Moke's antecedents had successful careers in the legal profession. His grandfather Charles Frederick Murray (1833–1904) and his great-grandfather, William Murray (1796–1870) had been both prosperous, London-based solicitors.

Charles Frederick, like his wife Catherine Georgiana, *nee* Tanqueray-Willaume (c. 1840–1932) and all but two of their children, was born in London. Charles' father William Murray,[7] born in Portsea, Hampshire, was the brother of a London barrister. Intriguingly, William's grandmother Susanna Branton signed the marriage register in 1788 with a mark, indicating that she was illiterate.[8] William Murray practised as a solicitor from 1830 to his death, and in 1856 he founded a law firm in the City of London. His son Charles, Moke's grandfather, educated briefly at Eton, joined him in 1858 and remained active in the firm until he died in 1904. William was elected to Parliament as a member of the Conservative Party in 1859 and served as an MP representing a Staffordshire constituency for the next six years. The family law-firm specialised in company law and survived under several names until 1953, long after any members of the Murray family worked in it.

Catherine Georgiana Murray, Moke's paternal grandmother,

---

7   William's wife Ann Maria Guppy, whom he married in 1824, died in 1839 "after years of affliction and suffering" according to *The Times*. The couple's Hampshire origins suggest that the Murrays' Scottish connection, if it existed, was already by the late 1700s fairly remote.

8   Letter to Moke from Valerie Murray, his ex-wife, 15 October 1986, written in Seville, Spain, where Valerie had moved with their daughter Louise in 1968. The letter is among Murray's papers in the Gurkha Museum, Winchester. No other correspondence between Moke and Valerie seems to have survived. It is unclear how Valerie gained access to this genealogical information.

was descended from the socially prominent Willaume and Tanqueray families who had emigrated from France in the 1680s as Huguenot refugees. Her father and her brother were successful solicitors in London. Some of the Willaumes were renowned in the early eighteenth century as gold – and silversmiths[9] while a century later a branch of the Tanqueray family led by Georgiana's uncle, Charles, made a fortune distilling and marketing the eponymous gin.[10] Branches of both families had established residences in Bedfordshire in the 1730s, soon after they stopped their metalworking in London. Over the years, the Tanquerays and Willaumes intermarried at least once. The family names were consolidated in 1848 when Catherine Georgiana's father, Thomas Butts Tanqueray (1807–1871) "took the surname of Willaume in addition to Tanqueray" from a childless cousin and was granted a composite coat of arms.[11]

Charles Murray and his wife, in other words, were charter members of the English upper middle class. Charles married "up" to a certain extent by joining a landed gentry family that used "Dymoke" as a middle name and had an officially approved coat of arms. The practice connected them at a considerable distance to a prominent Tudor figure, Sir Edward Dymoke (1508–1567), one of whose descendants had married a Willaume in Bedfordshire in the early nineteenth century. Since the 1860s, "Dymoke" has been used five times as a middle name by males in the Murray family.

Charles and Catherine Georgiana were married in the

---

[9] A David Willaume silver tankard valued at £4000 featured on the *Antiques Road Show* in August 2016. The Tanqueray and Willaume families had connected in London as early as 1708 when David Willaume engaged David Tanqueray as an apprentice goldsmith.

[10] See Olivia Williams, *Gin Glorious Gin: How Mother's Ruin Became the Spirit of London* (London: Headline Publishing, 2014). Tanqueray gin was first distilled in London in 1830.

[11] See J. Bernard Burke, *The Heraldic Register 1849–1850: With an Annotated Obituary* (London: Churton, 1850), 7.

Paddington district of London in 1862, when Charles' father was an MP. Charles was already working in his father's firm. The Murrays lived in Paddington for the next sixteen years. In 1878 the family moved to Epsom, Surrey, some fourteen miles south-west of London. Epsom has long been celebrated for its curative salts and for its racecourse that annually hosts the Derby, England's most prestigious horse race. The Murrays stayed there until Charles' death in 1904.

In Epsom, Charles, Georgiana, and their children lived in Woodcote Hall, where Moke's father, uncles and aunts grew up. The Hall was a spacious three-storey, mid-eighteenth-century manor house which included stables, barns, and nearly twenty acres of land.[12]

According to the 1881 census, Charles and Georgiana had eight children (four boys and four girls) and nine servants, including a footman. Ten years later, the census reported two more children and the same number of servants, while in 1901, four of the children, a son and three daughters, were still living in Woodcote Hall. Charles Murray paid £300 per year in rent.

It is easy to imagine (and also to oversimplify) the rhythm of the Murray family's life in the 1880s and 1890s. The Derby would have occurred on a selected Wednesday in June,[13] the foxhunting season would occupy several days a week in the autumn and winter, while most Sundays would probably have involved the family's attendance at the Anglican Church of Christ in Epsom. There would have been occasional musical evenings in Woodcote

---

[12] In the 1920s Woodcote Hall was broken up into flats and the surrounding acreage was subdivided and developed. Nikolaus Pevsner, *The Buildings of England: Surrey* (Harmondsworth, Middlesex: Penguin, 1962), 177, refers to Woodcote Hall as "large red brick, mid-Georgian, much pulled about".

[13] Henry James, *English Hours* (London: W. Heinemann, 1905), 13 ff, describes James' attendance at the Derby in 1874, a year before the Murrays moved to Epsom.

Hall, festivities at Christmas involving the household staff and shopping excursions to London. From local newspapers we learn that the Epsom Flower Show was held at least once in Woodcote Hall, which was also occasionally the site of Conservative Party celebrations.

Consciously or not, these ceremonies took place against the backdrop of the British Empire, then in its most prosperous, self-assured and influential stage. When Moke joined the Indian Army in 1932 the unquestioning self-assurance displayed by most English men and women throughout the empire (and in many homes like Woodcote Hall) was still strong but had been shaken by the catastrophic losses that the imperial forces, their allies, and their opponents had sustained in what was then known as the Great War. Growing political unrest was also challenging the empire's authority in India, but at that time few outsiders and even fewer servants of the Empire were prepared to predict its demise.[14]

Like his three brothers and five of his sisters Moke's father Edward Murray (1869–1940) was born in London. Like his brothers, he also attended Eton. Indeed, between 1878 and 1892 there was always at least one of Charles Murray's sons attending the College. As was common in those far-off days, however, the female Murrays probably did not receive much formal schooling outside the home, though several apparently married well.

Edward's older brother William (1865–1920) went on from Eton to Oriel College, University of Oxford, where he took a degree in law in 1887. Soon afterwards he joined his father in the family firm of Murray, Hutchins and Co. He stayed with the firm for the remainder of his life. Edward followed William to

---

14 A good introduction to the notion of Victorian tranquility is W. L. Burn, *The Age of Equipoise: A Study of the Mid-Victorian Generation* (New York: W.W. Norton, 1965). I'm grateful to Graeme Davison for this reference.

Eton and Oriel College but failed to take a degree.[15] "Going down" from Oxford was probably a deliberate choice on Edward's part, and it precluded his entry into the family law firm. I've discovered no evidence that he ever wanted to do so.

Edward's younger brother Frederick Dymoke Murray (1872–1901) had a distinguished career at Eton. After attending Sandhurst, he joined the Black Watch regiment (suggestive of a Scottish connection) and in October 1901, holding the brevet rank of major, he was killed at Bakenlaagte in the Second Anglo–Boer War, taking part in a rear-guard defence against overwhelming enemy forces. Before he died, Frederick was highly regarded by his military superiors.[16] Frederick is buried in Germiston, South Africa.[17]

The impact of Frederick's death on his parents and siblings must have been intense but it's impossible to document because no family correspondence from this period (or any other) is known to have survived.

Edward's youngest brother Herbert Willaume Murray (1875–1938) was still living at Woodcote Hall in 1901. Ten years later we know that he was he was, like Edward, a member of Lloyd's, the prestigious insurance group that provided substantial incomes for its members, who formed syndicates with specific blocks of capital and took particular risks. Edward and Herbert had probably invested in Lloyd's with money that they inherited from their father in 1904. Herbert moved to London at some point, married there in 1917 and died in 1938.

---

15   The 1891 census lists Edward as residing in Woodcote Hall and notes that he is "a student of law".

16   See Frederick's fulsome obituary in *Eton College Chronicle*, 14 November 1901. His name also appears on the Black Watch Monument in Edinburgh.

17   In late 1940 Winston Churchill referred to the Anglo–Boer conflict, in which he had taken part, as "the last enjoyable war". Andrew Roberts, *Churchill: Walking with Destiny* (London: Penguin Books, 2018), n. 32.

Above: Esther Murray 1872–1968

In 1899, when Edward, Moke's father, was twenty-nine years old he married Esther Beatrice Rumford (1872–1968), the daughter of prosperous neighbours, in Christ Church, Epsom. Esther's sister, Ethel Annie Rumford (1869–1939), had been married in the same church two years earlier to Herbert Canning (1848–1934), whose occupation in the marriage registry was listed as "gentleman." At the time Canning, an accountant, was secretary to several companies in the City of London including, most notably, Cecil Rhodes' British South African Company.

When Edward Murray married, he was still living in Woodcote Hall. In the marriage register, he jocosely listed his profession as "poultry farmer" instead of using the term "gentleman" that might have been expected at the church or by his father who witnessed the ceremony. Since leaving Oxford in 1891 without a degree the "poultry farmer" may have been something of a disappointment to his parents.

His wife's father, Joseph Kennerley Rumford (1842–1897), was a Londoner of relatively humble background who prospered in the insurance business. He had been the secretary and later the manager of several insurance companies in Hampstead, where the family lived, and also in Birkenhead. When he died in 1897, Rumford left an estate of £72,000, a sum roughly comparable with the £57,000 that Charles Murray was to bequeath in 1904.

Both sums would be worth twenty times as much today.

For most of Moke's lifetime the word "gentleman" was used in England as a social marker, but like many English terms denoting status ("class" is another) it evades precise definition. In his magisterial book *The English Gentleman*, Philip Mason notes that the *Shorter Oxford Dictionary* defines a gentleman as "a man of chivalrous instincts and fine feelings", while the *Concise Oxford Dictionary* proposes "a man of chivalrous manners and good breeding" as well as "a man of good social position". How terms like "chivalrous" and "good" are to be measured, displayed, or verified is not explained.[18]

George Orwell provides a vivid illustration in "The Spike", an essay about his time as a tramp in England in 1932. Then, still known as Eric Blair, he tells how a friendly fellow tramp, after hearing him talk, asked Eric if he was a gentleman. Eric's quintessentially English reply was "I suppose so". His self-confident demeanour and his middle-class vowels, it seems, were his undoing.[19]

As far as the Murrays are concerned, I think Edward, who grew up in the Victorian era, always considered himself and wanted to be viewed as a gentleman. The term seems to have had less resonance for Moke.

Edward's brother-in-law, Robert Henry Rumford (1870–1957), Esther and Edith's brother, was a concert singer whose musical career received a boost in the 1890s when he became known as Queen Victoria's favourite baritone. Robert's future wife was soon to be the renowned contralto Clara Butt DBE

---

[18] See Philip Mason, *The English Gentleman: The Rise and Fall of an Ideal* (London: André Deutsch, 1982). Martin Mulvihill (personal communication) suggests that "self-possession, which is implicitly boundless" is an essential part of being taken for a gentleman.

[19] George Orwell, "The Spike", in *Collected Essays* (London: Penguin, 2000), 7–14.

(1872–1936). Dame Clara had been born into a modest Bristol family. She showed promise as a singer and in the 1890s, part of her musical education was paid for with a stipend from the Queen. She met Rumford in 1897 and they soon began giving concerts together. With her booming voice, her impressive physical appearance (she was more than six feet tall), and her talent for showmanship Clara quickly became a renowned and popular singer. She and Robert were married in 1900 in a high-profile ceremony in Bristol Cathedral. Sir Arthur Sullivan, a friend of them both, composed an anthem for the occasion. A contemporary account relates:

> After ticket-holders to the number of 500 had been admitted the doors were thrown open to the public, and a scene of confusion followed. Women and children were mercilessly elbowed about in a surging, swaying crowd. Many screamed aloud, and dozens gained the interior of the Cathedral minus hats and bonnets and with clothes torn. It was a sight that can hardly be imagined, and it took many minutes before order could be restored. This was only done by closing the doors, but not until the building was full to the doors.[20]

At twenty-eight, Clara was a super star. In Windsor Castle two years later, keeping her maiden name, she debuted a revised version of the patriotic hymn "Land of Hope and Glory". The music came from Edward Elgar's orchestral suite *Pomp and*

---

20 *Daily Mail*, 26 June 1900. Jeffrey Richards, *Imperialism and Music: Britain, 1876–1953* (Manchester: Manchester University Press, 2001), 483, writes that Clara's marriage was the first to be celebrated in the cathedral in a hundred years. Of her overpowering voice, the conductor Sir Thomas Beecham once remarked in jest that when Clara sang in Dover she could be heard in Calais.

Circumstance, with lyrics provided by A.C. Benson.[21] In later years "Land of Hope and Glory" was often Dame Clara's signature song, delivered on occasion with the contralto draped in a Union Jack flag and at other times even outfitted, breastplate and all, as Britannia herself. Her patriotic singing occasionally moved her audiences to tears.

During the Great War, she gave and sponsored several fundraising concerts and pageants, which sometimes doubled as recruiting drives.[22] For the pageants, she occasionally enlisted Moke's sisters Eileen and Cicely (1906–2001) to play supporting roles. As a reward for her patriotic efforts, she was appointed Dame Commander of the Order of the British Empire (DBE) in 1920.[23]

For the remainder of her life, Dame Clara travelled the world giving concerts with her husband, supported by an entourage of twenty. In 1930–31, touring Asia and Australia, she and Rumford invited Moke's sister Cicely to join them and accompany them on the piano. Cicely's musicianship drew many favourable reviews. The 1931 tour was probably the high point of Cicely's professional life. It's possible that her tales about the tour whetted her young brother's appetite for adventure and may even have led

---

21 See Yvonne M. Ward, "'Gosh! Man I've Got a Tune in My Head': Edward Elgar, A.C. Benson and the Creation of 'Land of Hope and Glory'", *The Court Historian* 7, no. 1 (2002): 17–39.

22 Late in life, Moke recalled these pageants, which he had attended as a boy, and described efforts in the intervals to entice members of the audience into the armed forces. Liam Fox, interview with Anthony Barnett, Worthing, 11 August 2018.

23 The DBE order was founded in 1917, along with the parallel orders of OBE and CBE, which were reserved for men. To begin with DBE's rewarded "prominent British women" for their contributions to the war effort. The order, with its name unchanged, continues to be awarded today.

to his eventual decision to join the Indian Army.[24]

On 9 June 1910, Dame Clara's nephew by marriage Edward Dymoke Murray, the protagonist in what follows, was born at home in Beare Green, Surrey. He was the only male child in the family. At his sister Cicely's Epsom christening four years earlier, Moke's father had given this address and had been identified as "underwriter" by profession. The Murrays' oldest child, Eileen (1902–1994), although she was also christened in Epsom, had been born in Hampstead. Moke was christened in Christ Church Epsom in July 1910, and soon after his family moved to the Old Cottage, a two storey Georgian house in Mickleham, Surrey.

Above: Edward Murray (1869–1940)

From 1908 to 1913 Moke's father was Master of the Surrey Union Hunt, which had been founded in the late eighteenth

---

24   See for example *Sydney Morning Herald*, 21 March 1931 and *Daily Telegraph*, 24 March 1931. See also the Cicely B. Murray Collection of Dame Clara Butt. General Collection, Beinecke Rare Book and Manuscript Library, Yale University, which contains memorabilia from the 1931 tour. Dame Clara had urged Adela Verne, a renowned concert pianist, to train Cicely for the tour, and Verne's memoir contains excerpts from Cicely's letters to her from Asia.

century and flourishes today.[25] The hunt's kennels, then located in Bookham, were an easy cross-country ride from Edward's house in Mickleham. Edward's unpaid position as Master would have involved raising, training, and maintaining a pack of hounds as well as arranging meets; supervising a support staff, monitoring financial records; maintaining a stable of horses for the Master and his assistants; and negotiating with local farmers for permission to hunt over their land. The 1909 Boxing Day hunt, the *Surrey Mirror* reported, drew several hundred spectators to the send-off, including Edward's brother William and his wife who had come down for the meet from London.[26]

Late in life Moke told Liam Fox that his mother, Esther Murray, had been an enthusiastic fox hunter, riding side-saddle. Her rattan, bone-handled riding crop is among Murray's effects in Worthing, where Liam Fox showed it to me in October 2018. One side of the crop, I noticed, had been worn smooth from extensive use.

When Moke died in 2002 there were two identical, early twentieth-century tinted studio photographs of Esther among his unprepossessing collection of effects. One of them, like the riding crop, had probably been passed on to him in 1992 when his sister Cicely moved from her house in Worthing to a retirement home in Winchester. That Moke kept Esther's photograph among his modest collection of effects suggests that he was close to her. In his final years in Worthing, however, he rarely mentioned her

---

25   Edward Murray had been joint master of the hunt in 1907–08. I'm grateful to Julian S. Womersley, the current secretary of the Surrey Union Hunt for helpful information. See Julian Womersley, *The Surrey Union Hunt: Our History Unbuttoned* (Crawley: The Surrey Union Hunt, 2007). The *Surrey Mirror and County Post*, 3 December 1908, notes Murray's appointment "by acclamation" as the new Master of the Surrey Union Hunt. The article summarizes Murray's acceptance speech. Another speech at the meeting noted that the hunt cost £5000 a year to maintain. The sum was presumably raised from subscriptions.
26   *Surrey Mirror*, 30 December 1908, for a photograph of Edward.

and Liam Fox could not remember Moke ever talking about his father. He also never mentioned his son Colin, who was born, as we shall see, in Surrey in May 1936.[27]

For the 1911 census, Edward Murray gave his occupation as "Member of Lloyd's" but his work was with the hunt and several local committees. He was also a well-regarded member of Surrey society, renowned for his skills as a composer, amateur magician and after-dinner speaker. The same census shows that the Murray household in Mickleham consisted of five Murrays and four female domestic staff. Only two of the household (Moke and his father) were male. The effects of this gender imbalance on Moke's boyhood, if there were any, are impossible to assess.

Edward retired as Master of the Surrey Union Hunt in 1913 and soon after moved his family to what was then the Surrey village of Wimbledon, where Moke would receive his formal education.

---

27 Email from Liam Fox, 5 December 2018. The authors interviewed Colin Murray and his wife Bernice in Folkestone, Kent in 2018.

TWO

Moke's Boyhood and Early Military Career

By 1922, the Murrays had relocated to Putney, which is close to central London. They lived there until 1929, when they moved to Ripley, Surrey. The first two moves were probably connected with Moke's formal schooling, which began in Wimbledon and continued after 1924 in West Kensington, an easy commute from Putney.

It's not known when or why the Murrays decided to send their son to St Paul's School, but their choice of a preparatory school in Wimbledon that was known for sending boys on to St Paul's suggests that the decision must have been made during what was then called the Great War, when Moke was seven or eight. He attended Rokeby Preparatory School as a day boy in about 1918–24. The school had been founded in 1879 and still exists in the Canning Town district of London.[1] Back in Moke's day it had a hundred students, nine or ten of whom were boarders. One of its foremost alumni was the poet Robert Graves,

---

1 Fees at Rokeby in 2019 were £23,000 per year for day students and £36,000 per year for boarders (Justin Corfield, personal communication).

whose savage memoir of his public-school experiences and trench warfare in World War I, *Goodbye to All That*, was published in 1929 just as Moke was embarking on a military career.[2]

Rokeby has always been largely a day school, so Moke escaped the often-bruising experiences of boys of Moke's social position who were sent away from home, sometimes when they were as young as seven.[3]

In October 1922, his family's equilibrium was jolted when Edward Murray declared himself bankrupt in a Surrey court.[4] A year prior, he had described his occupation in the 1921 Census as a "Manufacturer of aluminium ware", suggesting the family's changing fortunes in the lead-up to his bankruptcy. We don't know the extent and character of Edward's debts, but the event almost certainly put an end to his being a non-working member, or "name", of Lloyd's. The bankruptcy was probably connected with Murray's syndicate at Lloyd's being found liable for a payment that soaked up most or all of his stake. In later life, Moke referred enigmatically on several occasions to the financial damage sustained by his father following the loss of a ship, in Murray's words, that was "coming from South Africa loaded with gold bullion".[5] Responding to a query on this issue, Justin Corfield, has written:

---

2 Robert Graves, *Goodbye to All That* (London: Jonathan Cape, 1929). Another Rokeby "old boy" was Agatha Christie's second husband the archaeologist Sir Max Mallowan (1904–1978). He wrote of the school in his memoirs, "I do not think that I received a better education anywhere and spent at least two years marking time at my public school thereafter."

3 See for example George Orwell, "Such, Such Were the Joys", in *A Collection of Essays* (London: Harcourt, 1946; and Henry Green, *Pack My Bag: A Self-Portrait* (London: The Hogarth Press, 1939).

4 *The Times* of 30 October 1922 lists Edward as a "gentleman, with no occupation" while the *London Gazette* of 10 November 1922 merely says "No occupation", suggesting obliquely that Edward's bankruptcy had at least temporarily rendered the term "gentleman" invalid.

5 Anthony Barnett's interview with Liam Fox, Worthing, 10 August 2018.

It sounds like the *SS Egypt*, which went down in 1922—actually on its way from England to India with gold bullion on board. It could be South African gold—more than likely. Although it went down in 1922, the gold was only recovered some years later. Once Lloyd's pays out for the loss of the ship, the wreck and anything on it belongs to Lloyd's. If it is not recovered quickly, then with less prospect of finding it, when the rescuers were contracted years later, Lloyd's might not have received as much back and of course there was the cost of the ship itself.[6]

It's uncertain what employment if any Edward subsequently took up. In January 1924 when Moke entered St Paul's School, Edward gave his occupation as "wine merchant", but I have not found any corroboration for this.[7] The ripple effects of the bankruptcy on the Murrays are impossible to document but his semi-public loss of income and respectability must have been bewildering and hurtful at least in the short term. Esther's inherited money, perhaps supplemented by assistance from the childless Cannings and Dame Clara probably saw the family through. Well into the 1930s, it seems, the Murrays' comfortable life style did not change substantially. How much of a breadwinner Edward managed to be in this period, however, is unclear.

---

6   The SS *Egypt*, carrying 294 crew and only forty-four passengers, sailed from London for Bombay on 19 May 1922. Its cargo, valued at over £1 million, included five tons of gold bullion and twenty tons of silver, destined for the Government of India. A day later, in heavy fog, the *Egypt* collided with a French cargo vessel, the SS *Seine*, and *Egypt* sank in half an hour. Eighty-six of the 338 people on board lost their lives. The wreck was not discovered until 1930 and by 1935 most of the cargo had been recovered. For details see Nigel Pickford, *Lost Treasure Ships of the Twentieth Century* (London: Pavillion, 1999), 175.

7   I'm grateful to Justin Corfield, who attended St Paul's in the 1970s, for helpful information about the school. Fees for day students at St Paul's in 2019 range from £6146 to £8101 per term, or close to £20,000 per year.

Between Spring Term 1924 and December 1928, commuting by bus from Putney, Moke was a day student at St Paul's School in West Kensington, London.[8] The academically prestigious school had been founded in 1509 on a site in London adjoining St Paul's Cathedral. In the 1920s it had about 700 students and was a favoured destination for boys proceeding from Rokeby. Only ninety boys were boarders. St Paul's put less emphasis on sport and was less snobbish than many equally prestigious public schools. Tuition when Moke attended the school was only 30 pounds a year, the same amount as his parents had paid at Rokeby.

The philosopher Sir Isaiah Berlin (1909–1997) attended the school when Moke was there[9] and the author Leonard Woolf (1880–1969) had been a student at St Paul's in the 1890s.[10] In *Sowing*, the first volume of his memoirs, Woolf wrote that while he admired some of the teaching at St Paul's and was good enough at games to avoid being bullied, he didn't recall his time at the school with pleasure. Instead, sixty-odd years after he left St Paul's, he wrote:

> The public school was the nursery of British philistinism. To work, to use the mind, to become a "swot"… was to become an untouchable in the public school caste system. Publicly to have confessed that one enjoyed any of these things would have been as impossible as for a respectable Victorian young lady publicly to confess unchastity and that she had enjoyed it.[11]

---

8   Justin Corfield, personal communication, March 2020.
9   Michael Ignatieff, *Isaiah Berlin: A Life* (New York: Metropolitan Books, 1998), 40–45.
10 Like Berlin and many other students at the school Woolf was a Jew. Ignatieff, 40. A 15 per cent Jewish quota went into effect at St Paul's shortly after Moke left the school. The imposition of the quota enraged Isaiah Berlin. It remained in force until the 1960s.
11 Leonard Woolf, *Sowing: An Autobiography of the Years 1880–1904* (London: Hogarth, 1960), 88.

At St Paul's, students in Murray's day elected to join one of four academic "streams"—Classics, Science, History, or Army/Engineering. Science with three streams of its own was the most popular one, followed by Classics, the stream favoured by students seeking scholarships to Oxford and Cambridge. The History stream enjoyed less academic cachet than Classics while the Army/Engineering stream was the smallest and academically the least prestigious. The stream was not limited to students hoping for a military career, but hardly any of them, it seems, went on to study at university.

It's possible that low marks on his entrance examination limited Moke's options at St Paul's, but Moke never expressed any regrets about opting for the military stream. He thus unwittingly became part of the symbiotic relationship that had developed in the late nineteenth century between the public schools and the British officer class.[12] The sociologist C.B. Otley has written that many English public schools became militarised in this period while the officer class, becoming more professional, came to reflect the public school training and male-oriented values that the vast majority of officers had absorbed during their early education. As public school administrators came to realise that thousands of their graduates would become officers in the army and the imperial civil service they adjusted aspects of their curricula accordingly, although at St Paul's and elsewhere training in Science and Classics still attracted the most gifted boys and enjoyed the most prestige.

Murray was a mediocre student at St Paul's but he was a

---

12 See C.B. Otley, "Militarism and Militarization in the Public Schools, 1900–1972", *British Journal of Sociology* 29, no. 3 (1978): 321–39 and also his "The Social Origins of British Army Officers", *Sociological Review* 18, July (1970): 213–39. I'm grateful to Andrew Hassam for these references. See also Jonathan Rutherford, *Forever England: Reflections on Race, Masculinity and Empire* (London: Lawrence & Wishart, 1997), esp. 11–38.

success in other ways. In his final year the teaching staff chose him to be one of St Paul's three senior prefects. These boys were selected on the basis of their clean records, their ability at sport, and their reliability. Moke also served as Quartermaster for the Officers' Training Company (OTC). All students, and not just those in the Army/Engineering stream, were required to join the OTC as cadets. He also belonged to the Music Society and was secretary of football (rugby). In his last two years he played in the First XV (rugby) and in the Second XI (cricket). A class note about departing students in 1928 remarked that he had been "an efficient and hard-working secretary. In the [rugby] scrum he always shoved hard and could be counted on to come up with the ball."[13]

In his final term at St Paul's, Murray ranked seventeenth in his class of twenty in the Army and Engineering stream. Over the years, his marks in the consolidated subject English and Divinity were considerably higher than his marks in other subjects, which were Science, Mathematics, French, Classics, and Drawing. He didn't opt for Higher Mathematics, it seems, and chose to take Classics instead.[14]

In early December 1928, Moke left St Paul's via what was then called Army 8, also known as Woolwich and Engineering. A few days later, he joined the London Scottish Battalion of the Territorial Army as a private soldier. The speed of this action suggests that he had planned it for some time. He spent the next twenty-five months as a part-time soldier. He was probably

---

[13] *The Pauline*, vol. XLVII, no. 313 (February 1929). See also *London Observer*, 28 November 1928, reporting on a match between Dulwich and St Paul's notes that "E.D. Murray was knocked out in the first half, stood out for St Paul's". Moke joined the Territorial Army on the following day. I'm grateful to Justin Corfield for this reference.

[14] The subjects that students in the Army/Engineering stream seem not to have contained any military content.

interested in obtaining a commission at some point but it's uncertain why he chose this unprestigious pathway to do so instead of enrolling in the military academies of Sandhurst or Woolwich, or why he waited eighteen months to apply for a commission. His poor marks at St Paul's and financial constraints in his family may have affected his decision but I suspect that he was simply reluctant at eighteen to take up further academic work or a full-time military life. Instead, it seems, he was happy to be soldiering in London on a part-time basis alongside men, most of whom had not attended a public school.

From the army's point of view, of course, good marks at school were less important than a potential officer's other skills, deportment, and accomplishments. By the time he left St Paul's Murray had already absorbed a range of valuable experience. As a prefect he had earned the respect of the school teaching staff. Teamwork, quick thinking (as in sport), a capacity for leadership, and being skilled at pleasing his superiors, all picked up at school, were to be persistent features of his military career. Unsurprisingly, perhaps, Moke was consistently popular with fellow officers and with the troops he commanded in India, Burma, and Malaya.[15]

Why did he become a soldier? He must have made the decision tentatively at fourteen, when he enrolled in the Army and Engineering stream at St Paul's. As far as future employment was concerned his Micawberish, financially unpredictable father was not an appropriate role model, and a career in "the City" probably had few attractions. Indeed, for a boy of Murray's class, with no capital to speak of and (as it turned out) few academic

---

15   Email from Lieutenant Colonel J. Cross, 7 April 2018. Cross, then in his nineties, served with Murray in Malaya in the late 1940s. On his retirement he became a Nepali citizen and lives in Kathmandu. Cross has written books about his career, the Gurkhas, and jungle warfare.

accomplishments, acceptable alternative options were very limited. Careers in the professions or the Church, for example, probably never tempted him and would have required a university education. He would probably not have considered a career in what was then referred to by people in his class as "trade". For Moke, given the things he was good at and the conforming pressures of his class, becoming a soldier and an officer was an almost inevitable choice.

To an extent this fitted into a fairly recent family tradition. His uncle Frederick's heroic death in South Africa may have provided some inspiration. Closer to home, Moke's first cousin Charles William Murray (1896–1915) had left Eton in September 1914 to volunteer for service. He was killed a year later as a nineteen-year-old subaltern five months after arriving at the front, cut down in a battalion-sized assault on a series of German trenches. Charles' battalion occupied these trenches briefly until they were forced to withdraw in the face of a German counterattack. Charles was killed at some point in the encounter and his body was never recovered from the battlefield. None of the survivors questioned after the attack remembered when Charles was hit or even seeing his body. Thirty-eight members of the battalion, including four other subalterns and a captain, lost their lives in the same assault.[16] Poignantly, the personal effects that Charles left behind when he set off on the attack included four rosaries, perhaps given to him by a Roman Catholic chaplain. The rosaries are the only indication I have seen of any intense religious faith in the Murray family. There is a modest memorial to Charles attached to his parents' headstone in the Christ Church Epsom cemetery.

Moke was only four years old when Charles was killed. Until

---

[16] Similarly, Rudyard Kipling's only son, John, an 18-year-old subaltern, was killed at Loos in March 1915, a mere two days after arriving at the front. See Nina Mortyris, "When Rudyard Kipling's Son Went Missing", *New Yorker*, 26 September 2015.

he was eight, what was to be called the Great War raged across the Channel and elsewhere in the world. Much later he remembered hearing the muffled sound of artillery barrages from France and Belgium when he was on holiday with his family in Bognor Regis.[17] Many of Moke's schoolmates would have lost relatives in the conflict and some of his teachers at Rokeby and St Paul's would have taken part in it. The Great War cast a shadow over Murray's extended family and his years at school.

In December 1920, while Moke was a student at Rokeby, authorities at St Paul's approved the installation of a set of wooden panels listing the names of 490 former students, known as Paulines, who had been killed or had gone missing in the war. The panels were installed in 1923.[18] The names listed comprised 18 per cent of the school's former students who had served in the armed forces. Of almost 200 public schools including several outside the British Isles whose records have been examined, St Paul's losses were the fourteenth highest.[19] Tellingly, subalterns such as Charles Murray comprised one-third of all the former public school students who were killed or went missing in action. A side effect of these losses was that Moke's sisters Eileen and Cicely found it difficult when they came to marriageable age in the 1920s to make friends with suitable young men, customarily a few years older than they were, drawn from the same now severely depleted social class. Like many young women of their generation, the sisters never married.

---

17   Anthony Barnett's interview with Liam Fox, Worthing, 10 August 2018.
18   Alexandra Aslett, email to author, 8 November 2017.
19   These statistics are drawn from the appendix to Anthony Seldon and David Walsh, *Public Schools and the Great War: The Generation Lost* (Barnsley, South Yorkshire: Pen & Sword Military, 2013); see also Anthony Seldon, "The Real Eton Rifles: The Heroism of Public School Boys in the First World War", *New Statesman*, 18 December 2013, <https://www.newstatesman.com/uncategorized/2013/12/real-eton-rifles>.

The human costs of war, starting with millions of dead young men on both sides, 953,104 of them from the British Empire dying in combat, and extending to the devastated friends, sweethearts, and families that they left behind, as well as the survivors whose minds or bodies had been wrecked in combat—sank into the collective mind of the British population in the 1920s, accompanied by an overwhelming sense of relief that the war was over.[20] At the same time the ongoing ethos of England's and the empire's public schools and what still seemed to many to be the permanence and necessity of the empire itself, like the monarchy, were to a large extent taken for granted by the British public.

By the time he left St Paul's Moke had absorbed these male-oriented assumptions and values without question. His consistently cheerful behaviour once he became a soldier suggests that he never doubted these assumptions and values, although as an old man he had some stray second thoughts about the full-blown righteousness of the empire.

Intellectually, Moke was a lively, observant, unadventurous creature of the class he had been born into, and of the values transmitted by his family, at school and during his military career. This consistent orientation permeates the narrative of his life.

In July 1930, a month after turning twenty, Moke moved within the Territorial Army from the London Scottish to the 12th City of London Battalion (The Rangers), whose recruits were drawn from the Holborn district of central London. At the same time, he applied for a commission. His application noted that he was living with his parents in Ripley, Surrey. He gave his

---

20   On this phenomenon approached from a literary perspective see Paul Fussell, *The Great War and Modern Memory* (New York: Oxford University Press, 1975) and J.M. Winter, *Remembering War: The Great War Between Memory and History in the Twentieth Century* (New Haven: Yale University Press, 2006); see also Charles F.G. Masterman, *England after War: A Study* (London: Hodder & Stoughton, 1922).

occupation as "school master", and his employer the Ancuit (i.e. Montessori) home school in nearby Stanmore.[21] It's unclear when he began this job, what it involved, or if it continued after he was commissioned. In any case, he never held another paying position in civilian life. His relatively prolonged time in the Territorial Army while he continued to live with his parents, also suggests that he was in no rush to take up full-time employment or to live independently of his family.

The process of obtaining a commission for someone of Moke's class and public school education was relatively easy. It involved taking a physical examination, obtaining a character reference from a master at St Paul's, being interviewed by a senior Territorial Army officer, and obtaining a pro forma approval for the transfer and application from the commander of the London Scottish. These were all easily obtained and the commissioning process went smoothly. Only ten days passed between Moke's submitting his application and becoming a subaltern or second lieutenant in the regular army.[22] He stayed with The Rangers until 31 January 1932, when he transferred to the Indian Army on a probationary basis as a second lieutenant (unattached). We do not know when or why he made this decision, but it was likely that he was opting for more exotic surroundings, higher pay, and a more adventurous life than staying in the Territorial Army or serving in a prestigious British regiment that would have involved some expenditure he was unable to afford. Moke had also reached a point where he was ready to leave his family.

Between the wars, the Indian Army consisted of roughly 150,000 Indian troops all stationed in the subcontinent, and

---

21 Information taken from E.D. Murray's personal records.
22 See *London Gazette*, 1 August 1930: "12th Lond. R.—Pte. Edward Dymoke Murray, from 14th Lond. R. (late Cadet C.Q.M.S., St. Paul's Sch. Contgt., Jun. Div., O.T.C.), to be 2nd Lt. 26th July 1930."

Above: Arriving in India (1933)

some 6,500 British soldiers. These included almost all the commissioned officers of the Indian regiments as well as the personnel of British regiments that were posted to India from time to time. The British regimental postings were attractive to officials in London because the Indian government financially supported these units in full.

Less than a week after his transfer, Moke sailed for India aboard HMT *Neuralia*. He took snapshots on the voyage that survive among his papers in the Gurkha Museum in Winchester.[23] Soon after he arrived, he was posted to the 2nd Battalion of the York and Lancaster Regiment in New Delhi. On 18 March 1933, it is recorded that Moke was a luncheon guest of the Viceroy, Lord Willingdon (1866–1940), possibly thanks to a family or professional connection that I've been unable to establish. For a 23-year-old recently landed subaltern, the luncheon must have

---

23 I'm grateful to Gavan Edgerley Harris, the director of the Gurkha Museum, for helpful correspondence and for his hospitality when I visited Winchester in September 2016 and again in March and September 2018. On the latter visits I benefited from the help provided by the Museum's deputy director Christine Bernath, its collections officer Doug Henderson, and its archivist Roy MacEwan. Henderson also responded helpfully to several emails in 2019 when I was unable to visit the museum.

been an unforgettable introduction to the splendour of the Raj. In Willingdon's day, Viceroy House, now the residence of the president of India, employed 6,000 servants.[24]

The York and Lancashire's duties were largely ceremonial but in May 1932 the regiment spent a few weeks on manoeuvres at Razmak in Waziristan. His year with the regiment marked the only time in Murray's career where he commanded British troops. He was to return there late in 1936 for two seasons of fighting insurgents in Waziristan. Until the outbreak of World War II, he took thousands of photographs that give a vivid picture of his activities and by extension some unexpectedly candid snapshots of the Raj. When he was not on manoeuvres, Moke played rugby for the regimental team and pasted clippings of the matches into a photograph album along with photographs that he took in Razmak and New Delhi. Negatives of more than 500 of the photographs that he took in India in the 1930s survived among his effects in Worthing.[25] Twelve of them are included in this book, pages 76-81.

Until the mid-1950s, shortly before he retired, Murray served with and commanded Nepalese Gurkhas in the Indian Army and Assamese irregulars in north-eastern India. In other words, for most of his military career Moke fitted snugly into the self-assured, hide-bound, all male context of the prestigious Gurkha Brigade, which was the only unit in the Indian Army whose recruits were not drawn from what are now India and Pakistan. The Gurkhas, all volunteers, came from the landlocked, quasi-independent kingdom of Nepal. They had joined the East India

---

24 *Times of India*, 19 March 1933. Because subalterns, as well as most civilians, were addressed as "Mr" it's impossible to tell if any other subalterns were among the Viceroy's reported luncheon guests. On the size of staff of Viceroy House, see Cannadine, *Ornamentalism*, 56.
25 His former neighbours Liam Fox and Monica Millest passed them along to Anthony Barnett in August 2018. They have since been developed.

Company's forces after the Anglo–Nepal Wars of 1814–16, when the company's officers noticed the enterprise and bravery of their Nepali opponents and began to recruit them among prisoners of war and deserters.[26] Gurkha units with British officers were active in putting down the Indian Rebellion in 1857 and for ninety years till the end of the Raj Gurkhas helped the British maintain order. After fighting in France, Turkey, and Mesopotamia in the Great War, Gurkha battalions participated in imperial policing and in the perennial conflicts in Waziristan in India's northwest in the 1920s and 1930s. More than 200,000 Gurkhas volunteered for service in World War II and in 1947 four Gurkha regiments that were absorbed into the British Army went on to fight in Malaya, on Borneo, and in the Falklands. The other six Gurkha battalions survive today in the Indian Army.

Towards the end of 1932, the 2nd Battalion of the 4th Prince of Wales' Own Gurkha Rifles (hereafter 2/4GR) vetted Moke. This battalion, first raised in 1886 by an Indian Army colonel named King-Harman, was cantoned in Bakloh, a salubrious hill station in the province of Himachal Pradesh, north-western India.[27] The battalion's deputy commander in 1933 was Lieutenant Colonel David Murray-Lyon (1890–1975), who may have been a distant relative of Moke's and therefore a family connection, but I've been unable to verify this. Murray-Lyon became commander of the battalion in April 1936, led it into battle in Waziristan in 1936–1938, and retired in March 1939. The Lieutenant Colonel,

---

26 See Mary Des Chene's magisterial study "Relics of Empire: A Cultural History of the Gurkhas, 1815–1987", PhD Dissertation (Stanford, Stanford University, 1991); For a breezier account see E.D. Smith, *Valour: The History of the Gurkhas* (Stroud: The History Press, 2016). Smith, a former Gurkha, served with Moke in Malaya.

27 See Ranald Macdonell and Marcus Macaulay, *A History of the 4th Prince of Wales's Own Gurkha Rifles, 1857–1937*, vol. 1 (Edinburgh: W. Blackwood, 1940), 91–132. Colonel King Harman, aged 94, was in Bakloh in February 1936 to celebrate the 50th anniversary of the battalion.

Above: Officers of the 2/4 GR (1935)

heavily decorated in World War I, returned to active service in 1942 as a Major-General, commanding an Indian Army division in Malaya which was torn apart by the Japanese. Murray-Lyon was relieved of his command and spent the remainder of the war as a prisoner in Singapore. Murray met him again, as we shall see, in 1953. The regimental history refers to him as a "great personality" whose departure from the battalion was "most affecting".[28]

Subaltern postings to Gurkha battalions were in high demand after the Great War, and in the 1920s the battalions introduced a vetting process for new officers.[29] Vetting required a candi-

---

28 James Nobel Mackay, *A History of the 4th Prince of Wales's Own Gurkha Rifles 1938–1948*, vol. 2 (Edinburgh: Blackwood, 1952), 5. Other battalion commanders failed to receive similar accolades.
29 John Masters, *Bugles and a Tiger* (New York: The Viking Press, 1956), 74. Between the wars, Masters writes, "Sikh and Gurkha units usually had three to four applicants for every vacancy". See also Gilmour, *The British in India*, 240.

49

date, usually a second lieutenant, to spend a week or ten days of leave as a guest of his preferred battalion. What was at stake was whether a candidate's prospective fellow officers and the battalion commander, who had veto power, felt at ease with the candidate, and had been able to assess some of his military, sporting, and social skills favourably during his visit. In the words of a former Gurkha officer writing about the process in the 1930s, "The object was to find out if the prospective candidate was the type who could 'muck in' and turn his hand to any job. The CO would say to his officers, 'Is this a chap you are prepared to live with?'"[30]

In those days at least, Moke was a clubbable person. His straight-forward, affable manner, his Territorial Army experience and his year of soldiering in New Delhi must have satisfied the battalion commander, Lieutenant Colonel B.F. Graeme, as well as Murray-Lyon and the other officers in the 2/4GR. He was welcomed into the battalion as a full lieutenant in March 1934 and acquired his nickname.[31]

In the 1930s, there were ten Gurkha regiments in the Indian Army, each with two battalions, a number that was to expand under wartime conditions.[32] Each battalion consisted of four companies, lettered "A" to "D" with three or four platoons in each company and three or four sections in each platoon. Companies "A" to "C" were infantry, while Company "D" was a machine gun contingent; all were commanded by British officers. Gurkha officers led the platoons, and non-commissioned Gurkhas commanded the sections. A fully staffed Gurkha battalion had some 800 troops

---

30   Tony Gould, *Imperial Warriors: Britain and the Gurkhas* (London: Granta, 2000), 217.
31   The appointment ended Moke's probationary status in the Indian Army. It is unclear what would have happened to him if he had failed the vetting process in 2/4GR.
32   For a comprehensive history of the Brigade of Gurkhas, see Des Chene, "Relics of Empire".

(all Gurkhas) and thirty-odd officers (all British).[33]

British and Gurkha officers and other ranks considered themselves to be the elite of the Indian Army; one author has compared then to the Brigade of Guards, the most prestigious unit in the British Army.[34] The anthropologist Lionel Caplan has written:

> In the course of the nineteenth century the Gurkhas came to regard themselves as a unit apart from the rest of the Indian Army. The brigade was deemed an elite corps and its officers took every opportunity to emphasize the superiority of their men to those of other Indian regiments ... [The former Gurkha officer] recalls that while a few other (non-Gurkha) regiments of the Indian army were barely tolerated, the British army 'lock stock and barrel', was [considered] useless.[35]

Indeed, aside from technological developments in such things as weaponry, electric power, and motor vehicles, the Battalion between the wars were shielded from much of the outside world. The memoirs of British officers describing their service in the 1880s and 1890s are almost indistinguishable from those compiled half a century later in terms of games, tiger shoots, mountaineering expeditions, the ritualised culture of the mess and periodic fighting in Waziristan, an inhospitable mountainous area straddling the current borders of Pakistan and Afghanistan. Using the word *Waziristan* allowed the British to paper over the fact that the combat area consisted of portions of British India and portions of the allegedly sovereign, perennially unstable state

---

33 H.D James and D. Sheil-Small, *The Gurkhas* (London: Macdonald, 1965), 9.
34 Raymond Callahan, "Were the Sepoy Generals Any Good? A Reappraisal of the British-Indian Army's Command in the Second World War," in Kaushik Roy (ed.), *War and Society in Colonial India: 1807–1945*, (New Dehli: Oxford University Press, 2010), 305–29
35 Caplan, *Warrior Gentlemen*, 37.

of Afghanistan. The border between the two, to put it mildly, was very poorly defined.[36]

Under the Raj, the views and martial virtues nurtured by the Gurkha Brigade and the lively competition among Gurkha battalions, on the one hand, and between the brigade and the rest of the Indian Army on the other, remained almost unchanged from one century to the next. As Caplan notes:

> Over the years each Gurkha regiment had elaborated a distinctive identity, through shaping its own history, developing exclusive conventions and rituals, acquiring its sacred trophies, and holding stereotyped images of their own and other Gurkha regiments, to say nothing of other army units.[37]

Two important elements of the Gurkhas' collective identity were that they came from Nepal while all company commanders and above in Gurkha units came from Britain prior to World War II. This unique admixture in the brigade of Gurkhas meant that British officers and Gurkhas, unlike their Indian and British counterparts, never served at home. Similarly, they were never called upon, as Indian soldiers sometimes were, to open fire on their own people.[38] An exception to the "never served at

---

36 See Michael Barthorp, *The North-West Frontier: British India & Afghanistan, A Pictorial History 1839–1947* (Poole: Blandford, 1982); and T. R. Moreman, "'Small Wars' and 'Imperial Policing': The British Army and the Theory and Practice of Colonial Warfare in the British Empire, 1919–1939", *Journal of Strategic Studies* 19, no. 4 (1996): 119, which states that unrest posed "the most insistent military problem" in British India. In March 2011, US president Barack Obama called Waziristan "the most dangerous place in the world". See Akbar Ahmed and Akins Harrison, "Waziristan: 'The Most Dangerous Place in the World'," Al Jazeera, 12 April 2013, <https://www.aljazeera.com/opinions/2013/4/12/waziristan-the-most-dangerous-place-in-the-world>.
37 Caplan, *Warrior Gentlemen*, 131; See also Gould, *Imperial Warriors*, 203, which refers to an "illusion of timelessness, of time standing still" in accounts of Gurkha life between the wars.
38 Gould, Imperial Warriors, 204.

Moke's Boyhood and Early Military Career

home" rule occurred in February 1934 when elements of 2/4GR including Moke were dispatched to Kathmandu, the capital of Nepal, to rehabilitate the city after an earthquake in which over 10,000 people died. Moke snapped dozens of photographs of the damaged city, now kept in the Gurkha Museum, that survived among his papers.

A consistent element in the British–Gurkha relationship was the British mythologisation of the Gurkhas as a martial race of trustworthy, courageous, and unflappable soldiers, who were capable, under orders, of a level of violence that was seemingly rare among British or most Indian troops.[39] Since the early nineteenth century "Johnny Gurkha" has occupied a privileged position in British military thinking and an admired, slightly scary place in popular mythology.[40] The recollections of British officers who served with Gurkhas often contain touches of sentimentality and wishful thinking as they document what they believe to have been the consistently fond rapport between themselves and the Gurkha soldiers. The paternalistic character of the relationship involved some good-natured infantilising of the Gurkhas by their supposedly fatherly British commanders, and also perhaps greater emotional commitment from the middle-class British officers than they had received, in many cases, from their own very distant fathers.[41]

In July 1935, after Moke had spent a year at Bakloh, Second

---

39 See Heather Streets, *Martial Races: The Military, Race, and Masculinity in British Imperial Culture* (Manchester: Manchester University Press, 2004).
40 General Wavell, cited by Des Chene, "Relics of Empire", 185, noted that Gurkhas were "probably among the best soldiers in the world if properly officered and trained, as they have been in the Indian Army". The term "Johnny Gurkha" seems to have come into use in World War I. The British equivalent was "Tommy Atkins".
41 Gilmour, *The British in India*, 240: "Officers who had served in Gurkha battalions invariably missed their 'grand little men' and often annoyed colleagues from other units by talking so much about them."

Lieutenant John Masters (1914–1983) was vetted for the battalion. Masters was the son of an Indian Army officer and had been born in India. In England, he had attended Wellington College and Sandhurst, where he won several prizes. His absorbing memoir *Bugles and a Tiger* (1956) recounts, among other things, his experiences in 2/4GR.[42] Unlike Moke, who left the battalion for good in early 1939, Masters stayed with 2/4GR through World War II and won a DSO in Burma. He transferred to the British Army in 1947 (while Moke stayed on with the Gurkhas) but resigned his commission a year later, when he migrated to the United States and became a best-selling novelist. Several of his novels are set in India before independence.[43]

Moke befriended Masters soon after he was vetted in Bakloh and acted as his mentor. Being six years older, Moke was more at ease with his colleagues and could help the newcomer get adjusted. At one point, Masters—then only twenty years old—was worried that he was too talkative and abrupt and was becoming unpopular with his fellow officers. He sought Moke's advice and was told, "Well, I shouldn't offer my opinions quite so often or so definitely, if I were you."[44] Masters was a competent, courageous officer, but also brash, self-serving, and opinionated. He was never especially popular with his Gurkha colleagues.[45] In 2018, Liam Fox told Anthony Barnett that though the two men were together for a while, Moke didn't like Masters very much, but "he told me that he [Masters] was a very good chap as an officer".[46]

---

42 Masters, *Bugles and a Tiger*, passim; See also Gould, *Imperial Warriors*, 216–17.
43 John Clay, *John Masters: A Regimented Life* (London: Michael Joseph, 1992).
44 Masters, *Bugles and a Tiger*, 136.
45 Gould, *Imperial Warriors*, 216–17; In 1937, Murray-Lyon's annual report on Masters, who had performed admirably in action in Waziristan, noted his high abilities but added, "He must learn to be less impetuous", Masters, *Bugles and a Tiger*, 239.
46 Liam Fox, interview with Anthony Barnett, Worthing, 11 August 2018.

Between the wars, life for young, single Gurkha officers such as Moke and Masters was pleasurable and undemanding, although training sessions could be exacting and all the officers, like their men, were expected to be in top physical condition. In *Bugles and a Tiger* Masters writes of a training session that he shared with Moke in 1935. On that occasion, the battalion's junior officers, working in syndicates, were asked to prepare a paper for a company-sized assault over a given landscape on a specific target. These exercises were known as TEWTs (tactical exercises without troops). Masters delivered his syndicate's plan hesitantly, with many pauses. Then Moke presented his plan, which was similar to Masters' but received higher praise. As Masters recalled, "I hung my head in shame. Here was the only sensible plan, coming out in short decisive phrases, with no ums and ers, carrying conviction, easy to understand."[47]

Occasional peace-keeping missions interrupted the battalion's time in Bakloh. In July and August 1935, for example, elements of 2/4GR including Moke and Masters were tasked with suppressing riots that broke out between Sikhs and Muslims in Lahore, 140 miles from Bakloh, and to maintain British control over the city.[48] In Lahore and elsewhere, Indian Army troops acted under standing orders "to use minimum force".[49] These orders had been set in place in the wake of the Amritsar Massacre in April 1919 in which two Gurkha platoons had taken part and hundreds of

---

47   Masters, *Bugles and a Tiger*, 118.
48   Several snapshots that Moke took at that time suggest that he also attended the annual races held by the Lahore Race Club.
49   Macdonell and Macaulay, *A History of the 4th Prince of Wales's Own Gurkha Rifles*, vol. 1, 90; David Omissi, The Sepoy and the Raj: The Indian Army, 1860–1940 (London: Palgrave Macmillan, 1994), 210 states that Gurkha troops were favoured by the British to quell civil and religious disturbances. Onassi adds that Gurkhas "regarded all Indians alike with mild disdain".

Indian civilians were killed.[50] In between these commitments, Indian Army officers took advantage of generous leave provisions that allowed for mountain climbing, exploration, big game hunting, and vacations in alluring locations such as Kashmir.[51]

---

[50] Kim A. Wagner, *Amritsar 1919: An Empire of Fear & the Making of a Massacre* (New Haven: Yale University Press, 2019). See also William Slim's engaging essay "Aid to the Civil", in his *Unofficial History* (London: Cassell, 1959), 73–98. On p. 77, Slim refers to a four-page Indian Army text, IAF D 908, "Action in Aid of the Civil Power for Dispersal of Unlawful Assemblies". Slim calls the document "a very serviceable handrail to steady on among the pitfalls of the law".

[51] On the pleasures of off-duty life for unmarried Indian Army officers in the 1930s see Masters, *Bugles and a Tiger*, 150 ff; Gilmour, *The British in India*, 444–83.

THREE

Moke's First Marriage

On 28 august 1935, in the nearby hill station of Dalhousie, which unlike Bakloh boasted a cinema, shops and a hotel, Murray acted as best man for a 2/4GR colleague, Lieutenant Henry Laslett (1906–?), who had joined the battalion at roughly the same time. The bride's parents came out from England for the wedding, which seems to have been quite a grand social occasion. Laslett resigned his commission soon afterwards.[1] Before the wedding Moke's friendship with Laslett and his fiancée had led to a holiday on a houseboat in Kashmir, where a photograph survives of him with a young woman named Ethel Catherine Ellery (1914–1987), known as Tim to her friends. This pleasing, uncomplicated life came to an abrupt end a month or so after the Laslett wedding when Moke learned that Tim was pregnant with his child. Tim continued to live with her parents in Sialkot, a city in the Punjab where her father's British cavalry regiment, the 13/18 Hussars, had been stationed since 1934, while Moke remained in Bakloh.

Tim and Moke were married in an Anglican church in

---

[1] Laslett is missing from the captioned group photograph of 2/4GR officers taken in December 1935 that is included in Masters, *Bugles and a Tiger*.

Above: On holiday in Kashmir (1935)

Sialkot in January 1936. A photograph of the newlyweds shows them emerging from the church, wearing unobtrusive civilian clothes under the swords of an eight-man guard of honour of British officers from the 13/18 Hussars, provided by Tim's father.[2] A few days later Tim and Moke sailed for England on Moke's eight months of accrued leave and their son, Colin Dymoke Rumford Murray, was born in Surrey in late May 1936. The date of Colin's birth suggests that Tim became pregnant at about the time of the Laslett wedding.[3]

Who was Ethel Catherine Ellery, known as Tim?

She was the third child of Lieutenant Colonel Alpha Ellery (1883–1955) and his wife Jane, *née* Jebson (1880–1969), known as Jessie, who was the daughter of a Yorkshire blacksmith. Tim was born in Scarborough, Yorkshire, probably at her maternal

---

2 For a colourful account of marriages and weddings in India under the Raj, see Gilmour, *The British in India*, 198 ff.
3 The officers were probably drawn from the 1/18 Hussars. I have been unable to identify the church. I originally thought that it was the Anglican Cathedral in Sialkot, but the cathedral bears no resemblance to the building in the wedding photograph. The cathedral still exists, in the district of Christian Town, Sialkot.

Moke's First Marriage

grandparents' home. At the time, her father was a trooper in the 18th Hussars, the same regiment in which his father, also named Alpha (b. 1854, in India) had served in the ranks. Alpha had met Jessie in the early 1900s when the 18th Hussars were posted in York. She followed him to his next posting in Ireland in 1907 and they were married there. When they married, Jessie, like Tim later on, was four months pregnant.

Alpha Ellery had joined the 18th Hussars as a teenaged trooper in 1900. He served in the South African conflict and was commissioned during the Great War, when he served as a quartermaster in France and Belgium. The regiment, under Queen Mary's patronage since 1910, consolidated with the 13th Hussars in 1922. By the mid-1930s, Alpha had reached the rank of lieutenant colonel.

In January 1936 when Tim Ellery married Moke, she was twenty-two years old, a fun-loving, probably under-educated girl, and a colonel's daughter. She seems to have fitted easily into historian Margaret Macmillan's thumb-nail sketch of the ideal British Indian wife: "A skilful lawn tennis player, a good dancer, a brilliant fabricator of chaff—that being the staple commodity of Indian conversation."[4]

As with the other women in these male-oriented pages, we rarely hear Tim's voice. In March 2018, her 81-year-old son, Colin Murray, stated that his mother never wrote any letters. What we know about her comes from a handful of recorded events; from Colin's vivid, but somewhat bewildered recollections (he told us that Tim "was not a loving mother"); a few photographs from

---

[4] Margaret MacMillan, *Women of the Raj: The Mothers, Wives, and Daughters of the British Empire in India* (Random House, 2007), 110. Tim's daughter-in-law Bernice Murray told us that a photograph of Tim on water-skis had appeared on the cover of an English-language weekly in India shortly before she met Moke.

Above: Moke and Tim's marriage (January 1936)

India in the 1930s; four affectionate letters that Moke wrote to Tim in August and November 1936, discussed below, and the fond memories of Colin's wife Bernice Murray, who befriended her mother-in-law in the 1960s.[5]

Tim's unplanned pregnancy and the marriage itself had placed serious crimps in Moke's military career. Indian Army lieutenants were unofficially forbidden to marry and the army

---

5   Bernice Murray, who was immensely helpful to the authors, died in November 2019.

Moke's First Marriage

provided no financial support to officers who married before they were thirty. The postponement of the marriage until Tim was four months pregnant suggests that Moke concealed the relationship and Tim's condition from his 2/4GR colleagues until the couple had married at some distance from Bakloh and almost immediately sailed away.[6] The couple planned to have their child in England and they intended to stay for some of the time in Godalming, Surrey, with Moke's parents, who had recently leased a ten-room house. They lived there with Moke's unmarried sisters and a couple of domestic servants.

On 23 January 1936 while the newlyweds were at sea Dame Clara Butt died of cancer in her home in Oxford. Her death occurred five days after Rudyard Kipling's and three days after the death of King George V. Many commentators at the time remarked on the coincidence of the deaths because the three of them had long been hard-working luminaries of the British Empire as it drifted into its almost unnoticed closing phase. The Bishop of London presided over Dame Clara's Oxford funeral service, which was attended by the Murray family minus Moke and Tim. For a larger memorial service in London on 10 February, Moke's parents and sisters as well as "Dymoke Murray" (but not his wife) were recorded as being in attendance.[7]

Alpha and Jessie Ellery had sailed from India in March. When they got to Godalming, they had to endure a collision

---

6   The subterfuge and its aftermath, discussed below, may explain why Moke told Liam Fox that his "first wife was not welcomed by the Mess". Anthony Barnett's interview with Liam Fox, 10 August 2018. Masters, *Bugles and a Tiger*, 151 quotes an Indian Army adage: "Subalterns may not marry, captains may marry, majors should marry, colonels must marry". Masters goes on to describe the constricted, snobbish and often melancholy life the wives of British officers led in outposts of the empire such as Bakloh between the wars.

7   *The Times*, 28 January and 11 February 1936. The *Western Daily Press* of 11 February 1936, unlike *The Times*, notes that "Dymoke Murray" attended the London service.

of incompatible worlds and antagonistic social classes. Part of the problem was that Colonel Ellery didn't spring, as Edward Murray and his son both did, from the so-called "officer class". Similarly, Esther Murray's father, Kennerly Rumford, had never been a blacksmith. When the older couples met, they must have soon discovered that they had almost nothing in common. What could Alpha and Edward talk about, after all, unless it was horses? Esther for her part would have failed to recognise the distinction that Jessie had earned, enjoyed and cherished as a colonel's wife in a prestigious cavalry regiment. Jessie, in turn, probably didn't find much to admire about Esther's pretensions or what Colin, repeating Ellery family lore, has called his father's "very snobbish" family.

An Ellery family legend related by Colin has it that when Edward Murray met Alpha, he asked the colonel on the quiet for a loan of cash. He was briskly rebuffed. The quasi-comical, shaming moment tells us a good deal about both Edward the gentleman, who "felt free to cadge", while Alpha had probably been trained as a boy not to lend money to strangers.[8]

On 26 May 1936, Tim gave birth to a boy in a private clinic in Guildford, Surrey. On the birth registry the baby's name was given as Colin Dymoke Rumford Murray. Tim and Moke were listed as living with his parents. It's uncertain where Moke, Tim and Colin spent the remaining months of Moke's leave, which ended in late August 1936. At that point Moke returned to India, by himself, to rejoin his battalion in Bakloh.

Eighty-two years later, when Bernice Murray was sorting out family papers in her attic in Folkestone, she came across four chatty, affectionate letters that Moke had written to Tim soon after they parted company in August 1936. Neither Bernice

---

8 Authors' interview with the Murrays, Folkestone, September 2017.

nor Colin had ever seen the letters, three of which were written on board ship. The fourth, undated, was sent from Waziristan, where an advanced party from 2/4GR, including Moke, had been posted in November 1936. He mentions in this letter that he had only recently arrived.

While Moke had been in England 2/4GR had been preparing to move en masse to the northwest for what turned out to be two arduous years of combat and manoeuvres. According to the battalion's official history, 'The battalion had been under orders for Razmak since the beginning of 1936 and throughout that year preparations for frontier service, including training for mountain warfare, had gone steadily forward.'[9]

Above: Lt E D Murray (1936)

---

9   Macdonell and Macaulay, *A History of the 4th Prince of Wales's Own Gurkha Rifles*, vol. 1, 92.

So when Moke wrote to Tim from Razmak, he knew that he would be stationed somewhere in Waziristan for at least the next two years. He had probably learned of these arrangements when they were in England, though how the newlyweds coped with the news or what plans they may have made at the time are not documented. Bernice Murray has written that Colin had found these letters distressing. As we shall see, he never knew his father, and the letters provided the first evidence he had seen that his parents at one stage had been happily married.[10] The letters make clear, as no other evidence does, that in the afterglow of his marriage and Colin's birth, Moke was in love with Tim (whom he mysteriously addresses as "Anne"), fond of their infant son and expressed his affection with ease. None of the letters, however, suggests that a family reunion was remotely on the cards.

The first letter, dated 23 August, posted from Malta, wittily describes Moke's brief sojourn in Paris and the train trip to Marseilles, where he boarded the SS *Rawalpindi* bound for Bombay through the Suez Canal. He thanks "Anne" for the telegram she sent to the ship on its departure, and mentions that a few of his fellow passengers had travelled with him and his wife from India on another ship in January 1936. As the *Rawalpindi* was approaching Malta, Moke hurried to complete his letter, telling her: "I have nothing more to say except I miss you and Colin terribly my sweet and love you more and more. Take care of yourself darling. Much love to you both."

Moke's second letter, posted from Port Said, tells "darling Anne" that he might purchase a "toupee" [*sic*] in Port Said, noting, "I left Marseilles [heading for Surrey with Tim in January 1936] wearing my bowler hat and umbrella and also boarded at Marseilles with them! I have a good mind to arrive in Bombay in

---

10   Colin Murray generously allowed the authors to quote from the letters.

them too!" He closes the letter "your loving Dymoke." The next undated letter, posted from Aden, was the last that Moke wrote from shipboard. Poignantly, in view of what happened later, he ends with a frank expression of his longing to be with his wife:

> There is absolutely nothing to write about, Sweet, except that I miss you terribly. I lie in that damn bunk of mine at night and just think! Give my love to Colin, bless him. Oh, Sweet, I long to kiss you again. All my love, Dymoke

The final letter in the batch, posted from Razmak, mentions an earlier letter to "Anne" that hasn't survived, but tellingly doesn't refer to any letters from her. I suspect that she didn't write any. Moke closes this one with a fond reference to Colin, the last that I encountered in my research: "Colin, I expect has grown out of all recognition—has he got any teeth yet? I hope he is good at nights now he has not got me to do things for him!! Such conceit!!'

No other letters from Moke to "Anne" have survived, but it's clear that in November 1936 he was very much in love with his wife. Nothing foreshadows the estrangement that took place at some point, or over a lengthy period, between the end of 1936, when Murray wrote from Razmak, and mid-September 1939 when Tim and Colin were living in a boarding house in Folkestone, Kent. This was close to her repatriated parents and not far from where Colin Murray lives today.

I've found no evidence that Moke and Tim ever saw each other again after August 1936. The absence of documentation makes the breakdown of the marriage, terminated by a divorce brought by Tim in 1947, an indissoluble mystery, although scattered evidence suggests that the breakdown was more painful and humiliating for Moke than it was for his wife. The historian Sally Low read this chapter in draft and commented:

Playing devil's advocate, who can blame Tim for not wanting to live the stifling life of an officer's wife in India, where she was possibly considered socially below par by the other wives, or to spend her youth at home in England looking after her son and waiting for an absentee husband. Impossible to know what her psychology was, but I am picturing a young woman feeling very trapped and not particularly interested in settling down to life as a single mother/semi-widow in her early 20s. Who can blame her, really?[11]

This assessment seems very plausible. After Tim Ellery was catapulted, perhaps alarmingly, into marriage and motherhood, at twenty-two, and her husband had returned to active service in India, she opted to be relatively free and reverted to being a daughter again.

Her parents, Alpha and Jessie Ellery, travelled to India in September 1936 on the same ship, the *Strathmor*, that had taken them to England in March. We know that Tim stayed in England at least until November of that year when she received Moke's letter from Razmak. Although shipping information is not available, it seems likely that Tim never returned to India but stayed in England, perhaps with Ellery relatives until her parents returned to England in 1938. In December 2022, after he had read the draft of this biography, Colin Murray told Anthony Barnett that the only information he disagreed with were the lines that suggested he had ever returned to India.[12] Instead, he seems to have settled with his mother in Folkestone at about the time her parents returned to India.

Meanwhile, in Razmak, the 2/4GR had been absorbed into a larger Indian Army formation for extensive manoeuvres and

---

11   Sally Low, email to author, 2 July 2019.
12   Anthony Barnett, personal communication, 14 December 2022.

combat. The transfer followed the "four and two" pattern of most Gurkha battalions, which served four years in their home base and then two years in Waziristan.[13] The long posting to the northwest separated Moke from his wife and child, because, as David Gilmour has written:

> Razmak, deep in Waziristan, was one of several "non-family" stations, sometimes described as the world's largest monastery it was 6,500 feet above sea level and surrounded by arc lights and a triple circle of barbed wire. Inside lived 5,000 troops, British and Indian. And 5,000 mules that drove men half-crazy with their braying.[14]

There is also no evidence that Tim and Colin ever lived as a family in Bakloh, where Tim would have received no financial support and where the other officers' wives, most of whom were least a decade older than she was, might not have made her and Colin feel at home.[15]

In October 1938, while Moke was fighting in Waziristan, the 13/18 Hussars were posted to England, where the regiment was scheduled to refit as an armoured unit, ending its 150-year association with horses and its nine-year-long sojourn in India. Colonel Ellery and his wife thus returned to England. Three months later Alpha and Jessie had settled in Shorecroft, a suburb of Folkestone, where as an army family the Ellerys had been posted in the 1920s. In late September 1939, if not before, we know that Tim was living nearby.

The information about Tim's whereabouts at that time is recorded in the National Survey of England and Wales, which

---

13 Masters, *Bugles and a Tiger*, 131–32. Masters was on leave again in 1938. See also Gould, *Imperial Warriors*, 216.
14 Gilmour, *The British in India*, 269.
15 Masters, *Bugles and a Tiger*, 162

was launched soon after World War II began. It sought to locate and identify everyone then residing in those parts of Britain in order to provide information for wartime measures, including plans for evacuation, rationing and redirecting manpower. The survey located Tim and Colin in a boarding house in Folkestone, near her parents.[16] At the same address it noted a woman named Jenny Bolton and her husband. Jenny was four years older than Tim but coincidentally the two young women shared the same birthday and it's tempting to think that they became friends. The same survey recorded Moke's parents living in Wrecclesham, Surrey, with one domestic servant. Edward is listed as "Private means late Master of Foxhounds"—clearly the way that he wished to be remembered.

On 1 June 1940, Colonel Ellery retired from the Army on the grounds of ill health, just as the 13/18 Hussars were being evacuated from Dunkirk, abandoning their brand new tanks. For the rest of their lives, once they had settled in England, Alpha and Jessie saw a good deal of Tim and Colin, who remembers them fondly. Unsurprisingly, perhaps, after their unpropitious encounter with Murrays, the Ellerys never saw them again. Tim spent the rest of her life in different parts of Kent, remarrying in 1947, three days after her divorce from Moke became final, and for a third time in 1956. According to Colin, she "knew that her third marriage was a mistake after only two weeks". She died in 1987 at the age of seventy-four.

After Colin and Bernice married in 1967, they saw a good deal of Tim. She and Bernice became good friends, but it seems

---

[16] The survey located Moke's sister Eileen managing a restaurant for its owners in Warwickshire. Murray's parents had moved to Wrecclesham, Surrey, in 1937 and were registered there. Cicely is not recorded in the Survey. This suggests that she was overseas in September 1939. I am grateful to Andrew Hassam for recovering the survey information.

that there was always an element of wariness in Colin's relationship with his mother. After Tim's third marriage broke down, she kept a framed 1936 photograph of Moke, a glamorous Gurkha lieutenant in his rifle-green dress uniform, on her bedside table. Although she apparently didn't want to forget him, Tim never tried to find out where he was, or even if he was alive.[17]

In July 1947, Tim and Moke's marriage was officially dissolved "by reason that Murray, the respondent, had deserted the petitioner without cause for a period of at least three years immediately preceding the divorce petition"—that is since April 1944.[18] Tim remarried almost immediately and her second marriage lasted for ten years. Colin Murray told us ruefully that his attractive, insouciant mother, who "loved dancing", had "enjoyed the war".[19] In those years, Colin was sent to boarding school and during the holidays when he was in Folkestone his mother often palmed him off on her parents for extended periods of time.

From 1941 until 1957, when Colin turned twenty-one, Moke paid his school fees at successive public schools: Hoe Place Preparatory School in Guildford, Surrey, from 1941 to 1947, and Allhallows School in Rousden, Devon from 1950 to 1953. Colin probably spent the years 1947–50 in Allhallows Junior

---

[17] In July 2018, Bernice Murray emailed Anthony Barnett and me a copy of this photograph. It shows him in dress uniform, resting one hand on the hilt of his sword. Since it is doubtful Moke took the uniform on leave to England it's likely that the photograph was taken in an Indian studio, perhaps shortly before his wedding.

[18] Bernice Murray scanned the divorce documents and sent them to Anthony Barnett and me in November 2018. Tim probably postponed suing for divorce to avoid the legal expenses that were involved. Similarly, Moke and his second wife, who separated in 1967, never bothered to get divorced.

[19] From a different perspective Murray told Liam Fox that for him at least "the war had been great fun". Interview with David Chandler, September 2018.

School.[20] It's unclear when or how Moke made these arrangements. According to Bernice Murray, Colin didn't find out about his father's sponsorship until he was in in his teens. But apart from making these financial arrangements, Moke had nothing to do with Colin. He never saw him, wrote to him or showed any interest in his whereabouts, achievements or well-being. A tentative effort on Colin's part to make contact in the 1960s, after he survived a severe automobile accident, never reached Moke or was ignored. Moke never mentioned Colin to his Worthing neighbours, and Colin and Bernice first learned of Moke's death when we interviewed them in Folkestone in 2018.

Moke probably felt that the relatively generous arrangements he had made for Colin's education were all that he owed to his estranged wife and child. His indifference and lack of curiosity must have been bewildering and hurtful to Colin, but the impasse failed to produce sufficient regret for either of them to try to create a relationship. Their contact seems to have come to an end less than a year after Colin's birth.

When Colin turned seventeen in May 1953, shortly before his father led a contingent of Gurkhas in the parade at Queen Elizabeth's coronation, he ran away from Allhallows and joined the Royal Tank Regiment as a trooper, consciously or not following the lead of his grandfather, Alpha Ellery, more than half a century earlier. Colin saw service in Suez, Aden and elsewhere until 1966 when he was honourably discharged as a sergeant. He refused at least one offer to apply for a commission. Colin also

---

[20] Hoe Place School was founded in 1928 and has survived under a variety of names. The school is co-educational now, but enrolled only boys when Colin attended it. The school's Surrey location suggests that the Murray family may have been helpful in selecting it, but Colin does not remember seeing them in the years when he attended the school. Allhallows, where Colin was on the rugby team and was relatively happy, was founded in 1515, and closed in the 1990s due to insufficient enrolments.

Moke's First Marriage

told us that in his first four years in the Army (i.e. until he turned twenty-one) his mother failed to set aside or forward any of the funds that Moke was still providing for him.

Anecdotal evidence suggests that the marriage breakdown had become bitter and vindictive before Tim sued Moke in 1947. Lieutenant Colonel John Cross, a retired Gurkha officer who had served with Moke in Malaya, whom I contacted about my interest in Moke, sent me an email, stating, 'A rumour was current among Gurkha officers in the 1950s that Murray had when much younger, married a bar-girl and so had a constant money problem for her maintenance.'[21]

When I replied to Colonel Cross, informing him of Moke's marriage to Tim, the colonel wrote that he'd never heard of Tim, and added, "Moke never talked to me about women." I think that the bar girl story originated with Moke before Cross met him in Malaya, probably while drinking with fellow students at the Indian Army's Staff College in Quetta in 1947.

Moke was part of the last British intake there between February and October. In Quetta, Moke was in administrative limbo, as negotiations continued among authorities in India, Britain and Nepal about the fate of the Gurkha battalions and their British officers after India gained its independence. Amid this uncertainty, while Moke had no idea where he would go next, his estranged wife sued him for divorce. By anecdotally transforming a fun-loving, shallow colonel's daughter into a nameless bar girl, Moke whited out his marriage and showed a certain disdain towards women as a whole that was probably shared with

---

21 Email from Colonel Cross, 7 April 2018. When on duty in London in the 1950s Moke told a fellow Gurkha officer, Alistair Rose, that his first wife had not been "acceptable to the Mess". Liam Fox, interview with Anthony Barnett, August 2018. It is uncertain when or how "the Mess" expressed its disapproval, but it seems unlikely that Tim ever spent any time in Bakloh, where she might not have been welcome.

many of his military colleagues.[22] The much vaunted public school ethos, after all, had almost no room for women, and the empire itself, in John Tosh's words, "was quintessentially a male arena, where men worked better without the company of women."[23]

That said, it seems clear that there was more to Moke's denigration of Tim in Quetta than can be blamed on his male chauvinism or cold-heartedness. He must have been hurt by Tim's failure to join him in India, and perhaps even more if she sailed from Sialkot for England with her parents in October 1938. Although Tim's application for divorce cited Moke's "desertion", the reverse seems more likely: Tim deserted Moke, perhaps understandably.

From a twenty-first-century perspective oriented towards the victims of mistreatment and abuse, Moke's behaviour towards Tim and Colin is hard to justify, even admitting that in England's upper middle class emotionally distant fathers seem often to have been the rule. Emotionally distant mothers such as Tim seem to have attracted less attention in scholarly literature. Her separation from Moke began in 1936, when she failed to take up residence in Bakloh, and this decision led on to the collapse of the marriage later. By 1941, when he started paying for Colin's schooling, Moke probably felt it was permissible (or the "done thing") to airbrush Tim, pay for Colin's education and get on with his faintly blotted military career.

---

22 Gould, *Imperial Warriors*, 220–22.
23 John Tosh, *A Man's Place: Masculinity and the Middle-Class Home in Victorian England* (New Haven: Yale University Press, 1999), 174.

FOUR

On the Fringes of Empire, 1937–1942

THE TROUBLES THAT LAY AHEAD FOR TIM AND MURRAY, of course, were unforeseeable. In September 1936, when Moke returned to India and hastened to Bakloh, he soon met up with Masters, who had also recently returned from leave. The two of them, joined by their 2/4GR colleague Lieutenant John Strickland, spent a convivial evening drinking orange-scented rum, a Gurkha standby, at the Gurkha Officers' Club. The three men were about to embark in combat service for the first time, this topic was clearly one that they discussed in the Gurkha mess. Murray probably knew that his marriage was approaching a new phase in his life that might not have included living with his wife and son. Whether or not he discussed this issue with his comrades-in-arms is impossible to say.

The time the three men spent together constitute a poignant imperial moment as they were about to embark on a major military campaign in a sustained defence of the Raj. They were made welcome by their subordinates at the Club, as they knew they would be, even though Gurkha officers were not allowed, except on rare occasions, into the British officers' mess. Fondly recalling the occasion twenty years later, Masters wrote: "We were there till very late and came away in the moonlight".[1] Although Moke and Masters fought together in 2/4GR in Waziristan in 1937, Moke disappears from Masters' memoir at this point.

Throughout 1937 and 1938, Moke played a small part in a massive British and Indian military campaign in Waziristan against an anti-British religious leader named Haji Mizali Khan (1897–1960), better known as the Faqir of Ipi. The Faqir's well-armed, highly motivated forces had repeatedly crossed into India to harass, pillage, kidnap and kill local, non-Moslem populations. Toward the end of 1936, in the brisk and self-confident wording of the 4GR's official history, we learn that the Faqir "fled to the territory of the Tori Kel Wazirs ... where he found little difficulty raising agitation against British authority, for the Tori Kel had long been nursing imaginary grievances against the Government."[2]

The campaign "represented the largest scale fighting carried out by the Army in India since the 1919–1924 operations."[3] Between November 1936 and the end of 1937, over 50,000 British, Indian and irregular troops, equipped with machine guns, artillery, RAF aircraft, motorized transport, light tanks, thousands of mules and a cavalry unit were pitted against an estimated 5,000 Waziris, armed with knives and rifles, a contempt for the Raj, a love of fighting, and an intimate knowledge of the desolate Waziri landscape. British and Indian forces never captured the

---

[1] Masters, *Bugles and a Tiger*, 181.
[2] Macdonell and Macaulay, *A History of the 4th Prince of Wales's Own Gurkha Rifles, 1857–1937*, 1:92–93. The 1938 Alexander Kordaa film, *The Drum*, set in the north-west frontier, casts Raymond Massey as a figure resembling the Faqir. Massey's brother had been Governor-General of Canada.
[3] T. R Moreman, *The Army in India and the Development of Frontier Warfare, 1849–1947* (Basingstoke: Palgrave, 2001), 166.

On the Fringes of Empire, 1937–1942

Faqir, and his forces, although they suffered hundreds of casualties, never formally surrendered.[4]

In his memoir, John Masters pathologized the Waziris as seemingly viewing war more as a sport but were perhaps not as barbaric as the British Raj made them out to be. In his interpretation of Waziri culture, he made the case that:

> The tribesmen looked on war as an honorable, exciting, and manly exercise. When they had no quarrel with the British or the Afghans they arranged one among themselves. Many of them clearly thought the Government of India organized Frontier wars on the same basis. At least, there seems no other reasonable explanation of the fact that when a campaign was over scores of Pathans [Waziris] used to apply to the Political Agents for the Frontier Medal with the appropriate clasp. I think this request was reasonable. As they pointed out, they were British subjects and they had fought in the battles so thoughtfully organized by the King Emperor Across the Seas. Indeed, without their co-operation, the war would have been a complete fiasco and no one would have got any medals.[5]

The conflict in Waziristan between the Raj and the Waziris prompted by the Faqir of Ipi was, in some sense, a game for both sides. In the case of the British Raj, it was part of the Great Game as the British Empire sought to secure the northernmost borders of the Jewel in the Crown against intrusion—through Afghanistan—by the Russian Empire. For the Waziris, if Masters' characterization is accurate, it was a habitual part of life on the frontier.

---

[4] In 1949–1953 in Malaya, Moke was once again part of an overwhelming Commonwealth force confronting a few thousand inspired, seasoned, lightly-armed guerrillas. See Chapter 9 below.

[5] Masters, *Bugles and a Tiger*, 212.

Snapshots from the Raj; a photo essay

Northwest Frontier 1937–1938. These photographs were taken (or organised) by Moke. An account of the provenance and subsequent history of them is on page 47.

On the Fringes of Empire, 1937–1942

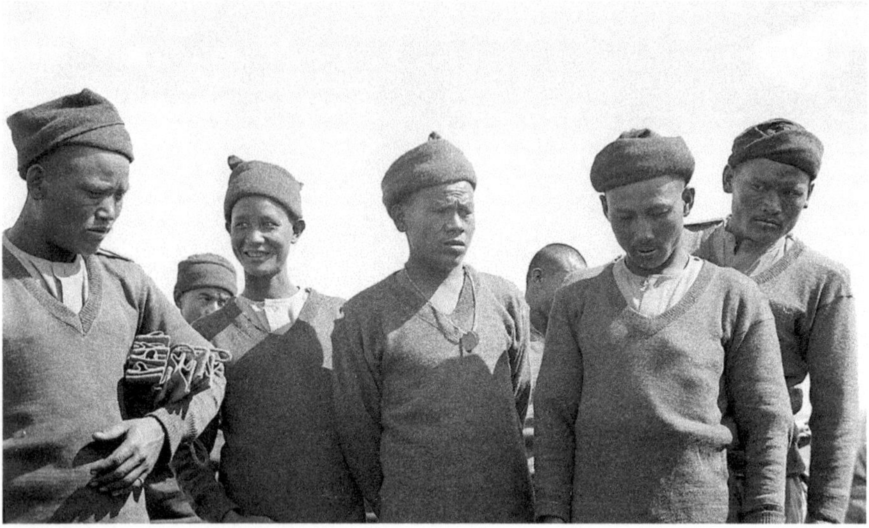

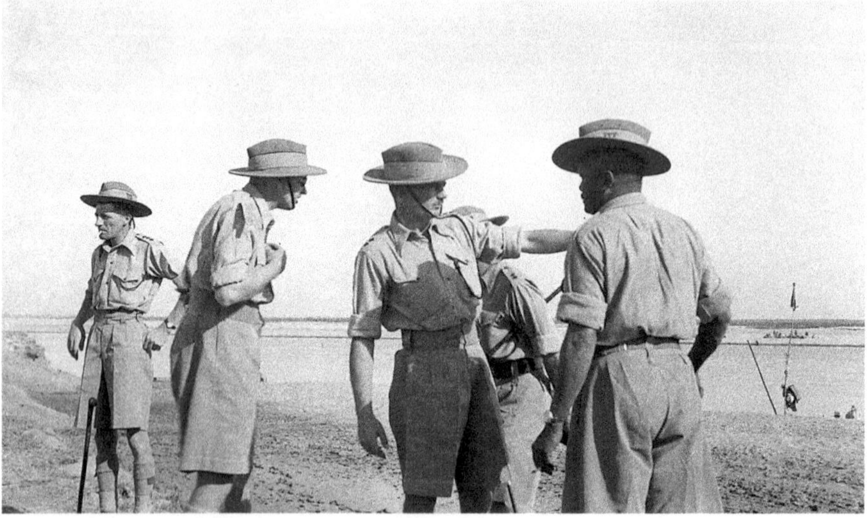

On the Fringes of Empire, 1937–1942

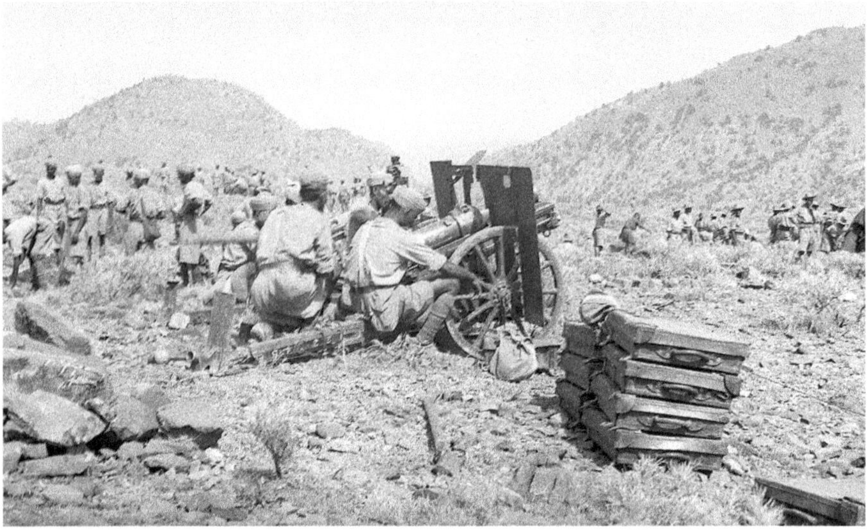

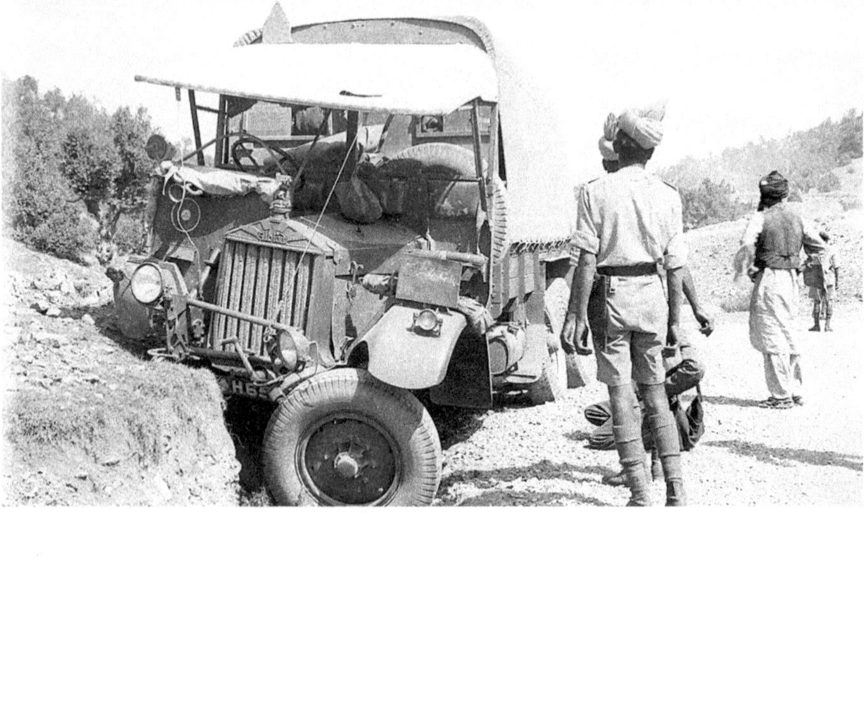

On the Fringes of Empire, 1937–1942

In 1937, when the campaign against the Faqir and his followers was entering its second year, 2/4GR went into action in April. On 26 June, "B" Company under Moke's command, engaged in combat and in the words of the official history "accounted for" over twenty of the enemy. On the same day, over a flat stretch of land, a squadron of Indian Army cavalry "charged, but the enemy retired to cover".[6] This may have been the last example of a British Army cavalry charge. It's worth remembering that at this point, the 13/18 Hussars were still unmechanized. The battalion didn't see any further action in the first eight months of 1938, but the regimental history tells us that "in September a notable operation was carried out in which the battalion played a prominent part". On the night of 11 September 2/4GR and other units formed part of a fast-moving column made up of Indian, Gurkha and British troops commanded by Lieutenant Colonel Murray-Lyon. In the words of the regimental history:

> We had an exciting battle for the Pakkalita Sar (better known as the Crag). We were advanced guard at the time and expected trouble at this spot, so the CO stopped when we came to it and prepared a proper fire plan and registered our guns before launching "A" Company under Lieutenant E.D. Murray into the attack.[7]

In what the regimental history calls "a very smart bit of work" no one in the company was killed, but Moke, along with two Gurkhas, was lightly wounded. He recovered from his wound to lead the second exercise two weeks later. In the two sorties, "A" Company suffered no fatalities, while its men killed an estimated

---

[6] Moke's colleagues Masters, Strickland, and Fairweather commanded 2/4GR companies at different stages of the 1937 and 1938 campaigns.
[7] Mackay, *A History of the 4th Prince of Wales's Own Gurkha Rifles 1938–1948*, 2:12–14.

thirty-five Waziri. Moke's personal copy of the second incursion report, which he submitted a week later, has a note in his handwriting that reads, "As I passed through Battalion Headquarters the C.O. [Murray-Lyon] murmured, 'Well done A Company'. This was great praise for 2/4GR."[8]

Moke's campaign ribbons indicate that he was mentioned in despatches for his work in Waziristan in 1937–1938. I suspect that the award was connected to one or both of these incursions, which is the most likely explanation for why Moke kept his written reports among his papers.

In January 1939, probably at his request, Moke transferred from 2/4GR to the Assam Rifles, a force of Gurkha battalions with police responsibilities that was maintained by the Assam provincial administration on the eastern edge of India.[9] By then, Tim was almost certainly back in England with Colin and her parents. Although no documentation survives, I am fairly certain that when someone informed Moke that his wife and child had left India for good, he may have found the prospect of continuing in 2/4GR in Bakloh uncongenial. He probably also opted for higher pay in Assam and a dramatic change of scene. The Assam Rifles, founded in 1835, was the oldest paramilitary force in India, one that existed as part of the Indian Army's responsibility to act in 'Aid of the Civil Power' as part of internal security considerations alongside its jurisdiction in conventional warfare and

---

8   Mackay, marginalia.
9   Murray's military records suggest that in 1940 he established a formal connection with 6GR but he never seems to have served in that Battalion's home base of Abbottabad.

policing the North-West Frontier.[10] Reporting to civil authorities rather than to military ones, its mission was to maintain order along India's forested eastern frontier, an area known generically as Assam. Pay was higher in the Assam Rifles than it was in regular Gurkha units, because living conditions were for the most part correspondingly harsh.

Between 1 April and early September 1939, six platoons of the Assam Rifles were assigned to maintain order on the oil fields near the company town of Digboi during a long, intermittently violent strike.[11] Two months earlier, in February, approximately 6,000 workers at the Digboi oil fields and refinery had formed a union, encouraged by Congress politicians hostile to the Raj, including Nehru.[12] The Assam Oil Company management, who were British, recognized the union but refused to deal with it on substantive issues. In early April, after presenting an ambitious list of claims, the workers went on strike, initially for a week. The claims included unconditional recognition of the Assam Oil Company Labour Union, low wages, the retrenchment security of services, good quarters to all workers with due regard to the number of family members, forty-four hours of work in a week for all workers including medical staff, sweepers, production department, chowkidars and Bungla servants, service rules with provisions for gratuity, old age pension, one month privilege

---

[10] Daniel Marston, *The Indian Army and the End of the Raj* (Cambridge: Cambridge University Press, 2014), 37–38. For more on the Indian Army's internal security role, see Srinath Raghavan, 'Protecting the Raj: The Army in India and Internal Security, 1919–1939', *Small Wars and Insurgencies*, 16, no. 3 (2005): 253–79; Gyanesh Kudaisya, '"In Aid of Civil Power": The Colonial Army in Northern India, 1919–1942', *Journal of Imperial and Commonwealth History*, 32, no. 1 (2004): 41–68.

[11] Dipankar Banerjee, "Working Class Movement in Assam Assam Oil Company Workers Strike of 1939" (PhD, Gauhati University, 2000), 97.

[12] Ditee Moni Baruah, "Assam Oil Company and the Labour Strike in Digboi, 1939", *Vidyasagar University Journal of History* 8 (2019): 161.

leave, festival leave.[13] Soon afterwards, prodded by its leaders and by Indian nationalists elsewhere, the union voted to extend the strike indefinitely. At that point the management began replacing strikers with workers brought in from outside, which exacerbated the situation, and six platoons of Assam Riflemen were sent to maintain order and to guard the oil fields and the administrative buildings.[14]

At around 9:00 PM on 17 April 1939 a section of Assam Rifles under Moke's command was set upon by several hundred strikers, many of whom were armed with heavy sticks. The riflemen fired a volley into the crowd, presumably on Moke's orders, killing two strikers and wounding four.[15] The subsequent official inquiry, convened two days after the incident by the Congress-controlled Assam government, revealed that Moke himself had fired a shot that killed a middle-aged oil worker named Chanu Ahir. The inquiry produced a 32-page typewritten report that has not survived.[16] Moke and seventy-two other witnesses testified at the inquiry. The examining magistrate, in his report, ruled that all the shots had been fired in self-defense.

In his final years in Worthing, boasting that he was an

---

13   Bijoy Gogoi, "Organized Labour Movement in Assam: A Historical Study between the Period of Two World Wars," *International Journal of Humanities & Social Science Studies*, May 2017, 455.
14   Banerjee, "Working Class Movement"; Ditee Moni Baruah, "Polity and Petroleum Making of an Oil Industry in Assam, 1825–1980" (PhD, Indian Institute of Technology Guwahati, 2014), 176–88, https://www.gyan.iitg. ac.in:8080/xmlui/handle/123456789/576. See also *Times of India*, 16 May and 27 June 1939. On conditions in Digboi in the 1930s – a company town with two clubs for Europeans — see Gilmour, *The British in India*, 298.
15   "Digboi Firing Justified," *The Statesman* 15 May 1939. Supporters of Congress rejected the magistrate's unpublished findings at the time and condemned *The Statesman* for being consistently pro-British.
16   Banerjee fails to cite the report in his copious bibliography, although on the basis of second-hand information about it he rejects its findings out of hand and accuses the examining magistrate, probably justly, of anti-striker bias.

excellent shot, Moke told Liam Fox that during the Digboi strike he had shot and killed an apparent ringleader, firing at 200 yards in a monsoon downpour. When Fox asked him why he had killed the man, he replied, off-handedly "Because he was a bad hat" — dredging up a phrase from *Boys' Own Paper* that he had probably absorbed in his youth.[17] Keeping the peace for the Raj, and British companies, occasionally involved killing unruly people. On this occasion it seems likely that Murray fired at point blank range using his revolver. In the rainy darkness an accurate shot at 200 yards would have been all but impossible to make, and the enquiry heard from witnesses that Moke, before he fired, had been hit on the head by a staff wielding striker. Moke also told Liam Fox that soon after the affray, Nehru called openly for his arrest. I don't believe that he made this up, but I've been unable so far to locate any documentary evidence for the accusation.

No further casualties occurred for the remaining four months of the strike, which attracted wide attention in India, where Gandhi, Nehru, and the Congress leaders supported it, and in London, where critical questions were raised in the House of Commons. On 12 June 1939, for example, John Jagger (Labour) raised a question to the Under-Secretary of State for India:

> Whether he can make a statement about the use of troops against strikers in the oilfields of Assam; in particular, whether they opened fire on the strikers without previous warning; whether any civil officials were present when the firing took place; whether they gave advice or instructions; and whether the troops were asked for by the Provincial Government?

In response, the Under-Secretary Lieutenant-Colonel Muirhead (Conservative) asserted:

---

[17] The journal appeared between 1879 and 1967.

No troops have been employed in connection with the strike at Digboi. The subsequent parts of the question do not, therefore, arise. A patrol of the Assam Rifles, however, was involved on 18th April in a shooting incident in which three persons were killed and five injured, apart from injuries to members of the patrol. The Assam Rifles are police, and their actions are within the responsibility for law and order of the Provincial Government.

I suspect that following the inquiry Moke was shifted elsewhere for his personal safety. Following his encounter with the strikers, and after killing one of them, he was awarded the Indian Police Medal (for Gallantry). From a 2023 perspective of course, the gallantry of the encounter is hard to perceive. It must be remembered, however, that other methods of crowd control than gunshot were not widely available at the time. He was proud of the decoration and told Liam Fox that he believed he was the only Indian Army officer to have received it. The Digboi strike ended in September 1939 when World War II began in Europe and the Assam oilfields were taken over by the Indian government. None of the strikers were reinstated. Since independence, the strike has achieved iconic status from nationalist Indian writers and the casualties have been treated as martyrs.[18]

I have been unable to find out much about Murray's activities with the Assam Rifles in 1940 and 1941. We know that he shifted his Gurkha parent unit from 4GR to 6GR in January 1940 and that he was promoted to captain six months later, and to major in 1942. In January 1940, Moke's father Edward died in Wrecclesham, Surrey where he and his wife had moved in 1937. There's no evidence that he and Moke were ever close and Moke's Worthing neighbor Liam Fox does not recall Murray ever

---

18   Banerjee, "Working Class Movement," passim.

mentioning him. By mid-1941 Moke was serving as adjutant of the 3rd (Naga Hills) Battalion of the Assam Rifles, posted to the town of Kohima, just inside Assam, where he worked closely with the Naga tribespeople who inhabited the area. He also became familiar with the alluring, mountainous, heavily forested landscape around the peaceful villages of Imphal and Kohima, where a series of ferocious battles were fought by Allied and Japanese forces between April and August 1944.

In an email, Doug Henderson, the collections officer at the Gurkha Museum wrote that he was unable to locate any material in the museum archives related to the activities of the Assam Rifles in Assam in 1940–1941.

In the early days of December 1941, the Second World War finally arrived in Southeast Asia and for most of the next four years Moke was swept up in the fighting, emerging as a decorated lieutenant colonel and colonel mentioned in despatches.

FIVE

Moke's War

On 7–8 December 1941 Japanese forces attacked the US naval base at Pearl Harbor in Hawaii, the US protectorate of the Philippines, the British colony of Hong Kong and most of mainland and insular South East Asia. The combined air, sea and land attacks were launched from bases established earlier in the year—with French permission—in what was then called French Indochina. The first Japanese action against Burma occurred on 11 December 1941, with the capture of an airfield at Victoria Point.[1] In mid-January 1942, the Japanese 33rd and 55th divisions invaded Burma from Thailand, a month before the fall of Singapore.[2] Both divisions had extensive combat experience in China and Moke would encounter elements of the 55th Division in Cambodia in October 1945.

When the so-called Pacific War began, Moke was the adjutant of an Assam Rifles unit operating in the Assamese region of Imphal and Kohima. Both towns were to be the sites of decisive

---

1   James Lunt, *A Hell of a Licking: The Retreat from Burma 1941–2* (London: Collins, 1986), 80.
2   Moke would later accept the surrender of elements of the 55th Division in Phnom Penh in November 1945. See Chapter 8 below.

battles in 1944. Moke, now a captain, had been posted to the area at the beginning of 1940 during what was called the Phony War in Europe.

Fighting was severe around the Burmese capital Rangoon, but by the middle of March 1942, the British, Indian and Chinese troops in the colony were in a hard-fought but humiliating 900-mile retreat towards China and the Indian border, pursued by well-trained, well-led and highly aggressive Japanese forces. The retreat was the longest in British military history and cost some 1500 British and Indian army lives.[3]

The speed, brutality and thoroughness of the Japanese attacks took local people and their colonial patrons by surprise. Non-colonised Thailand, which had a pro-Japanese regime, surrendered almost at once. Over the next two months (February–March) Hong Kong, Singapore, Malaya and the Netherlands East Indies fell and more than 80,000 Dutch, British, Indian, American and Australian servicemen had been taken prisoner. Fortunately for the Allied cause, the monsoon broke in April and slowed the Japanese advance.[4] Between March and June 1942 thousands of exhausted Allied troops and perhaps as many as 400,000 civilian refugees crowded along the Assamese–Burmese border, where they joined some 100,000 British and Indian Army troops who had been hastily brought in to block a Japanese invasion of India.[5] In these chaotic weeks, units of the Assam Rifles,

---

3   Louis Allen, *Burma: The Longest War 1941–45* (London: Dent, 1984), 639. Allen links the relatively low number of Allied casualties to the skilful generalship of Major General William Slim, an important figure in what follows. Slim arrived in Burma on 9 March 1942, three days after the fall of Rangoon.
4   For a detailed narrative of the retreat see Allen, *Burma*, 1–90; Warren Alan, *Burma 1942: The Road from Rangoon to Mandalay* (London: Continuum, 2011); Lunt, *A Hell of a Licking*, passim.
5   Hugh Tinker, "A Forgotten Long March: The Indian Exodus from Burma, 1942", *Journal of Southeast Asian Studies* 6, no. 1 (1975): 10.

including Moke's, did what they could to assist the rag tag horde that was flooding out of Burma into Assam. In 1942–44 neither the Japanese nor the Allies chose to mount a full-scale offensive.

In May 1942 Moke was transferred from the Assam Rifles to a newly formed irregular unit known as V Force that had General Wavell established a month earlier, at what was probably the lowest point in Allied military fortunes in South East Asia. Wavell conceived of V Force as a clandestine, intelligence-gathering formation that would operate in six zones along the India–Burma border. V Force units were expected to "harass the Japanese lines of communications, patrol enemy occupied territory, carry out post-occupational sabotage and provide post-occupational intelligence".[6] The ominous phrase "post occupational" suggests that Wavell feared and had to prepare for the possibility of a successful Japanese occupation of much of Assam. In this case V Force units were expected to stay behind.

The first commander of V Force was Brigadier A. Felix-Williams, who had led paramilitary forces on the Northwest Frontier in the 1930s. Later in the year V Force came under the command of the 23rd Indian Division that had recently been posted to Assam. This division was led by Major General Reginald Savory (1884–1980), an energetic, forward-looking

---

6 Anonymous, "The Story of V Force: The Phantom Army of Burma", *Indian Army Review*, November 1946. An abridged version appeared in *Military Review* in 1947; According to Adrian Fort, *Archibald Wavell: The Life and Times of an Imperial Servant* (London: Jonathan Cape, 2009), 296, V Force was the brainchild of Captain Peter Fleming, who was attached to Wavell's staff. Until the 1960s Peter was much better known than his younger brother Ian. Peter had conceived of similar units operating after a successful German invasion of Britain.

officer who soon befriended Moke.[7]

Before V Force came under Savory's command, each V Force sector had five British officers, four platoons of Assam Riflemen (all Gurkhas) and up to 1000 locally recruited tribesmen. Moke's first V Force unit, the 3rd, served the towns of Imphal and Kohima as well as the surrounding heavily forested landscape, an area he had come to know intimately before the war. By the end of 1942, however, V Force units had been broken down into small, self-sufficient detachments posted systematically across 9000 square miles of the heavily forested terrain of eastern Assam.[8]

Regarding his time with V Force, Moke wrote to Anthony Barnett in 1982 that no history of the unit existed, "but there should be one. It was three years [sic] of constant laughs." Moke did not elaborate, but an anonymous essay about V Force published in India in 1946 survives in his papers that mentions him twice. I suspect that he wrote it. Towards the end of 1942, the essay relates, Moke briefed General Wavell for half an hour about V Force activities. Wavell, famously a man of few words, replied, "Good. Remember I back you. Commission your own officers. If you need help, let me know. Good night."[9]

---

[7] See A.J.F Doulton, *The Fighting Cock, Being the History of the 23d Indian Division 1942–1947* (Aldershot: Gale & Polden, 1951), 46. According to Doulton, in October 1942 an ill-informed V Force officer had spread a "wild rumour" that 1000 Japanese troops were approaching his outpost. From then on V units had more personnel and operated in demarcated areas of responsibility. Also, when Savory's division arrived in Assam, Savory issued an order describing the purpose of the 23rd Division as (a) stop the Japanese invading India, and (b) defeat them.

[8] Anonymous, "The Story of V Force", 11.

[9] Anonymous, "The Story of V Force", 11. An independent unit such as V Force inevitably attracted eccentrics. In a letter to Moke dated 6 May 1983 Ursula Betts writes of a V Force colleague "known to the troops as the Bearded Major who travelled around with a Chinaman, a wireless telephone set that went straight to GJQ in Delhi and a squad of Naga porters".

An intrepid British ethnographer named Ursula Graham Bower, later Betts (1914–1988), had been living since 1939 among the Naga tribespeople of Assam. In August 1942 she was recruited to V Force with the rank of captain. For the next two years she commanded a V Force unit in Assam, as did several other civilians, all male, who had pre-war experience in the region. As a regular soldier, Moke was the exception in V Force rather than the rule.[10] Bower was an alert observer with an intimate knowledge of Assam, its landscape and its people. She adapted quickly to her new, quasi-military role. In her sprightly memoir, *Naga Path*, she wrote that in 1943 her V Force unit consisted of "150 native scouts, 1 service rifle, 1 shotgun and 70 muzzle-loaders".[11] Units such as hers and Moke's, or the one commanded by Ursula's future husband Tim Betts, were never equipped for battle. Instead, they were intended to provide intelligence by messenger and radio to British and Indian units about Japanese troop movements in their respective areas.

Bower and Moke had met socially in Kohima in 1940. They went their separate ways after that and in 1942–44 their V Force units were not contiguous. They renewed their acquaintance by mail in 1976 but they didn't meet again until 1983, when a letter from Betts mentions how good it was to see Moke "after all these years". Moke kept seventeen letters from Ursula Betts among his papers as well as the drafts of three letters that he wrote to her.[12] These amiable exchanges, discussed in Chapter Eleven,

---

10   Anonymous, "The Story of V Force".
11   Ursula Graham Bower, *Naga Path* (Murray, 1951); See also Paul Cheesright, "Queen without a Throne: Ursula Graham Bower and the Burma Campaign", *Asian Affairs* 45, no. 2 (2014): 289–99; C.A. Bayly and Tim Harper, *Forgotten Wars: The End of Britain's Asian Empire* (London: Allen Lane, 2007), 202–4, 354–55.
12   The Moke–Betts correspondence began in 1976, seems to have broken off until 1983 and ended in 1986, two years before Ursula's death.

give us welcome glimpses of a self-confident, middle-aged Moke in conversation with an outgoing, intelligent person whom he admired and was fond of.[13]

In "Some Notes to Amuse Myself", a light-hearted typescript that Moke assembled in the 1980s, now housed in the Imperial War Museum, he wrote: "At the end of 1942, I was pushed off to England after three monsoons under the banana leaf."[14] Moke's temporary absence from V Force appears in his military records as "war leave". In fact he travelled to London to accompany his severely wounded V Force colleague Captain Bruce Sutherland, who was to be awarded a Military Cross by King George VI in Buckingham Palace. Sutherland's citation, reprinted in *The Times*, reads as follows:

> Encountering such strong opposition that farther progress of his patrol became impossible he ordered his men to hide in the jungle while he went forward alone. He penetrated deep into enemy territory and surviving much danger and hardship returned with information of the highest value. Captain Sutherland's attempt to save his men, however, was unavailing for they were later found gagged, mutilated and dead, tied to trees in the jungle.[15]

Sutherland wore a prosthetic leg. In "Some Notes", describing the ceremony at the palace, Moke recalled that his companion stumbled and almost fell as he backed away after receiving the medal. The King reached out and steadied him.

---

13 I am grateful to Doug Henderson, the collections officer at the Gurkha Museum, for locating these letters among Murray's papers.
14 "Some Notes to Amuse Myself", typescript in Murray's papers held by the Imperial War Museum. I am grateful to the IWM for their assistance when I visited the museum in 2016 and 2017.
15 *The Times*, 8 December 1942. I'm grateful to Andrew Hassam for finding this reference.

When he was in England, Moke probably visited his widowed mother in Wrecclesham, Surrey, where she was living with her daughter Eileen. It's tempting to think that they spent Christmas 1942 together. There's no evidence that Moke made contact with his estranged wife Tim and their son Colin, who were living in Folkestone near Tim's parents. Nevertheless, during his time in England Moke may have finalised the arrangements intended to finance Colin's schooling. He was back "under the banana leaf" in February 1943, commanding a substantial V Force post on the Assamese bank of the Chindwin.

At this time a limited, idiosyncratic Allied offensive into Burma was taking shape. It involved recently assembled units called Long Range Penetration Groups or LRPGs, nick-named Chindits. With Wavell's support the Chindits had been training in India for several months. They were inspired and led by Brigadier Orde Wingate (1903–1944), a charismatic, talented and perhaps mentally unstable leader, whom a recent author has compared to Captain Ahab in Melville's novel *Moby-Dick*.[16] Like many others in this book, Wingate had been born in India. He had earned DSOs in Palestine in the 1930s (where he came to Wavell's favourable attention) and in Abyssinia in World War II. In both cases, Wingate was convinced that he was doing God's work. In his view LRPGs would consist of several columns of Chindits supplied by air that could penetrate what Wingate called "the guts of the enemy" and inflict substantial damage before marching back to safety.

Wingate's proposal appealed to many, starting with his patron General Wavell, and dismayed others, including General William Slim (commander of the Burma Corps), but as Louis Allen has

---

16 F.J. McLynn, *Burma Campaign: Disaster into Triumph, 1942–45* (New Haven: Yale University Press, 2014), 270.

written, Wingate's first proposed excursion, code-named Longcloth, had three overriding virtues: "it had *panache*, it had glamour, it had *chic*".[17] These three words didn't match anything that British and Indian forces had accomplished in the Burma theatre so far.

Longcloth was launched into Burma on 14 February 1943, shortly after Moke had returned to duty with V Force. Before the columns marched off General Wavell addressed them in a simple ceremony in which he wished the men well. In a poignant reversal of military custom he gave, rather than returned, a salute.[18] Longcloth, as planned, lasted for about three months. The eight Chindit columns suffered heavy casualties and inflicted little significant damage on Japanese troops or installations. On 27 April, Acting Brigadier Bernard Fergusson (1911–1980), a Black Watch officer seconded to the Chindits, arrived at the west bank of the Chindwin with some exhausted survivors of his Longcloth column. Crossing to safety, several Gurkhas, unable to swim, drowned in the wide, swift-flowing river. Of the 318 men who had set out with Fergusson only ninety-five survived the campaign and the river crossing. Another twenty-nine survived as prisoners of the Japanese. All the other Longcloth columns suffered as severely. Nonetheless, the operation surprised the Japanese and showed that British Commonwealth forces were capable of penetrating deep into Burma and that General Slim, Wingate's immediate superior, might be preparing for offensive action.[19]

---

17   Allen, *Burma*, 119.
18   Wilfred Burchett, *Wingate Adventure* (Melbourne: Cheshire, 1944), 26; For similar accounts see David Halley, *With Wingate in Burma* (W. Hodge & Co.: Glasgow, 1945), 52; Allen, *Burma*, 122. Allen refers to the ceremony as involving "a few embarrassed words of farewell" from Wavell, who must have believed that the Chindit columns would sustain heavy casualties. They did.
19   William Joseph Slim, *Defeat into Victory* (London: Cassell & Co., 1956), 172. Slim calls Longcloth "an expensive failure".

Moke's War

In his upbeat elegantly written book about Longcloth, Fergusson notes the "kindness he received from Colonel Murray and his officers" when Fergusson and remnants of his column reached Moke's outpost on the Chindwin.[20] It is tempting to imagine Moke's mentioning family connections with Eton and the Black Watch. In "Some Notes" Moke recalled: "Fergusson and what remained of his column spent that first night at my headquarters. He held a Thanksgiving service the next morning [which was Easter Sunday] on a hill just above."[21]

Wingate himself crossed the Chindwin further downstream two days later with a handful of soldiers minus several Gurkhas who drowned in the river. Murray continues, "Before he went on, I had the signal honour of having Wingate held under arrest by my concealed guard [who found him] rummaging in my office." Moke met Wingate soon afterwards, apologised for the arrest and offered him some whisky, only to learn that the exhausted brigadier, born into the Plymouth Brethren, was a teetotaller.

One day later Wingate left for Imphal, where he stayed briefly with General Savory, the commander of the 23rd Indian Division. In terms of what happened to Wingate and his reputation soon afterwards, Savory's diary for 1 May 1943 records that once Wingate had bathed, shaved, rested and borrowed a uniform from Savory, "the first question he asked was: 'Does this mean a court martial?'"[22] Wingate's "gut reaction" to Longcloth, in other words, was that it had been a colossal failure for which he might be held criminally responsible. Nothing substantial

---

20 Bernard Fergusson, *Beyond the Chindwin* (London: Collins, 1955), 239. It is tempting to think that Moke had a chance to tell Fergusson about his own Etonian, Black Watch uncle who had been killed in the Boer War.
21 Moke Murray, "Some Notes to Amuse Myself".
22 Savory papers, National Army Museum. London. I am grateful to Ms Sarah Hume for her assistance when I visited the museum in 2018. I've not seen Wingate's anxious query published elsewhere.

had been accomplished, and Wingate had lost one-third of his men. General Savory, an early supporter of the Chindits, assured Wingate that he would not be punished. Indeed when Wingate reached New Delhi, where he was to prepare his report, he was quickly made to realise that Longcloth could rapidly and convincingly be refigured into a powerful (if mendacious) tool for British propaganda. Instead of being court-martialled for Longcloth, Wingate was awarded a second bar to his DSO.[23]

Wingate's bellicose and self-serving report on Longcloth attracted Prime Minister Churchill's enthusiastic attention. The prime minister, like Wingate (but unlike Wavell) had a low opinion of the Indian Army's fighting abilities. He was pleased by what he saw as a welcome *British* military success.[24] Churchill summoned Wingate to London and invited him to attend the upcoming Allied Conference, code-named Quadrant, that took place in Quebec in August 1943. Wingate was a star performer at Quadrant and won substantial support for the next Chindit operation, code-named Operation Thursday, which was scheduled for early 1944. Wingate died in a plane crash on 25 March 1944, ten days after the ultimately successful excursion had begun.[25]

In September 1943 immediately after Quadrant, Wavell became Viceroy of India, a move that had been in the works for

---

[23] For some bleak assessments of Longcloth by participants at the time, see Julian Thompson, *Forgotten Voices of Burma: The Second World War's Forgotten Conflict* (London: Ebury Press, 2009), 61–108. Of the 4800 DSOs awarded in World War II, only fifty-three were awarded to a single officer for the third time.

[24] Churchill's multi-volume history of World War II plays down the Indian Army's contributions and those of General Slim. See Raymond Callahan, "Did Winston Matter? Churchill and the Indian Army, 1940–1945", in Patrick Rose and Alan Jeffreys (eds), *The Indian Army, 1939–47: Experience and Development* (London: Routledge, 2017), 60–67.

[25] The command of Operation Thursday passed to Brigadier Walter "Joe" Lentaigne, a 2/4GR officer who had been at Bakloh with Moke and Masters in the 1930s. Lentaigne was unaffected by Wingate's charisma and Slim considered him to be a much safer pair of hands.

some time, although he was not Churchill's first choice for the position.[26] General Claude Auchinleck (1884–1981), an Indian Army officer, replaced Wavell at India Command. A month later, Slim took command of the 14th Army, which he later led to victory. As part of the reshuffle, a new organisation called the Southeast Asia Command or SEAC was established in New Delhi, led by Lord Louis Mountbatten (1900–1979), the self-promoting, quick-witted naval officer who was favoured by Churchill for the new position. Mountbatten was a second cousin of the king.[27]

Meanwhile, many of the British soldiers posted to Assam complained bitterly about what they called "the 3 Ms"—malaria, monsoon and (poor) morale. Moke and his V Force colleagues, on the other hand, seem to have kept malaria at bay, didn't complain about the climate and they don't seem to have suffered from poor morale. They were far from home and had no idea what was expected of them.[28] On 22 May 1943, Wavell issued a General Order to officers of under his command. The order was written to provide guidance to officers when they tried to explain to the soldiers serving under them the rationale for fighting in Assam and Burma. From the scholarly, restrained and much-admired

---

26 Churchill's first choice was Anthony Eden. He reluctantly supported Wavell's appointment, and the two men never developed a good working relationship. Churchill pointedly failed to attend Wavell's state funeral in 1950.
27 SEAC moved to Kandy, Ceylon, in April 1944 and to Singapore in September 1945. By then, its responsibilities had been extended to include French Indochina south of the 16th parallel and the Netherlands East Indies.
28 George MacDonald Fraser, *Quartered Safe out There: A Recollection of the War in Burma* (London: HarperCollins, 1993), is a stirring autobiographical account of life in the ranks of a British regiment in Burma. See also Alan Allport, *Browned off and Bloody-Minded: The British Soldier Goes to War 1939–1945* (New Haven: Yale University Press, 2015), 66 ff., which deals with experiences in Burma.

author, the Order was surprisingly roughly worded:[29]

> It is the duty of all officers to explain to the troops, British and Indian, the reasons for the necessity for the speedy defeat of Japan, the character of the Japanese, their treachery, cruelty, lust, dishonesty, arrogance and godlessness need to be described.

Wavell probably felt that racialist phrases like these would resonate among restless and reluctant British troops and nudge them into concerted action. During the cascading Japanese victories in 1942, and after learning about the Japanese treatment of Allied prisoners of war, Wavell and most of the soldiers he commanded were fully prepared to dehumanise the Japanese. Throughout World War II the idea that the Japanese were barely human was widely held in Allied circles.[30]

V Force units, were fully engaged both with the enemy and with local Nagas, with whom dealings always involved issues of negotiated trust. In 1983 when the author Harry Seaman interviewed Moke about his activities in the war, Moke recalled:

> We always thought the Nagas would remain loyal throughout: in that we were right. Though we never completely trusted the Kakis we thought they would never actively move to harm us.

---

29 A copy of the General Order is in General Savory's papers in the National Army Museum in London. See also Bernard Fergusson, *The Battle for Burma: Wild Green Earth* (London 1946), 122: "Nevertheless, we must not forget that he is a barbarian". Fergusson, *Beyond the Chindwin*, 122; For a discussion of similar demeaning views see Allen, *Burma*, 611 ff.
30 For a sweeping and persuasive analysis of this issue, see John W. Dower, *War without Mercy: Race and Power in the Pacific War* (New York: Pantheon Books, 1993).

In that we were wrong.[31]

In June 1943 Moke's work with V Force over the preceding twelve months earned him an OBE for distinguished military service.[32] The poorly typed text of the recommendation for the award gives an excellent summary of his accomplishments in 1942–43:

> The work done by this officer during the period under review has been beyond praise; with very limited forces at his disposal he has been responsible for keeping a constant watch from TONEE to HOMALEN. His patrols have been constantly and aggressively active penetrating as far as MAINGKAING on the SYN (?) River and to the neighbourhood of SITSAWK and TONMAKING bringing valuable information. He has worked up a valuable intelligence service in the Chindwin opposite HOMALIN. All this has been done with a detachment of 4 Assam Rifles and V Force irregulars assisted by only one [company] of regular troops. He has infused the officers and men under him with his own fighting spirit and they have responded nobly and usefully.

General Savory recommended Moke for the award, shortly before he transferred to a command in New Delhi, where he took charge of infantry training the Indian Army. After Moke had received the award, Savory wrote him a letter addressed to

---

31 Harry Seaman, *The Battle at Sangshak, Prelude to Kohima* (London: Leo Cooper, 1987), 35–37; R.J. Travers, "The Battle of Sangshak", *The Kukri: The Journal of the Brigade of Gurkhas*, 2001, 12–13 notes that because of the delay imposed on them by the battle of Sangshak, "the Japanese arrived at Kohima a week late and half starved".

32 The order was founded in 1917 and is awarded to civilians as well as to members of the military. Moke did not engage the Japanese in combat, for which, like Sutherland, he would have been eligible for a Military Cross. For her work with V Force, Bower was awarded a slightly less prestigious CBE.

"My dear Moke" that survives in Moke's and in Savory's papers. It reads in part:

> I remember so well the early days when the Burma Army came through and what difficulty we had in getting information and how even then when you were just starting you filled with much efficiency so many gaps in our system. Then during the last monsoon V Force started going forward and undertook many patrols, at first up to the Chindwin, then beyond it, later penetrating deep into the enemy along the Uya.
>
> There is no doubt that the ascendancy, which we established over the Kabaw Valley after the withdrawal of the Burma Army was largely due to the aggressive patrolling activities of V Force.
>
> I have always had complete confidence in you. I have noted that anything I ordered would be done and done well. I felt at times that I had to restrain you but that as you know though contrary to my inclinations is in accordance with policy.[33]

Savory closed his letter by noting that in the previous two months, Murray and his V Force colleagues had "penetrated east of the Chindwin [i.e. into Burma] farther than anybody".

Savory's diary indicates that on at least three occasions in 1942–43 he visited Moke's V Force unit, dined with him, and came away favourably impressed, referring to Moke on one occasion as "a very gallant commander of V Force on the Chindwin". The two men probably became as close friends as their differences in age and rank allowed. In September and October 1945, as we shall see, Moke was to attract similarly favourable attention

---

33 Letter from Reginald Savory to Moke Murray, 12 May 1943, Savory Papers, Army Museum.

from his divisional commander Major General Douglas Gracey (1894–1964), a crucial figure in the chapters that follow. Moke's reply to Savory's letter survives in Savory's papers. Typed in red ink on a crumpled sheet of paper, it reads in part:

> I write to thank you most sincerely for the letter you wrote me on giving up command of your division. I can assure you that it is very greatly appreciated by me, and by my officers and men to whom I have communicated its contents. What we have done, I can very truthfully say has been done with the object of doing our stuff for the fighting commander who commanded us. What aggressive attitude we may have adopted was inspired by, if I may use your nickname without any disrespect, "Tiger" Savory.[34]

Moke went on to request Savory's assistance in getting him free of what he called the "rut of V Force", claiming that he would be "left behind in the advance into Burma when it comes".

Savory's reply to Moke, if there was one, has not survived. When the letters were exchanged Savory no longer commanded V force and it's unlikely that the general or his successor would have considered moving Murray from a position where he was doing so well. Moke remained in V Force until March 1944, as we shall see. "When he received his OBE, Moke was an acting lieutenant colonel, officially attached to 6GR, General Slim's old regiment, on loan successively to the Assam Rifles and V Force".[35] According to the 4/10GR's official history, he was also temporarily commanding "A" Company of that battalion—almost certainly the "regular company" mentioned in his OBE citation. In June 1943 "A" Company and the remainder of 4/10GR were

---

34 Letter from Moke Murray to Reginald Savory, 12 May 1943, Savory Papers, Army Museum.
35 Information derived from Moke's military records.

absorbed into General Gracey's 20th Indian Division. In August 1944, Moke formally joined this division and 4/10GR in the closing phases of the battle of Imphal. At that point he became second in command of the 4/10GR.

In *The Battle of Sanshak*, Harry Seaman, a veteran of the battle, writes about V Force and Moke, whom he introduces as "a Scot and a kinsman of the Dukes of Argyll".[36] But Moke must have been pulling Seaman's leg about being a Scot and was in any case more likely to have been related (at some distance) to the Duke of Atholl, head of Clan Murray. Rather breathlessly, Seaman continues:

> Murray was by all accounts yet another of those aggressively gifted leaders which Scotland produces in remarkable profusion for quasi-guerrilla warfare ... Murray's intelligence and pugnacity called down equal measures of praise and restraint from his superiors. The Japanese for their part paid him the compliment of placing a stupendous price upon his head.[37]

In "Some Notes" Murray wrote that in 1943 the price on his head, and on those of two V Force associates, had been set by the Japanese at 10,000 silver rupees. He added: "That these rewards were never claimed is a fitting tribute to our friends the Nagas." Elsewhere in "Some Notes" he writes that early in 1944 he told a group of assembled Nagas: "for the last 100 years or so we have been trying to stop you head hunting. So long as they are Japanese heads you may take as many as you like."

At that time the British Commonwealth forces comprising

---

36 Seaman, *The Battle at Sangshak*. As a Gurkha lieutenant, Seaman had taken part in the Battle of Sangshak, in a village north-east of Imphal. In preparing his book, he interviewed Ursula Betts, among others, and travelled to the scene of the battle. See also Allen, *Burma*, 210–27.

37 Seaman, *The Battle at Sangshak*, 36. Moke must have read this passage with pleasure but one wonders what is meant by the phrase "all accounts".

the 14th Army under General Slim, and the Imperial Japanese Army, were gearing up for offensive action. From a range of intelligence sources Slim was aware that Japan was planning a major offensive in the middle of March 1944, while he was planning one for later in the year. The Japanese offensive began a week earlier than expected, just as Operation Thursday was getting under way.[38] Rather than launch his own offensive prematurely Slim opted for an initially defensive strategy that aimed to block the Japanese advance into Assam, to inflict heavy casualties, and bomb the enemy's overstretched lines of supply. In his vividly written memoir *Defeat into Victory*, General Slim divided the 14th Army's campaign in 1944–45 into four distinct cases: concentration, attrition, counteroffensive and pursuit, at which point the Japanese forespoke and, "snarling and snapping, was hunted from the field".[39]

Early in March 1944 Moke was commanding an 18-man V-Force post in the Angouching Hills that straddled the border between Burma and Assam. The outpost was equipped with the only radio transmitter in the region that was powerful enough to reach Slim's 14th Army headquarters in Imphal. The radio was so heavy that it needed two hours to dismantle and two mules to take it anywhere.[40]

Local Kuki tribesmen, whose untrustworthiness Moke later mentioned to Seaman, informed the Japanese about his V Force post and on 14 March as part of a general Japanese advance into Assam, a company of Japanese infantry under Captain

---

38 Slim, *Defeat into Victory*, 389.
39 Slim *Defeat into Victory*, 296.
40 Seaman, *The Battle at Sangshak*, 60. This information must have come from Moke.

Susiumu Nishida overran it.⁴¹ Robert Lyman has claimed that everyone in the post but Moke was killed but this statement is unsourced. From other accounts we know that Moke, although wounded, managed to escape on foot by himself, after sending a radio message to Imphal saying that his post had been overrun.⁴² Two days later after trekking through the jungle Moke was picked up by an Indian Army patrol with a jeep that took him to safety. At that point before he received medical attention Moke passed his earlier message along to headquarters in written form. Unfortunately this message never reached its destination. Moke's wound probably prevented him from delivering it in person.⁴³

Moke's trek, it seems, soon became the stuff of legend, and in a letter written in 1976 Ursula Betts teased him about it, referring to his "legendary retreat from Sanshak in March 1944 … I cannot remember if you ambushed 35 Japs in 37 miles or 37 Japs in 35 miles; I think you will dispute the figures, but the impression remains!"⁴⁴

It seems likely that in his brief, perilous and solitary trek Moke steered clear of making any contact with the Japanese. The five-month gap in Moke's military record, between being ambushed on 14 March 1944 and joining 4/0GR and the 20th Indian Division in August, suggests that his wound was serious

---

41 Nishida had made a courageous, undetected reconnaissance of the voluntary British troops around Kohima with a small Japanese patrol in October 1943: Allen, *Burma*, 202.
42 Robert Lyman, *Japan's Last Bid for Victory: The Invasion of India, 1944* (Barnsley, South Yorkshire: Praetorian Press, 2011), 46; Tim Betts, a colleague of Moke's in V Force, who later married Ursula Bower, made a 70-mile trek from his outpost to Kohima in early March. See Fergal Keane, *Road of Bones: The Epic Siege of Kohima* (London: Harper Press, 2010).
43 In an email dated 19 October 2018 Liam Fox wrote: "The colonel had a scar on his head and I asked about it. He nonchalantly shrugged it off as a grenade or shrapnel injury." A serious head wound would have required hospitalisation and a period of convalescence.
44 Ursula Betts, letter to Murray, 2 May 1976.

enough for him to be evacuated to India for treatment.

In 1984, forty years after his outpost had been overrun, Moke met Susumu Nishida, the former Japanese lieutenant, who had led the attack, in London. Susumu was visiting England with a delegation of Japanese war veterans.[45] Recalling the meeting in "Some Notes", Moke wrote: "[Susumu] was ordered to put my headquarters out of action, and he did in a way but we delayed the [Japanese] advance for 24 hours."[46] In the 1990s Moke told Liam Fox that a few days before the Japanese ambush he and Susumu had encountered each other by chance not far from the V Force outpost. Neither of them had fired for fear of being mowed down by a concealed, larger force. Instead, they glanced at each other for a moment before melting back into the forest. When they met in 1984, Murray asked Susumo how many of his men had been nearby. "A company", the Japanese officer said, and asked Moke the same question. Moke replied, "There were three of us."[47]

The Battle of Sangshak that opened a few days later in late March 1944 was on balance a British-Indian defeat but several authors, following Seaman's lead, have argued that it postponed the massive offensive into India that the Japanese commanders had in mind. It also gave General Slim time to airlift an entire Indian division into the frontier area. In the following months Slim's 14th Army, composed of Indian, British and Commonwealth units, held off and then defeated the Japanese, first at Kohima and then in the prolonged and costly battle of Imphal, in which Moke's Gurkha battalion played a minor role.

---

45   In a letter to Moke dated 6 June 1984, Ursula Betts deftly refers to Susumo as "our former Jap opposite number".
46   Murray, "Some Notes to Amuse Myself".
47   Barnett's interview with Liam Fox, Worthing, September 2018. Moke also told Fox that when he met the Japanese captain, he decided not to shake hands.

Louis Allen has written, 'Imphal was not a single engagement but a complex set of battles lasting five months ranging from the banks of the Chindwin to the road beyond Kohima, well inside Assam.'[48]

In these battles, the Japanese lost more than 20,000 men. British and Indian casualties were also heavy. Roughly one-third of all 10GR's casualties in World War II occurred in these encounters.[49] Fighting was often at close quarters and in June 1944, during the battle of Imphal, Slim wrote privately to a friend:

> The fighting has been very intense and deadly, a great deal of it hand to hand ... What we find is that we can kill the first 50 per cent of a Jap formation comparatively easily because they attack and counter-attack thus giving us our opportunity. It is the second 50 per cent and especially the last 25 per cent, who cause us our losses and who hold us up. They dig in and have to be literally prized out and killed individually in the bitterest kind of fighting imaginable. That fighting is going on now, continuously.[50]

For the next fifteen months with pauses induced by the monsoon, the 14th Army took the initiative and recaptured Burma in a triumphant, meticulously executed and extremely violent campaign that put paid to the humiliations Allied forces had endured in South East Asia since 1942.

The 20th Indian Division, formed in India in April 1942, played a key role in the Burma campaign, with Moke embedded

---

48 Allen, *Burma*, 191.
49 In World War II, 10GR suffered some 4000 casualties (1013 killed, 2958 wounded). Roughly one-quarter of these casualties occurred during the battle of Imphal.
50 Cited in T.R. Moreman, *The Jungle, the Japanese and the British Commonwealth Armies at War, 1941–45: Fighting Methods, Doctrine and Training for Jungle Warfare* (London: Frank Cass, 2005), 140.

in it. The division was commanded until its dissolution in 1947 by General Douglas Gracey (1894–1964), who later became an important figure in Moke's life. Like Slim, Gracey was a Gurkha officer. Along with Alpha Ellery, John Masters, George Orwell, and Orde Wingate, Gracey had been born in India, where his father was a civil servant. Harry Seaman, who served under Gracey in Burma, has written:

> [Gracey was] of medium height, with a barrel chest and a strong, mawkish face marred by a shattered cheekbone, the heritage of a shooting accident in his youth. With his Labrador dog always at his heels, he spoke and sounded like a cross between a pirate and an archetypical English country gentleman.[51]

Gracey and Slim were friends, and Murray told Barnett that "he would have done anything for them". Both generals were hard driving, talented, unpretentious and confident commanders, fair and popular with their troops and their immediate subordinates. For the rest of 1944 and for the first eight months of 1945 the officers and men of the 20th Indian Division, including Moke and his colleagues in 4/10GR, were in almost constant contact with the enemy. In the closing phases of the campaign the battalion drew special praise from Gracey. As Professor T.O. Smith has written:

> On 5 March [1945] the 20th Indian Division's artillery crossed the Irrawaddy … at the same time, the 4/10 Gurkha Rifles attacked and took the village of Talington. Gracey was most pleased with the battalion's success: "My heartiest congratulations and thanks for the brilliant and successful

---

51 Seaman, *The Battle at Sangshak*, 33. For similarly high praise of Gracey from several men who served under him, see Peter M. Dunn, *The First Vietnam War* (London: C. Hurst, 1985), 61 ff.

battle. This is the finest victory and the best killing of the campaign so far."[52]

The 4/10GR, one of three Gurkha battalions in the division, was a special favourite of Gracey's and after the war the battalion was awarded the division's dagger Banner (depicting a hand grasping a dagger) as the best battalion in the division.

Until the closing weeks of the war nearly all Japanese soldiers, following what they called the cult of *bushido*, were unwilling to surrender or be taken prisoner. When a Japanese unit was surrounded, its soldiers often killed their wounded colleagues before committing suicide en masse. Moke and the forces of the 4/10GR observed a poignant example of this behaviour on the night of 30–31 January 1945, following the defeat of a small Japanese force in the village of Letkapin. Moke's battalion encircled the village and was waiting for daylight when they hoped to accept the surrender of any survivors. Instead, as S.N. Prasad, the historian of the Indian Army in the Burma campaign recorded:

> The [4/10] Gurkhas watched by moonlight as the survivors of the village, about twenty-five Japanese officers and men, committed suicide by walking fully armed and equipped into the river. Many of their wounded were thrown in by their comrades.[53]

---

[52] T.O. Smith, *Vietnam and the Unravelling of Empire: General Gracey in Asia, 1942–1951* (Houndmills, Basingstoke, Hampshire: Palgrave Macmillan, 2014), 26. It must have been at this point, if not before, that Murray was mentioned in dispatches and came to General Gracey's favourable attention. In 2023, it is impossible not to be shocked by the lackadaisical phrase "best killing", two words that epitomise the horrors of warfare through the ages.

[53] S.N. Prasad, *Official History of the Indian Armed Forces in the Second World War: Reconquest of Burma*, vol. II (Calcutta: Combined Inter-Services Historical Section (India & Pakistan), 1959), 232. See also *100th Brigade War Diary*, entry for 1 January 1945, which notes that "24 Japs leap into river. [We] watched them drown", TNA WO 172/7135.

Prasad adds that in the operation at least 150 Japanese were killed, while Gurkha casualties were "negligible". This lopsided ratio of Japanese to Indian Army deaths recurred consistently in the closing months of the war, and exposes the intensity of the campaign phases. The Japanese, it seems, literally fought themselves to death. Slim's 14th Army was a finely tuned, well supplied and merciless killing machine. Assessing the 4/10GR's performance in the Burma campaign, E.D. Smith, a former Gurkha officer, writes:

The 4/10GR had been dubbed "The non-stop Gurkhas" by the military correspondent of the *Times*, earned at the end of 1944 when they crossed the Wainggy. During fourteen days and nights in the middle of February 1945, the battalion was to win its finest victory. Having captured the village of Talingon the battalion found itself attacked repeatedly by the Japanese. At times it looked as if the Gurkhas would be overwhelmed by superior numbers but they stood fast with their CO showing great courage to bring down artillery "defensive fire" close to and even on company positions. Between 16 and 26 February the 4/10th lost 50 killed and 127 wounded ... but they virtually wiped out the counter-attacking 16th Japanese regiment by inflicting 953 casualties, which include at least 500 killed.[54]

To Moke, who assumed command of the battalion in June 1945, replacing Lt Col Parbury, the commander mentioned in the preceding passage, these months of intense combat and high responsibility must have been exhilarating. But in mid-September, three months later, General Gracey abruptly ordered him and a

---

54   E.D Smith, *Britain's Brigade of Gurkhas* (Havertown: Pen & Sword, 1983), 139; of this campaign, Slim later wrote, "[The] breakout of the 20th Division was a spectacular achievement which only a magnificent division, magnificently led, could have staged after weeks of the heaviest defensive fighting": Slim, *Defeat into Victory*, 473–74.

skeleton crew to Saigon. From 1 July 1945 we have an endearing, sidelong glimpse of Moke in the memoirs of Brigadier Miles Smeeton (1904–1988), later a renowned yachtsman and environmentalist. A delegation of Japanese officers was en route to Smeeton's headquarters to arrange a ceasefire and to discuss the possibility of surrendering their troops. The meeting was to be held in the local Gurkha headquarters, which occupied a small railroad station. In Smeeton's words:

> The railway station was built on solid piles, and a vertical ladder through a trap door in the floor reached the only room of any size. The young Gurkha colonel [commanding 4/10GR] as usual had an idea. There was a small alcove of the room … and he suggested that they hang an army blanket over the door, so that I might conceal myself behind that and when the Japanese officers were suitably aligned, I could sweep in from behind the blanket … and take my seat behind a table. Anyway, that is what we did.[55]

In September 1945, when fighting had stopped, Moke would almost certainly have agreed in the jargon of the day, that his had been "a good war". Between May 1942 and the Japanese surrender, Moke had been decorated for meritorious service and had been mentioned in despatches. He had escaped with his life from a Japanese ambush, and he'd come to the favourable attention of two British generals. Most importantly, in the dying days of the Raj, Moke achieved what must have been the goal of every Gurkha officer, namely the chance to lead a Gurkha battalion in combat. This fact alone made the war "good" for him.

Whether World War II and the Burmese segment of it had

---

[55] Miles Smeeton, *A Change of Jungles* (London: Hart-Davis, 1962), 511. I am grateful to Craig Reynolds for tracking down this reference.

been "good" is another question entirely, and an important one discussed by many writers. As Robert Lyman brilliantly evokes in the title of his study of the hard-fought battles there, the Burma campaign was a 'war of empires' that served as a crucible through which Britain, Burma, India, and Japan were transformed in its aftermath. Both the British and Japanese Empires lost power and influence, the former in a more drawn-out affair than the latter while both Burma and India would gain independence shortly after the war and one after the other.[56] Yet, whether or not Burma was a "good" war was probably never a question that Moke would have asked himself. Besides, he believed that his activities in it constituted the high point of his career.

In Worthing towards the end of his life, when he needed two canes to walk and was consuming at least a bottle of Bell's Scotch whisky a day, Moke spent much of his time hunched over large-scale maps of Burma and Assam, revisiting the landscapes that he had fought over, first in V Force and then as second command and subsequently commander of the Non-Stop Gurkhas of 4/10GR. Moke's Worthing neighbour Liam Fox remarked that the years Moke spent fighting in Assam and Burma were the ones that he was proudest of and spoke about most often.

The alcoholism that suffused so much of Moke's postwar years may have been designed to lessen the effects of an undiagnosed post-traumatic-stress disorder, but I doubt it. In his conversations with Liam Fox at least, Moke always spoke about his time in combat with pleasure and nostalgia. I suspect that he drank as much as he did in the last decade of his life because he was a creature of habit, and as old age, resentments and solitude crowded in on him he probably couldn't think of anything better to do.

---

56   Robert Lyman, *A War of Empires: Japan, India, Burma and Britain, 1941–45* (London: Bloomsbury, 2021).

SIX

Southern Vietnam and Cambodia in World War II

O N 13 SEPTEMBER 1945, LESS THAN TWO WEEKS AFTER Japan's formal surrender in Tokyo Bay, General Douglas Gracey and elements of the 20th Indian Division arrived in Saigon, the capital of the French colony of Cochin China, now part of the modern-day Socialist Republic of Vietnam. Neither Moke nor General Gracey had ever visited French Indochina. They had only very sketchy notions of its history and culture. On the basis of the scanty intelligence that he had received, Gracey seems to have believed that his mission would be unproblematic and relatively short-lived. He was badly mistaken.

Gracey's and Moke's activities in Saigon are dealt with in the following chapter, while this chapter deals with Murray's mission to Cambodia that extended from early October 1945 to the closing days of the year. Here I seek to provide a historical sketch of French Indochina, and especially Cochin China and Cambodia.

For much of the war, Indochina had been under Vichy French following the establishment of the collaborationist regime in the metropole under German patronage. In June 1940, the leaders of the French Third Republic capitulated to the Germans and signed over full powers to Marshal Philippe Pétain. He assumed the leadership of the French State, better known as 'Vichy France', named for the town from which it soon operated in collaboration with the Germans. Vichy authorities then assumed control of Indochina. Despite their differences, they never declared war on Japan, Germany's ally in Asia. French authorities ended up negotiating a modus vivendi that lasted until the Japanese *coup de force* on 9 March 1945, discussed below.[1] The agreement allowed Japan to station troops in French Indochina while France remained in day-to-day administrative control. In this respect, for most of World War II, what happened in French Indochina differed sharply from what happened in other colonies in the region that had been defeated and occupied by the Japanese. A consequence, of course, of the Vichy collaboration with Nazi Germany.

By August 1941, more than 100,000 Japanese troops were garrisoned in French Indochina. Because the colonial administration, army and police remained on duty, the French managed to keep nationalist forces throughout the region—not yet well-armed or organised in a significant fashion—under observation and restraint. This included the bloody repression of a communist-led revolt in southern Vietnam in 1940.

In December 1941, however, Japan opened the Pacific stage of World War II by seizing the American Pacific and attacking the European and American colonial presence in Southeast Asia, using their Indochinese bases to invade Burma, Thailand, and Malaya. The pro-Japanese Thai government surrendered at once and remained in place but Japan speedily defeated British and Indian forces in Malaya, captured Singapore, ousted the Americans from the Philippines, and, as we have seen, forced

---

1 A formal agreement was signed between Japan and the Vichy regime in Vichy on 29 July 1941. The French text can be accessed in Box 6/13, Gracey Papers, Liddell Hart Centre for Military Archives, King's College London.

British and Indian units (and tens of thousands of civilians) in Burma to retreat ignominiously towards India en masse.[2]

On 25 June 1944, General Charles de Gaulle's powerless regime-in-exile in Allied-liberated North Africa belatedly declared war on Japan. Some courageous men and women in French Indochina had already secretly shifted their allegiance away from the Vichy government in France and the stridently pro-Vichy administration in French Indochina, but these poorly organised *résistants* had no capacity to remove anyone from office, while French military units in the region were unprepared and probably unwilling to take on the Japanese.[3] Moreover, the *résistants* were thousands of miles from any military or political support.

In this evolving context, and in terms of what happened later, the events of 9 March 1945 are crucial. That evening, Japanese officials throughout the region, expecting Allied landings at any moment and distrustful of local French intentions, carried out a relatively bloodless *coup de force* codenamed Operation Blue Moon. The plan was to intern most French troops and all French officials in Indochina and to replace them with indigenous officials, in

---

[2] For the history of French Indochina in World War II, see Eric T. Jennings, *Vichy in the Tropics: Petain's National Revolution in Madagascar, Guadeloupe and Indochina, 1940–1944* (Stanford: Stanford University Press, 2002); Jean Decoux, À la barre de l'Indochine: Histoire du mon gouvernement general, 1940–1945 (Paris: Plon, 1949) (an exculpatory account); and Paul Isoart (ed.), *L'Indochine française 1940–1945* (Paris: Presses Universitaires de France, 1984). See also Sebastien Verney, *L'Indochine sous Vichy: Entre révolution nationale, collaboration, et identités nationales, 1940–1945* (Paris: Riveneuve éditions, 2013); and John Tully, *France on the Mekong: A History of the Protectorate in Cambodia 1863–1953* (Lanham, MD: University Press of America, 2003), 263–86.

[3] For information about French resistance in Indochina, see André Gaudel (pseudonym of Louis Malleret), *L'Indochine française en face du Japon* (Paris, 1947); and Julien Legrand, *L'Indochine à l'heure japonaise* (Cannes: Impr. Ægitna, 1963).

theory at least. Allied code-breakers translated the Japanese *diktat* that was given to local rulers. It included the chilling sentence, "We are by no means employing compulsion in this matter but compliance will minimize the shedding of blood."[4]

According to the Norwegian historian Stein Tønnesson, the Japanese had been planning such a *coup* since September 1944 when the Vichy regime collapsed and de Gaulle had taken power in Paris. From then on, the French in French Indochina were living on borrowed time.[5] In March 1945, as the Japanese *coup* unfolded, a few thousand French troops posted in Tonkin under General Camille Sabattier (1892–1966) managed to escape on foot to China and a handful of French officials in Laos and Cambodia took to the forest. The thousand-odd French troops from the 1ᵉ *régiment d'infanterie de marine* [1st Marine Infantry Regiment] stationed in Saigon put up no significant resistance and were easily interned.

Three French-installed rulers in French Indochina were affected by the Japanese *coup*. They included Emperor Bao Dai (1913–1997), set up as the ruler of the protectorates of Annam and Tonkin, comprising what are now central and northern Vietnam; Norodom Sihanouk (1922–2012), the King of Cambodia; and Sisavong Vong (1885–1959), the King of Luang Prabang in Laos. The Japanese informed these rulers that their realms were now independent. In the French colony of Cochin China where there was no local leader, the Japanese assumed control over its administration. They only relinquished power to local authorities in mid-August 1945.

---

4 Dixee R. Bartholomew-Feis, *The OSS and Ho Chi Minh: Unexpected Allies in the War against Japan* (Lawrence, Kansas: University Press of Kansas, 2006), 131–32.

5 Stein Tønnesson, *Vietnam 1946: How the War Began* (Berkeley: University of California Press, 2010), 21.

King Sisavong Vong, a fervent Francophile, delayed responding to Japanese orders for almost a month. He was rewarded for his loyalty in 1946 when the French named him king of a united Laos. Bao Dai, on the other hand, was quickly drawn to the idea of independence. After a few days, Norodom Sihanouk succumbed to Japanese pressure.[6]

Contemporary records suggest that nearly everyone in French Indochina (except the French, of course) welcomed the unexpected Japanese gift. In the Vietnamese-speaking segments of the colony, where anti-French nationalism was well developed, the *coup de force* set in motion a series of widespread, uncoordinated uprisings of nationalists with conflicting allegiances and different points of view. The uprisings took place primarily in the North and met with little or no Japanese opposition.

In the northern two segments of what would later become Vietnam, nationalist unrest in the summer of 1945 quickly came to be dominated by the well organised, Communist-controlled Viet Minh nationalist front created in 1941. In Tonkin and Annam, the evolving, almost bloodless unrest—later labelled the August Revolution—led to the Viet Minh controlling wide swathes of territory. This took place amid a ruinous famine in which an estimated 1.5 million people starved to death especially in the centre and the north.[7] The August Revolution ended on 2 September 1945 when the Viet Minh leader, Ho Chi Minh (1890–1969), proclaimed before a huge crowd in Hanoi that Vietnam had gained its complete independence. The incoming regime named itself the Democratic Republic of Vietnam or

---

6 The sequence of events is discussed in chapter seven. See Norodom Sihanouk and Jean Lacouture, *L'Indochine vue de Pékin* (Paris: Éditions du Seuil, 1972).
7 On the famine, see Geoffrey C. Gunn, *Rice Wars in Colonial Vietnam: The Great Famine and the Viet Minh Road to Power* (Lanham: Rowman & Littlefield, 2014). The famine did not affect Cambodia or southern Vietnam.

DRV. On the same day, Japan had formally surrendered to the Allies.[8]

In sharp contrast, nothing of the kind occurred in Cambodia, where nationalism, such as it was, focused on loyalty and obedience to the king rather than on opposition to the French. In Cochin China the situation was also very different, as Shawn McHale has shown in his recent book, while Vietnamese opposition to a French return to power was all but unanimous, in the south, the Viet Minh found it difficult to consolidate their control or manage the behaviour of anti-French resistance.[9]

The story of how the Japanese imposed independence in Cambodia between early March and mid-October 1945 is crucial to understanding Moke's mission to the kingdom. The region was less violent than its Vietnamese neighbour, where the twentieth century emperors installed by France were seen as puppets and were never widely popular. Cambodia's untested 22-year-old king, like his forebears, occupied a larger place in his subjects' thought world than the French ever did as we shall see.

The news that Sihanouk had openly welcomed independence—whatever the unfamiliar term implied—was accepted by the population, just as they had accepted the French Protectorate, at least since the early 1900s, because it had been approved by three successive kings. Unsurprisingly, nearly all of the same people followed Sihanouk's lead seven months later in September 1945 when the young king, bowing sensibly to force majeure, welcomed the return of French protection. Armed resistance to France in Cambodia, when it broke out in the late 1940s, took place under systematic Vietnamese patronage without any

---

8   Tønnesson, *Vietnam 1946*, 3.
9   See Shawn F. McHale, *The First Vietnam War: Violence, Sovereignty, and the Fracture of the South, 1945–1956* (New York: Cambridge University Press, 2021).

backing from Phnom Penh or the royalty. It seems that for most of the colonial period (at least after King Norodom died in 1904) Cambodian nationalism, by and large, meant reverently respecting the monarch and being indifferent to the French.

In March 1945, following the *coup de force*, dozens of Japanese and French soldiers died fighting in the provincial city of Kompong Cham. The Japanese takeover of Phnom Penh went more smoothly but was not unopposed.[10] The French ethnologist Eveline Porée Maspero (1907–1988) had lived in Phnom Penh since 1930. On 9 March 1945, she recorded in her journal, "We heard the stuttering sound of machine guns, rifle fire and heavier explosions that must have been from grenades—coming from all sides."[11]

In his memoir Sihanouk writes that shortly before 9 March he had been warned by acting *Résident Supérieur* André Berjoan (1903–1990) that some kind of Japanese *coup* was imminent. In the event, Berjoan urged Sihanouk to take refuge in the Résidence, the spacious Art Deco building that six months later, ironically, would become Moke's headquarters. In Sihanouk's words, "He invited me to die beside him in his house, along with the Protectorate that named me King."[12]

On the evening of 9 March, once the *coup* had begun,

---

[10] See David P. Chandler, *The Tragedy of Cambodian History: Politics, War, and Revolution since 1945* (Chiang Mai: Silkworm Books, 1994), 14–26; Other acts of French resistance to the 9 March decree, especially in Vietnam, are cited in Jean-Michel Hertrich, *Doc-Lap !: l'indépendance ou la mort* (Paris: Jean Vigneau, 1946), 119–34.

[11] Porée Maspero Journal, entry for 10 March 1945. I am grateful to the late Mme Porée Maspero and her husband the late Guy Porée for their hospitality in Mormoiron (Vaucluse) in 1977 and 1983, when I was able to consult her vivid, unpublished journals.

[12] Norodom Sihanouk, *Souvenirs doux et amers* (Paris: Hachette, 1981), 117. See also Cambodia's *Journal Officiel*, 14 March 1945, a 33-page text that sets out in some detail, in excellent French, the establishment of the independent government.

Sihanouk asked his chauffeur to drive him to the Résidence. They turned back when they heard machine-gun fire. Instead of returning to the Palace, the King took refuge in a nearby Buddhist *wat*. He returned to the Palace in the morning and was informed by Japanese officials that Cambodia was independent.

Sihanouk formally declared the kingdom's independence two days later. He claims in his memoir that court astrologers chose the date.[13] His royal proclamation—almost certainly drafted in French by the Japanese diplomats accredited to the king—read in part: "In view of the circumstances the King assumes the Presidency of the Council of Ministers, a prerogative given to the *Résident Supérieur* by a Royal Ordinance dated 11 July 1887." On the same day another royal proclamation clarified what had taken place:

> All of the treaties and conventions that established the French Protectorate of Cambodia are repealed (*abolis*) as of the date of this Declaration. As a consequence the Kingdom of Kampuchea is henceforward in a state of independence.

On 18 March in another royal decree the king amplified his previous statements, "The government of Japan and the Supreme Command of the Japanese Army has decided, as of 9 March 1945, to defend Indochina by themselves against the enemy."[14] The unnamed "enemy", of course, included the encircling forces in faraway Gaullist France, as well as local French military personnel and *résistants*, whom the Japanese had interned. But most of all, it was a reference to the military forces of the Allied Powers—predominantly American and British—that were tightening the noose around the Japanese-controlled Pacific.

---

13 Sihanouk, 121.
14 *Journal Officiel du Cambodge*, 12 March 1945, 1.

In the following weeks, the new Cambodian government issued a series of laws and decrees that renamed some streets in the capital to honour national heroes and abandoned French-sponsored efforts to Romanise the Cambodian alphabet and to adopt the Gregorian calendar. These ostensibly modernising proposals had enraged the conservative, influential, and anti-French Buddhist *sangha*, or monastic order.[15] Other decrees left the French language in place as the language of government and kept in force all French regulations "provided they [were] not incompatible with the fact of independence".

The new government changed the country's name in French from Cambodge to Kampuchea, reflecting the word's pronunciation in Khmer. The regime also made Khmer the primary language of teaching in the kingdom's primary schools and established a National Guard.

Between March and November 1945, Cambodian authorities promulgated 155 laws (*kram*) and 390 administrative decrees (*kret*). The bureaucracy's smooth, largely Francophone performance without any French participation was a credit to its members' training, a tribute to their competence and a muted rebuke to the French colonial project in the sense that a French presence appears to have been no longer necessary.[16] When the French returned to power at the end of the year they allowed three-quarters of the laws and nearly 90 per cent of the decrees to stand. The only ones that they rescinded were those devoted

---

15   Chandler, *The Tragedy of Cambodian History*, 15.
16   Chandler, *The Tragedy of Cambodian History*, 17.

to the declaration and celebration of Cambodian independence.[17] These were replaced with holidays such as Bastille Day, that were imported from metropolitan France, an action that could only be described as either the product of colonial blindness or being deeply out-of-touch on the part of the returning French.

On 12 March 1945, a seven-man Council of Ministers took office in Phnom Penh. Most of its members had served in the previous council and several remained prominent in Cambodian politics well into the 1950s. None had any anti-French credentials. Instead of reporting to a French Résident Supérieur, however, the newly assembled council reported to the Japanese Supreme Advisor, Kanichiro Kubota (1902–1977), a career diplomat who later returned to the area in the 1950s as Japan's ambassador to South Vietnam.[18]

As the new Cambodian government gathered momentum and self-confidence, it continued to generate, distribute and archive many of the same documents and reports that had been required by the colonial regime. One of these was the monthly Report on the Internal Security of Cambodia issued by the National Police. Several of these reports from 1945 survive in the Cambodian National Archives. Like the previously French-sponsored documents, they assess "nationalist activity" as a threat to the status quo, and find it most intense among the so-called Annamite (i.e. Vietnamese) minority. As for the Cambodian population, a report from June 1945 states with unconscious

---

[17] On the laws and decrees, Chandler, *The Tragedy of Cambodian History*, 17 ff. Research based on documents in the French colonial archives in Aix-en-Provence. Further evidence for the new regime's bureaucratic efficacy comes from the Cambodian National Archives in Phnom Penh, which I visited for several days in 2016. I am grateful to the competent and companiable archive staff for their help.

[18] In *Souvenirs doux et amers*, 112, Sihanouk praises Kubota for his "tact" and his "impeccable French".

irony that nationalist activities among the Khmer "have been almost nil, given the fact that Cambodians are satisfied with the independence of their country".[19]

A report from the same month provided a thumbnail sketch of the anxious French community in Phnom Penh:

> [In the past month] French men and women often gathered in the streets, they had discussions that stopped when any Indo-Chinese approached. They cherished their rancour. Many of them have stopped hoping for a quick recovery, while others have abandoned their contempt for the Indo-Chinese who have taken their positions.[20]

At the end of May, Japanese officials brought the Cambodian nationalist Son Ngoc Thanh (1907–1977) back from Japan, where he had lived in voluntary exile since 1942 after evading arrest for sponsoring an anti-French demonstration in Phnom Penh.[21] He had become fluent in Japanese.

Son Ngoc Thanh was born in Cochin China, the son of a prosperous Vietnamese father and a Cambodian mother. The province of his birth, Tra Vinh, included a substantial Khmer-speaking minority.[22] In 1933, after being educated largely in France, Son Ngoc Thanh came to live in Cambodia and worked

---

19 NAC, Situation Report, June 1945.
20 NAC, Political Report, June 1945.
21 On Son Ngoc Thanh's career, see Matthew Jagel, "Son Ngoc Thanh, the United States, and the Transformation of Cambodia" (PhD Dissertation, Northern Illinois University, 2015); Penny Edwards, *Cambodge: The Cultivation of a Nation, 1860–1945* (Honolulu: University of Hawaii Press, 2007), 341 ff. Sihanouk states misleadingly that Thanh arrived in Phnom Penh a week after the *coup de force*, rather than more than two months later: *Souvenirs doux et amers*, 114.
22 On the Khmer minority in southern Vietnam today see Philip Taylor, *The Khmer Lands of Vietnam: Environment, Cosmology, and Sovereignty* (Singapore: Asian Studies Association of Australia in association with NUS Press and NIAS Press, 2014).

as a public servant. From 1936 to 1942, while he was attached to the Buddhist Institute in Phnom Penh, he co-edited a Khmer language weekly newspaper, *Nagara Vatta (Angkor Wat)*, which set out a modest reform agenda and was read by thousands of educated Khmer. In 1942 the paper assumed a subdued pro-Japanese stance and was banned after an anti-French demonstration in July. Thanh himself, partly via the paper, had become well known and was popular with many members of the Buddhist *sangha* and the kingdom's literate population. At the time, his half-Vietnamese ethnicity did not seem to trouble his supporters.[23]

The May 1945 "Monthly Report" noted that "the return of Son Ngoc Thanh from Tokyo and the news that His Majesty is going to entrust him with important functions has inspired great joy in Cambodian circles".[24] Soon after he arrived in Phnom Penh, at Japan's insistence, he became Cambodia's first foreign minister. On paper, the new ministry resembled its counterparts elsewhere in the world but as Sihanouk later pointed out, the supposedly independent Kingdom of Kampuchea never received diplomatic

---

23 On *Nagara Vatta*, see Ben Kiernan, *How Pol Pot Came to Power: A History of Communism in Kampuchea, 1930–1975* (London: Verso, 1985), 41 ff; Edwards, *Cambodge*, 216–21, 225–28, 236–39; the paper reappeared in May 1945 following the return to Cambodia of its former co-editor, Pach Chhoeun, who had been imprisoned on the penal island of Poulo Condore for his role in the 1942 demonstration. See Bounchan Mol, *Kuk Niyobay* (Phnom Penh: Apsara Press, 1971). When it reappeared in 1945 *Nagara Vatta* was periodically censored for its "severe" (probably republican) views. Copies of the paper from this period are missing from the Cambodian National Archives.

24 Ironically for students of Cambodian history, the report was signed by Police Commissioner Sam Sary (1908–1962?), an intimate of Sihanouk who opposed the prince in the 1950s (as did Son Ngoc Thanh), went into exile and died under mysterious circumstances in the early 1960s. His son Sam Rainsy (1949–) led opposition to the Cambodian government in the 1990s and beyond.

recognition from any country, including Japan.[25]

Instead, as the Cambodian *Journal Officiel* noted, the ministry's primary task would be to maintain "relations with the Japanese authorities".[26] In this regard, the government minister Nhiek Tioulong writes in his unpublished memoir that the council welcomed the appointment of the Foreign Ministry, because friction had often developed between Cambodian farmers and Japanese military officials who were requisitioning their rice and other crops. It was hoped that Thanh could play a mollifying role.[27]

In June 1945 the Japanese allowed Thanh to travel to Saigon, where he suggested to some bemused and powerless local authorities that two provinces of Cochin China with substantial Khmer populations—including Tra Vinh where he had been born—be returned to Cambodian jurisdiction. The Vietnamese taking over in Hanoi were in no position to agree.

On 20 July 1945, several thousand Cambodians paraded past King Sihanouk and what the king's chronicle referred to as "officials large and small" to commemorate the anti-French 1942 demonstration that Thanh and Pach Chhoeun had sponsored.[28] For the next few months, 20 July assumed the status of a national holiday.

Shortly before dawn on 10 August, after atomic bombs had been dropped on Hiroshima and Nagasaki, a group of eleven

---

25   Norodom Sihanouk, *Action royale pour l'indépendance du Cambodge 1941–1955* (Phnom Penh: Penn Nouth, Doyen du Haut Conseil du Roi, 1959), 5. The evidence that Sihanouk opposed French protection with any vigour before 1952 is sparse and unconvincing.
26   *Journal Officiel du Cambodge,* July 1945.
27   Porée Maspéro Journal, entry for 15 August 1945. See also Geoffrey C. Gunn, *Monarchical Manipulation in Cambodia: France, Japan, and the Sihanouk Crusade for Independence,* Nordic Institute of Asian Studies Monograph Series, no. 141 (Copenhagen, Denmark: NIAS Press, 2018), 260.
28   Sihanouk, *Action royale,* 6.

127

young Cambodians located, rounded up and imprisoned the entire Council of Ministers, except for Son Ngoc Thanh. A few of the *coupistes* were armed, and one of them shot and wounded a junior minister, Nong Kimny, who managed to escape. After forcing their way into the palace, the young men made the king sign a document that demanded changes in the Council of Ministers.

In his unpublished memoir, Nhiek Tioulong, the mayor of Phnom Penh at the time, asserts that Thanh had not been informed of the *coup* beforehand.[29] This seems unlikely. Nearly all the young men involved in it had worked closely with the Japanese, who were still, even in this uncertain, liminal period, supportive of Thanh. The *coupistes* wanted dramatic changes in the way Cambodia was governed. They were particularly displeased that the Council of Ministers included so many mediocre men who had happily served the French.[30]

The historian Ben Kiernan has called the *coup* "a clarion call to anti-French resistance", but material from the Cambodian archives suggests that it passed almost unnoticed at the time.[31] Its participants were quickly arrested and the imprisoned ministers released. Three of the *coupistes* escaped from prison before they could be tried. As Kiernan points out, they were later active in the anti-French resistance. The eight remaining prisoners were soon indicted for the crime of *lèse majesté*.

Son Ngoc Thanh, although perhaps not the instigator of the *coup*, emerged as its beneficiary and at that point, if not before, he

---

29 Tioulong would play an important role in Cambodian politics in the 1950s and 1960s.
30 Porée Maspéro Journal entry for 11 August 1945 reports that printed notices had circulated in Phnom Penh on the 10th declaring that "the King continues to amuse himself while the people suffer".
31 Kiernan, *How Pol Pot Came to Power*, 30. The issues of *Cambodge* that may have reported the *coup* (dated 11, 19 and 15 August 1945) were missing from the Cambodian National Archives when Michael Vickery was doing his research in 1963 (Michael Vickery, email 22 November 1989).

lost the confidence of the king and of Sihanouk's parents, who were appalled by the threat to the throne that the *coup* presented. Urged on by the Japanese, however, Sihanouk named Son Ngoc Thanh Cambodia's first prime minister five days after the *coup*. A new, ten-man Council of Ministers, markedly less pro-French than its predecessor, took office shortly afterwards.[32]

Thanh's becoming prime minister is treated in most histories of Cambodia (including mine) as abrupt and Japanese-inspired, as it certainly was, but it also proceeded in an orderly bureaucratic fashion, as shown by the four pages of fastidiously worded decrees that appeared in the *Journal Officiel* of 16 August 1945. The decrees set out and limited the roles that a prime minister would play in a kingdom that still had neither a constitution nor an elected parliament.[33]

In mid-August, Thanh asked the Japanese to take over the electric power plant in Phnom Penh and ordered "the reinforcement and surveillance of frontiers". A flurry of other documents that ordered the mobilisation of the Garde Nationale (disarmed by the Japanese shortly after the 9 March *coup*) and reinforced the police were issued in succeeding weeks. However, nothing resembling a full mobilisation ever took place, probably because Khim Tit (1896–1975), the newly installed minister of defence, had quickly come to think that a French return to power was both imminent and desirable, and that taking up arms against them would not succeed.

Under the new arrangements Sihanouk's uncle, Prince Sisowath Monireth (1909–1975), became Supreme Councillor to the council, replacing Kubota. Monireth was the eldest son of King Sisowath Monivong (r. 1927–41). He had served as an

---

32 T.O. Smith, "A British Interlude: Allied Peace Enforcement, 1945–1947", in *Cambodia and the West, 1500–2000* (London: Palgrave Macmillan, 2018), 67–114.
33 *Journal Officiel du Cambodge*, 16 August 1945.

officer in the French army and the Foreign Legion. He was hard working, upright and competent, but in spite or perhaps because of these qualities the French in 1941 had preferred to name his nineteen-year-old nephew as king. They viewed Sihanouk as a more pliable, unquestioning servant of French imperial interests than Monireth might have been.

With hindsight the French decision not to offer Monireth the throne in 1941 marked an intriguing road not taken in Cambodian history. It's possible and even likely that Monireth would have been a genuinely constitutional monarch, unlike his nephew, and that the ripple effects of his law-abiding, somewhat aloof personality would have profoundly affected the course of Cambodian politics—a world without Sihanouk, in other words— in the 1950s and 1960s. In the summer of 1945, Monireth, like most of the Cambodian elite, supported the idea of independence, although he certainly knew that the French would soon return in force. He was prepared to negotiate with them. Son Ngoc Thanh was not.[34] The young Sihanouk would bend with the changing winds that the end of World War II had introduced.

By mid-August 1945, Thanh knew that the war was coming to an end and with it the protection that the Japanese continued to give to his regime. Nevertheless, on the day after he took office as prime minister Thanh called for continuing cooperation with Japan and what he called the *'jaune'* (jaune) inhabitants of South East Asia.[35]

---

34 See Tully, *France on the Mekong*, 252–53. In late October after the French returned to power, Monireth dissolved the Council of Ministers and reconstituted its members into a committee to negotiate with France. Monireth and his colleagues drove a relatively hard bargain but the agreement that they reached in early 1946 fell short of prolonging or foreshadowing Cambodia's independence. For a helpful discussion of this issue see Gunn, *Monarchical Manipulation in Cambodia*, 80 ff.
35 *Journal Officiel du Cambodge*, August 1945.

Soon afterwards, Eveline Porée Maspero made an entry in her journal that displays a level of empathy that's rare in this relentlessly forward moving, male-dominated account:

> Just now I heard the singing in a minor key of Japanese troops and I went [outside] to watch them. It was raining—not the joyous rainfall of a real storm but a low-paced rainfall, coming after a day of greyness. Two small detachments were passing by at a rapid pace, rifles on their shoulders, officers to the side. And suddenly I found all this very sad. These men who perhaps had never wished for a war, exiled for years far from their families, were leaving now after their defeat headed for a ravaged country.[36]

On 24 August, while the Japanese were negotiating the final details of their surrender to the Allied powers, Thanh addressed the Council of Ministers, in a session chaired by Prince Monireth:

> Given the delicate situation in which Kampuchea finds itself, it's necessary to show us firmly resolved to maintain our independence. An active program of propaganda will be set in motion ... to encourage the entire population to display their unshakable will not to depend on any other nation.[37]

Thanh went on to stress that resistance to the French would not be based on violence but would be "purely and simply a moral resistance"—whatever that meant. His remarks were unanimously approved. Later in the protracted meeting, Prince Monireth struck a more realistic note. The minutes of the meeting record:

> [Prince Monireth] noted that the Allies will soon arrive here to execute the clauses of the armistice treaty, disarmament

---

36 Porée Maspero Journal, entry for 19 August 1945.
37 *Journal Officiel du Cambodge*, 24 August 1945.

in particular. Our country will be occupied and we will have to bear the consequences of that occupation. To accomplish our obligations it will be in our interest to remain calm and to prove our capacity to govern ourselves ... it will be necessary also, for the preservation of an independent Kampuchea to be ready to negotiate with the Allies if they agree to it.[38]

In effect, the prince was reading writing on the wall that was illegible to many of his colleagues. He was telling them, as politely as he could, that Cambodia's days as an independent country were numbered, that the French were returning in force and that resistance to them would be unproductive.

It's impossible, seventy-eight years later, to question Thanh's sincerity (or Monireth's) or to avoid the conclusion that no one in the Council of Ministers wanted the kingdom to revert to French "protection". Instead, contemporary records suggest that most Cambodians were pleased by what they understood about independence and hoped somehow that it would continue after the departure of the Japanese. As yet, however, reflecting the *attentisme* of their young king, the Council of Ministers and the population at large were unprepared and unready to resist the French by taking up arms. No military preparations for doing so had been made.

At the same time, documents in the Cambodian National Archives suggest that even at the end of August, after Japan had indicated its willingness to surrender, mass, non-violent enthusiasm for independence could still be generated at the government's insistence in the Cambodian countryside. On Sunday the 26th following orders sent to them the week before by the Council of Ministers, Cambodia's provincial governors sponsored pro-independence demonstrations throughout the kingdom. One was also

---

38 *Journal Officiel du Cambodge*, 24 August 1945.

planned for the capital. At the Council of Ministers meeting on 20 August, the recently installed Minister of Education, Nhiek Tioulong, noted that:

> To avoid incidents on the occasion of the demonstration planned for next Sunday, he had informed the French that it was a question of a patriotic demonstration organised by the people and authorised by the government that has as its unique objective to show the firm determination of Cambodians to remain independent. The demonstration is not directed at any nation and so the French have no reason to be disturbed by it. When these explanations were given, the Governor of the city asked [French citizens] to remain calm when the parade goes past their houses.[39]

Tioulong makes the point that the parades were to be obedient celebrations of the status quo, that is, national independence approved by the king—rather than demonstrations against the French. In this way they differed significantly from the anti-French, pro-independence demonstrations that occurred in Saigon, Hanoi and elsewhere in Vietnam in 1945.

Detailed reports about the Cambodian demonstrations survive in the Cambodian Archives from the provinces of Kompong Chhnang and Kampot.[40] In his report, the governor of Kompong Chhnang called the demonstration in his province "grandiose", and went on to say, "Thousands of Cambodians, along

---

[39] Minutes of Council of Ministers Meeting, 24 August 1945. Nhek Tioulong had remained governor of the city for a time after taking on the portfolio of minister of education. For this meeting Son Ngoc Thanh gave the chair to Prince Monireth.

[40] Porée Maspero, Journal, entry for 27 August 1945 notes that a pro-independence parade had taken place in Phnom Penh the day before, but documents for this parade and for parades on most of the provinces are missing from the archives.

with delegations of Chinese and Annamites took part in the demonstration bearing national flags and banners and cheering, in unison, 'Long Live Independent Cambodia'."

Assembling in front of the governor's mansion where a triumphal arch had been erected, a large, orderly crowd heard the governor give an "informal talk" that praised the new government, the independence of Kampuchea, the king and the Buddhist religion. He closed by saying the staged, enthusiastic event lasted for almost four hours.[41]

In the Kampot celebration, an estimated 2000 people marched in an orderly fashion to the office of the governor, Pho Proeung (who became an important political figure in Cambodia after 1955). Proeung praised their patriotism in a welcoming speech. The celebrations were carefully orchestrated, to be sure, and even though the participants were accustomed to doing what they were told it's hard to assert they were insincere, or brainwashed, in expressing fondness for what they knew or imagined about independence. The alternative, preferring French protection, probably did not occur to them, perhaps because the idea doesn't yet seem to have crossed King Sihanouk's mind, to say nothing of the Council of Ministers.[42]

On 2 September, Son Ngoc Thanh extended diplomatic recognition to the Democratic Republic of Vietnam (DRV) that had been established on the same day in Hanoi. He invited the Viet Minh–dominated Provisional Administrative Committee in Saigon to send a representative to Phnom Penh. Thanh must have known beforehand that the date of Ho Chi Minh's declaration of independence would be chosen to coincide with Japan's formal surrender in Tokyo Bay. His swift, quasi-diplomatic action

---

41 See also Gunn, *Monarchical Manipulation in Cambodia*, 270 ff. As far as I know, Gunn's is the first published account to cite these documents.
42 Neither of the surviving reports mentions the French.

exhibited what General Gracey later called his "pro-Annamite" stance. It was one justification for his later departure from office under French pressure.

The very next day, in a bizarre attempt to legitimise himself and the Kingdom of Kampuchea even further, Thanh declared that in a recently held national referendum 541,000 citizens drawn from an alleged electorate of 674,048 male Khmer had formally agreed with the proposition that they were happy to be "as free as they were under Jayavarman with the temples of Angkor Wat". Of the completed ballots, he announced, one ballot was reported as blank and another allegedly gave a negative response.[43]

No such referendum could possibly have taken place. The size of the so-called electorate was probably consistent with heads of family tax records maintained by the central government but Cambodians had never voted for anything, communications between the capital and the provinces were often intermittent, and the "results" (announced within forty-eight hours of the alleged referendum) were risible. Nonetheless they provided Thanh, it seems, with statistics that he wanted to believe and that genuine independence, expressed by the Cambodian people, could be conjured up out of thin air.

In mid-September, a French major named Gajean with the *nom de guerre* Gallois and seven military associates parachuted into Cambodia as the "official representatives" of the recently installed French government in Paris. Other agents of the French government were parachuted into Vietnam and Laos at this time; Gallois had been born in Cambodia and had family connections

---

43 Information on the referendum is drawn from Edwards, *Cambodge*, 8 and 15 September 1945 (Michael Vickery's notes). See also Chandler, *The Tragedy of Cambodian History*, 25–26; Tully, *France on the Mekong*, 397; Gunn, *Monarchical Manipulation in Cambodia*, 270 ff.

in the French bureaucracy there. He was far from being an ardent Gaullist and made a poor impression on some French residents including Eveline Porée Maspero, who noted in her journal that she thought he was "completely mad" apropos of nothing.[44] Like Moke later on, Gallois quickly befriended Cambodia's defence minister Khim Tit, whose outspoken hostility to Thanh, according to Nhiek Tioulong's unpublished memoir, had made recent council meetings "particularly stormy".[45]

Unlike their French military colleagues who had parachuted into Tonkin only to be arrested and imprisoned by the Viet Minh, Gallois and his colleagues were treated politely, but Japanese authorities kept them away from the Council of Ministers and the palace. Son Ngoc Thanh refused to see him. Until the end of September, Gallois pestered Sihanouk with letters suggesting that he send a delegation to meet Admiral Georges Thierry d'Argenlieu (1889–1964), de Gaulle's appointed High Commissioner for French Indochina, who was then in India waiting for transportation and for orders from Paris. The admiral's letters reached the king via Khim Tit.[46] In October, Sihanouk replied to the third of Gallois' importunate letters. After acknowledging the previous ones and their repeated, identical request, the king continued:

---

[44] For Gallois's meeting with members of the French community, see Porée Maspero journal, 18 August 1945. Only two in the audience repeated Gallois's cheery *"Vive de Gaulle"*. In the same entry, Poree Maspero calls Son Ngoc Thanh a *pirate arriviste*.

[45] Khim Tit had been brought into the Council of Ministers after the 10 August *coup* to take up the new portfolio of Minister of Defence. As the governor of Kampot, he had been markedly pro-Japanese, but by mid-September he had drifted away from Thanh's circle. See Khim Tit, 'Un épisode de l'histoire contemporaine du Cambodge', *Réalités Cambodgiennes*, 16 June 1967, a self-serving memoir.

[46] De Gaulle authorised d'Argenlieu, a fervent, narrow-minded supporter, to restore French control over Indochina before negotiating with any local people. See Philippe Devillers, *Paris Saigon Hanoi: Les archives de la guerre 1944–1947* (Paris: Gallimard/Julliard, 1988).

We ask the Admiral to inform us if the delegates we designate to send to Calcutta and then to Chandernagore will be considered delegates of an independent country. Cambodia recovered its independence after the events of 1945, independence registered by Kram No 3 NS, promulgated on 13 March 1945.

We are disposed to treat with France and to have friendly relations with France in political, economic and cultural matters. Nonetheless, these should not threaten the independence of our country.[47]

Despite his growing hostility to Son Ngoc Thanh and his awareness of shifting power relations in the region, Sihanouk and his close advisers (including his parents) were still unwilling to challenge the prime minister or to take an openly pro-French stand until there were adequate French forces in Cambodia to control the actions of the Japanese, neutralise "Annamites" and support the king's realistic, but altered position. Revealingly, Son Ngoc Thanh's quixotic call at a Council of Ministers meeting on 7 October for armed resistance against France met with no support.[48]

On 9 October 1945, Moke arrived in Phnom Penh as the Supreme Commander of Allied Forces in Cambodia, with the mission of maintaining order and accepting the Japanese surrender. Before he came to Cambodia, however, Moke spent two weeks in Saigon under General Gracey, helping elements of the 20th Indian Division to deal with a full-blown anti-colonial insurgency. This dramatic segment of Murray's life is covered in Chapter 8.

---

47   See Sihanouk, *Action royale pour l'indépendance du Cambodge 1941–1955*, 6.
48   See Khim Tit, 'Un épisode'. At the meeting, his last as prime minister, Thanh also proposed relocating the government to Kompong Cham. If driven from there, Thanh suggested moving to the Vietnamese province of Tay Ninh. He seems to have become disconnected from reality. On the following day Khim Tit travelled secretly to Saigon to ask Allied authorities to depose Thanh.

SEVEN

Gracey in Saigon

Although Allied forces had captured the Burmese capital Rangoon on 3 May 1945, in the final days of July, 4/10GR under Moke's command were still fighting the Japanese. While the soldiers of the 20th Indian Division, including Moke, could sense that the Burma campaign was almost over, they suspected that the war would continue in Malaya, where Singapore, the Netherlands East Indies and French Indochina all remained in Japanese hands. But of course they were totally unaware of the atomic bomb that would effectively end the war by 15 August when Emperor Hirohito formally surrendered.

Unbeknownst to Moke and his divisional commander General Douglas Gracey, at the end of July 1945 the Allied leaders met in Potsdam, a suburb of Berlin. Neither France nor the Netherlands was invited to attend. Alongside many more complex agreements, the Allied delegates took a decision in relation to French Indochina that would affect the 20th Division from Gracey on down and would have a major impact on Moke in an individual capacity. This decision concerned the process of surrender by Japanese forces. It was agreed that British and Indian troops of the Southeast Asia Command (SEAC) under

Lord Louis Mountbatten would accept Japanese surrenders in South East Asia outside the Philippines, with the exception of those in French Indochina above the 16th Parallel, just below the former imperial capital of Hue, where the Chinese were to be in charge.[1] Although Chinese troops had played a checkered role in the Burma campaign, their supreme commander, Chiang Kai Shek (1887–1975), had insisted via his American allies that China should take part in accepting Japanese surrenders in South East Asia. As the historian F.S.V. Donnison has noted, the decision to reward Chiang's desire 'was made to save the Generalissimo's face and could not but have, and did have, the most adverse effect upon arrangements for the re-establishment of French authority throughout the territory'.[2] The US had supported Chiang during the war and saw him as part of a broader policy of keeping China firmly in the American camp.

Mountbatten was summoned to Potsdam on 28 July to be informed of these arrangements, which expanded SEAC's jurisdictions to include the Netherlands East Indies and French Indochina. He was also told in confidence about the atomic bomb, but not about when or where one or more of them might be dropped. This news lent urgency to post-war planning but Mountbatten was enjoined to keep it secret 'for the time being'. Because the existence of the bomb was so closely concealed, its devastating use in Hiroshima and Nagasaki on 6th and 9th August, and the sudden Japanese collapse in mid-August, took Allied forces in South East Asia completely by surprise.

Back at his headquarters in Colombo, Mountbatten moved

---

1. Mark Andrew Lawrence, "Forging the Combination: Britain and the Indo-China Problem, 1945–1950", in M.A. Lawrence and Fredrik Logeval (eds), *The First Vietnam War: Colonial Conflict and Cold War Crisis* (Cambridge, MA 2007), p. 112, calls this "minor agenda item" a "significant British victory".
2. F.S.V. Donnison, *British Military Administration in the Far East, 1943–1946* (London: Her Majesty's Stationery Office, 1956), 404.

swiftly to deal with issues raised at Potsdam that related to French Indochina. Probably acting on advice from his newly-appointed associate General Slim, he chose General Gracey's 20th Indian Division as the unit that would accept the surrenders south of the 16th Parallel. One factor in the selection, aside from the Division's location relatively nearby in Burma, was that by August 1945 it contained only a handful of conscripted British personnel.[3] These men, throughout Southeast Asia, were scheduled to be repatriated as quickly and as efficiently as possible, in a program ineptly code-named Operation Python.[4] As Daniel Marston argues, one of the new developments with the Indian Army's role in their campaigns in French Indochina and the Netherlands East Indies was that there was no support from the British Army, a consequence of manpower shortages not only of frontline troops but support staff as well. Whereas the previous model was to have a British battalion in each Indian Army brigade, in 1945 and 1946, the Indian Army operated without any British battalions.[5]

Gracey learned about his own mission, code-named Operation Masterdom, when he was on home leave and the 20th Division was winding down its fight against the Japanese. The general returned to Burma on 31 August, bringing the news of the Division's imminent transfer to French Indochina. By then, the war was effectively over. Nevertheless, the American general Douglas MacArthur (1880–1964), who was to preside over the

---

[3] British units attached the 20th Division were withdrawn and their soldiers repatriated beginning in June 1945. The handful of British soldiers who came to Saigon with Gracey were all technical specialists. The remaining personnel, aside from the officers, were Indian or Gurkhas.

[4] Daniel Marston, "The 20th Indian Division in French Indochina, 1945–46", in Patrick Rose and Alan Jeffreys (eds), *The Indian Army, 1939–47: Experience and Development* (London: Routledge, 2017), 200.

[5] Marston, *The Indian Army and the End of the Raj*, 37–38.

formal Japanese surrender in Tokyo Bay on 2 September, had decreed to Mountbatten that no Allied troops could move into Japanese-occupied areas in Southeast Asia before the formal surrender had taken place.[6] MacArthur's order played into the hands of anti-colonial forces throughout the region and in particular in the Netherlands East Indies and the northern portion of French Indochina.[7] This was exacerbated by the exclusion of the French and Dutch from acting as Allied Powers in Allied Order No. 1, which resulted in the Japanese refusing to follow orders issued by French and Dutch officers parachuted into occupied territory since they were not vested with command powers.

The political situation in the French colony of Cochin China was more fluid and fractious than in the north, where several anti-colonial forces groups competed with the Communist-dominated Viet Minh movement for followers and control.[8] These included a significant Trotskyite faction, two anti-French religious groups and an anti-colonial party that was receiving support from Japan.[9] On 25 August Emperor Bao Dai, who had proclaimed Vietnam's independence in March, abdicated the throne and declared his loyalty to the incoming Viet

---

6   See Geraint Hughes, "A 'Post-War' War: The British Occupation of French-Indochina, September 1945–March 1946", *Small Wars & Insurgencies* 17, no. 3 (2006): 267.
7   Peter Neville, 'Britain in Vietnam: Prelude to Disaster, 1945–6', *Military History and Policy* 27 (London: Routledge, 2007), 71: "We can only speculate about how events might have been altered if Gracey's division had arrived in Vietnam three weeks earlier than it did."
8   Shawn F. McHale, *The First Vietnam War: Violence, Sovereignty, and the Fracture of the South, 1945–1956* (New York: Cambridge University Press, 2021), chap. 1.
9   See Van Ngo, *Revolutionaries They Could not Break: The Fight for the Fourth International in Indochina 1930–1945* (London: Index Books, 1995), esp. 95–110; Milton Sacks, "Marxism in Vietnam", in Frank N. Trager (ed.), *Marxism in Southeast Asia: A Study of 4 Countries* (Stanford: Stanford University Press, 1965), 109–34 contains a sympathetic account of the Trotskyites in Saigon.

Minh-controlled regime in Hanoi. A few days earlier the emperor had written to General de Gaulle who had just taken power in Paris:

> You have suffered so much in the last four years not to understand that the Vietnamese people who have two thousand years of history and an often-glorious past do not want and cannot support any foreign domination or administration ... You would understand better if you could see what is happening here, if you could feel this desire for independence, which is in everyone's heart.[10]

The emperor's heartfelt letter was ignored. Under de Gaulle, France had no intention of loosening its group on any of its possessions and protectorates, and specifically on those men and women whom France called her "children" in French Indochina.[11] The general remained in command of the French government until he resigned unexpectedly in January 1946. When de Gaulle sent his officers to Indochina, he made it explicitly clear to them that their mission was to restore antebellum French sovereignty over the territory by any means necessary, including deadly force, setting the scene for the bloody conflicts that would engulf Indochina for the next three decades.

Incidentally, during the closing months of 1945 the French and British authorities never used the words "Vietnam" and "Vietnamese", terms which implied a unified, historical nation, perceived as stretching south from the border with China to include all of Cochin China. The French had banned these terms as inflammatory. They resurfaced in Bao Dai's declaration of

---

10 See Philippe Devillers, *Histoire du Vietnam de 1945 à 1952* (Paris: Éditions du Seuil, 1952), 124 for the full text.
11 Gilbert Pilleul and Institut Charles de Gaulle (eds), *Le Général de Gaulle et l'Indochine, 1940–1946: Colloque* (Paris: Plon, 1982), 103.

independence in March 1945 and in documents produced by the Democratic Republic of Vietnam (DRV) and by other anti-colonial elements in the second half of 1945. Documents produced by Gracey, Moke and by French and Cambodian officials, on the other hand, refer consistently to the Vietnamese as "Annamites", depriving them at a linguistic level of what they considered to be their nationhood and their recently proclaimed independence.[12]

In Hanoi at 2.00 pm on 2 September 1945, just as the Japanese were surrendering in Tokyo Bay, the leader of the Viet Minh movement, Ho Chi Minh (1890–1969), speaking before an enormous crowd in Hanoi, declared Vietnam's outright and complete independence from France. The new regime called itself the Democratic Republic of Vietnam or DRV.[13] Ho's speech was radioed to the south where a Southern Region Provisional Administrative Committee, uneasily dominated by a Viet Minh faction had been set in place by authorities in Hanoi a couple of weeks before. The committee had been forewarned of Ho's proclamation and its members scrambled to organize appropriate celebrations in central Saigon.

Unfortunately, the radio connection with Hanoi was hard to establish and very few people of Saigon were able to hear Ho's address. Nonetheless a celebratory parade, involving perhaps as many as 20,000 people, some of them in quasi-military formations and lightly armed, proceeded joyfully up what had been Rue Catinat, temporarily renamed (in Vietnamese) Paris Commune Street. When the procession reached the Catholic cathedral, shots rang out; the crowd scattered and several French citizens including an aged, pro-Vietnamese Catholic priest lay dead. There were

---

[12] See Christopher E Goscha, *The Penguin History of Modern Vietnam* (London: Penguin, 2017).
[13] The DRV became the Socialist Republic of Vietnam (SRV) in 1975, after it was victorious in the Second Indochina War.

few if any Vietnamese casualties but the Viet Minh-sponsored police swiftly arrested more than 200 French men and women who had been watching the procession.[14] These prisoners were released later in the day but the fervent anti-colonial behaviour of the crowd, later downplayed by many French observers, foreshadowed extensive instability ahead. Indeed, as a sympathetic reviewer of Christopher Goscha's recent history of Vietnam has pointed out: "September 2, 1945 marks less the birth of a nation than the start of overlapping and intersecting wars."[15]

Soon afterwards General Gracey was officially named Commander of Allied Land Forces in French Indo-China, operating south of the 16th parallel. His military superior was his friend General Slim, who commanded Allied forces throughout the region. Both generals reported to Mountbatten, who reported to the recently installed Labour government in London and to British authorities in New Delhi. Gracey was ordered to accept the surrenders of an estimated 70,000 Japanese troops in Cochin-China, southern Annam, Cambodia and parts of Laos; to maintain or restore law and order, and to repatriate Allied prisoners of war. An unstated but fully understood aspect of his orders

---

14   Devillers, *Histoire*, 97. See also Christopher Goscha, "This Is the End? The French Settler Community in Saigon and the Fall of Indo China in 1945" (unpublished, n.d.). I am grateful to Goscha for providing me with a copy. On 22 September, a Viet Minh spokesman, Dr Bac, told Krull that the French had opened fire and that fifteen Vietnamese had been killed. No other sources, including those sympathetic with the Viet Minh, confirm Bac's statements; For a vivid eyewitness account of the event, see Jacques Le Bourgeois, *Saigon sans La France: Des Japonais au Viet-Minh (Souvenirs)* (Paris: Plon, 1949), 78 ff; See also McHale, *The First Vietnam War*.
15   Gerard Sasge, "Review of Vietnam: A New History, by Christopher Goscha", *H-France* 17, no. 19 (October 2017), <https://www.h-france.net/vol17reviews/vol17no194sasges.pdf>. Certainly, fighting against the French occurred in Cochin-China more than it did in the north, where officials were eager to maintain, friendly relations with France, for the time being. It's likely that the violence described below occurred without backing from the DRV.

was that the British government expected the French to return to the region and resume control in the not-too-distant future.[16]

The historian Daniel Marston has noted that Gracey was specifically asked:

> To report on Indochina's lines of communication, airfields, and the port of Saigon; open river and sea approaches to Saigon; using Japanese resources, reduce size of Japanese HQs as soon as possible; and maintain liaison with the French local government.[17]

These tasks were all straightforward except for the concluding phrase, for since 9 March 1945, as we have seen, there had been no "French local government" in Cochin China with which Gracey could maintain liaison. Instead, the occupying Japanese forces had allowed the newly established Vietnamese authorities in Saigon to maintain order until Gracey and his troops unceremoniously pushed the local authorities aside. The Viet Minh-controlled Committee had no official standing with Gracey, Mountbatten or the British government and Gracey didn't meet formally with the Committee's representatives until 2 October, only a few days before a substantial number of French troops came ashore in Saigon and altered the balance of power in the region dramatically.[18]

On 4 September, two days after Japan's formal surrender and

---

16 See The National Archives of the United Kingdom (hereafter TNA), WO 203/5444, South East Asia Command: Military Headquarters Papers.
17 File 4/2, 30 August 1945, Gracey Papers, Liddell Hart Centre for Military Archives, King's College London in Marston, "The 20th Indian Division in French Indo-China, 1945–46", footnote 26. See also File 4/2ALFSEA Op Directive no 8, 23 August 1945, Gracey Papers, Liddell Hart Centre for Military Archives, King's College London.
18 Peter M. Dunn, *The First Vietnam War* (London: C. Hurst, 1985), 171–72. According to Dunn, Gracey's chief of staff, Brigadier Maunsell, met with members of the committee on two occasions in September.

nine days before Gracey landed in Saigon a seventeen-man contingent of American soldiers attached to the US Office of Strategic Services (OSS) arrived there under the command of Major Peter Dewey (1916–1945). The OSS mission was "to protect US property, locate and assist American POWs and gather intelligence on southern Indochina".[19] It's unclear what "gathering intelligence" was meant to involve and Gracey had unsuccessfully opposed any OSS presence in Saigon, given the long-standing US interest in Indochina since even before 1945. He had managed to reduce the size of the mission from a proposed fifty men to seventeen. The day after he arrived in Saigon, Gracey met Dewey and urged him to stop gathering intelligence and to break off his contacts with the Provisional Committee. Dewey, who never acknowledged Gracey's authority, refused to do so, and never shared any of the OSS unit's findings with Gracey or his staff.[20]

In north Vietnam meanwhile, another OSS contingent headed by Major Archimedes Patti had made friendly contact with Ho Chi Minh and the Viet Minh leadership. Patti openly supported Vietnam's recently proclaimed independence.[21] However, others within the OSS contingent were more circumspect about Ho Chi Minh, choosing instead to assist the French in their reconquest on the basis that it would be preferable to secure American interests in the region.[22] Over the next few weeks, the OSS contingent's communications from Cochin China with Washington and with its headquarters in Colombo,

---

19 David P. Chandler, R. B. Cribb, and Li Narangoa (eds), *End of Empire: 100 Days in 1945 that Changed Asia and the World*, Asia Insights 8 (Copenhagen, Denmark: NIAS Press, 2016), 178. See also Ronald H. Spector, *Advice and Support: The Early Years of the United States Army in Vietnam, 1941–1960* (New York and London: Free Press ; Collier Macmillan, 1985), 64 ff.
20 Spector, *Advice and Support*, 65.
21 See Archimedes L.A. Patti, *Why Viet Nam? Prelude to America's Albatross* (Berkeley: University of California Press, 1980).
22 I am grateful to Christopher Goscha for this insight.

Ceylon, were anti-colonial and pro-Viet Minh, largely a reflection of Patti's personal beliefs more so than that of the intelligence officers on the mission as a whole.

The arrival of General Gracey by air on 13 September was captured in a photograph taken by a renowned European photo-journalist named Germaine Krull (1897–1986), who had flown in from Rangoon the day before with a handful of other journalists to cover it.[23] The general had been preceded by the 80th Brigade's headquarters contingent, a battalion of Indian soldiers, two platoons of French Marines and a company of Gurkhas from 1/1 GR. At the Japanese-administered airport of Saigon, Gracey and his entourage were met by a British colonel named Cass—Gracey's intelligence officer in the weeks ahead—as well as a handful of Western journalists, two Japanese Generals, a Vice Admiral and a dozen other Japanese officers. The photograph of the people assembled to welcome him does not include anyone resembling a DRV delegation, but we know that four members of the fifteen-member Provisional Committee were there to welcome Gracey. The General paid no attention to them or to anyone else, after shaking a few Japanese hands as he made his way to Saigon.[24]

The photographer Germaine Krull was a fervent Gaullist

---

23 Germaine Krull, "Diary of Saigon, Following the Allied Occupation in September 1945" ([c. 1945]), Box Folder 7, Douglas Pike Collection and Vietnamese Archive, Texas Technical University. The document was anonymously translated from French. I am grateful to Christopher Goscha for sending me a copy. The Institut Charles de Gaulle in Paris holds Krull's postwar reports from South East Asia. Most of the reports are unpublished. See Kim Sichel, *Germaine Krull: Photographer of Modernity* (Cambridge, Mass.: MIT Press, 1999).

24 The Trotskyite faction of the committee refused on principle to greet the Allied mission and was angered by the expressions of support for the Viet Minh faction that were already coming from the Soviet Union. The Viet Minh dealt with the Trotskyites severely in succeeding months.

and a lifelong friend of André Malraux, but she seems to have been unaware that de Gaulle had no intention of recognizing the allegedly independent states of Indochina. As she wrote:

> Gracey's arrival resembled that of that of any high official. The only thing I noticed was the marked contrast in demeanour between the Japanese bowing obsequiously with eyes cast downward, and the British erect and supercilious. The General spoke a few words to the interpreter and without a glance at the Japanese, got into his car and drove off with his staff. The British had arrived to take over. There was not a single Frenchman at the airport.[25]

Gracey's chief of staff, Brigadier Maunsell, later recalled having glimpsed the Provisional Committee's Viet Minh delegation at the airport. "We didn't know who they were," he said. "They were just a little group that turned out later to be the Viet Minh".[26] The general's official car, *faute de mieux*, was the Japanese commander's Chrysler convertible driven by a Japanese chauffeur. Driving into the city the general would have noticed banners welcoming the British and flags of the United Kingdom, the United States, the newly established DRV and the Soviet Union. There were no French flags on display; the Vietnamese had deliberately reminded their former colonisers that they were not Allied Powers. On that same afternoon Krull described her own impressions of the city. Rue Catinat with its shops and cafes, she wrote, was "the kind of attractive street that one might find in any small French provincial town". In the nearby Palais de Gouvernement, the Provisional Committee, soon to be expelled, had set up its headquarters. Krull wrote:

---

25 Krull, "Diary of Saigon, Following the Allied Occupation in September 1945".
26 Dunn, *The First Vietnam War*, 152, citing Dunn's 1977 interview with Maunsell.

All the Allied flags were on display there with the glaring exception of the French. Of course, there was the familiar red one with the yellow star of the Viet Minh.[27] Annamite soldiers stood guard at the entrance. Their uniform was a combination of Japanese and pre-war French. They carried guns and watched closely all French passersby. However, there were not many of these, and the few who had to go through that part of town glared furiously at the guard. Magnificent cars bearing the Viet Minh emblem kept driving up and there was an incessant activity of coming and going at the door. Great banners reading "Down with Imperialism" and "Slavery is over" were everywhere. Everywhere, that is, except the Rue Catinat.[28]

Gracey had not been briefed about the Provisional Committee and he had very sketchy information about the eleven-day old Democratic Republic of Vietnam that had assumed power in Hanoi. His most consistent source of information about Indochina was derived almost entirely from the French, particularly Colonel Jean Cédile (1908–1984), de Gaulle's recently arrived personal representative in Cochin China. Cédile had parachuted into the countryside near Saigon on 24 August, and was imprisoned by the Japanese until 1 September as he was not recognised as an 'official' representative of the Allied Powers. He was an experienced colonial administrator although he had no previous experience in Indochina, and unlike most of the French inhabitants of Saigon, was also a fervent Gaullist. On his release, he had immediately contacted the Provisional Committee, but he never had anything substantial to offer them.[29]

---

27   In 2023, this was still the flag of the Socialist Republic of Vietnam.
28   Krull, "Diary of Saigon, Following the Allied Occupation in September 1945".
29   In what follows I have drawn on Christopher Goscha's unpublished paper "This is the End? The French Settler Community in Saigon and the Fall of Indochina in 1945".

Gracey had received no intelligence about the widespread hostility that had developed between the Vietnamese and the local French population, which Cédile and others had observed in Saigon on 2 September and less dramatically ever since. Cédile downplayed this antagonism and Gracey had certainly not been warned to expect any organized armed resistance. Using a platoon of Gurkhas, the general moved swiftly to remove the Provisional Committee from its offices in what had once been the palace of the French governor general.[30] The committee shifted its personnel without incident to Saigon's Hotel de Ville, but on the following day Radio Vietnam broadcasting from Hanoi noted that "the English mission has violated the sovereignty of the Democratic Republic of Vietnam by occupying the offices of local officials".[31] The move soon provoked a massive anti-British demonstration generated with great speed by local authorities. Their capacity to bring thousands of their supporters into the streets, long before the existence of cell phones, should have been a warning to the British but they failed to heed it. To Phok Siv, a Cambodian police official, who had just returned from visiting Saigon, it was obvious. In an interesting document dated 14 September 1945 and titled "From the cafés", he recorded that "the new Communist governmental regime is far preferred by the Vietnamese".[32]

Gracey was slow to acknowledge the Communist affiliation of the Viet Minh, although Germaine Krull, who had been a member of the French Communist Party in the 1930s, easily recognised their leaders in Saigon as dedicated Communist

---

30 Because this peremptory action was so clearly political, and outside Gracey's remit, Neville, *Britain in Vietnam*, 77 refers to it as "odd". Its *brusquerie* foreshadowed much of Gracey's subsequent behaviour.
31 *Voix de Vietnam*, monitored in Phnom Penh, 2 September 1945.
32 NAC, 'From the Cafés', Report by Phok Siv, 14 September 1945.

patriots and the Provisional Committee as a Communist front. The General was also unaware of the fragmented and toxic character of local politics in Saigon, which had led to a split in the committee between a Trotskyite element favouring armed action against the French and those taking orders from Hanoi that discouraged armed resistance at this time. The DRV leadership also had the non-Communist, anti-French Cao Dai and Hoa Hao factions to contend with. The split, partially repaired later on, explains why only four members of the committee had been at the airport to meet the British general.

As an accredited French war correspondent, Krull easily gained access to a range of French sources in Saigon while her anti-colonial stance gained her entrée to members of the Provisional Committee. Krull came away from these meetings favourably impressed by the committee members' dignity, patriotism and self-assurance. At the same time, she was dismayed by the racism, rancour and entitlement displayed by the French residents of the city.[33] In contrast, Gracey had had no orders or inclination to greet or honour the committee's delegation at the airport. Indeed, as Peter Neville has written, "his orders had spelled out that only French authority was to be recognized".[34]

Many American writers and some British ones have treated General Gracey harshly, starting with Ellen Hammer in the 1950s and followed by Barbara Tuchman, George Rosie and others later on. These authors have accused the general of being a *pukka sahib* who held rigid, imperialist views and personally set in motion the First Indochina War (1945–1954) that soon engulfed Cochin-China. The Swedish-American scholar Fredrik Logevall, for example, has written that Gracey was "an unreconstructed

---

33 Krull, "Diary of Saigon, Following the Allied Occupation in September 1945," 14
34 Neville, *Britain in Vietnam*, 96.

colonialist, born in the empire [who] had spent his whole career in the Indian Army."[35] Logevall fails to note that reconstructed colonialists (whatever that phrase might mean) were scarce or non-existent in 1945.[36] Like many other writers he suggests that a more peaceful solution to issues in Cochin China was readily available to Gracey.

Yet he and other writers hostile to Gracey fail to suggest what such an arrangement might have involved, what pressures there were on anyone to make it, or how it would have worked. They ignore the fact that Gracey was obeying, and sticking to the orders he had been given. Moreover, the British general was terribly understaffed while attempting to broker some semblance of a settlement between the DRV and the French settler community, both of whom were becoming increasingly hostile and belligerent not just against each other but against the British military authorities as well. Instead, they seem to be dismayed that the general failed from the start to honour Vietnam's supposedly uncontested independence, and to accept the legitimacy of the Provisional Committee that had been formed less than a month before he arrived.

These authors expected Gracey to take an open-minded, anti-colonial position and seem aggrieved that a British general of Gracey's generation didn't share America's overriding, postwar anti-colonial priorities, or American *post hoc* regrets about what happened later in Vietnam. As the former Indian Army major Philip Malins stated in the American TV series *Vietnam: A Television History*:

---

35 Fredrik Logevall, *Embers of War: The Fall of an Empire and the Making of America's Vietnam* (New York: Random House, 2012), 113.

36 For a detailed account of Gracey's career and a discussion of his critics, see T. O. Smith, *Vietnam and the Unravelling of Empire: General Gracey in Asia, 1942–1951* (Houndmills, Basingstoke, Hampshire: Palgrave Macmillan, 2014).

Gracey was not in a position to hand over French Indochina on his own personal whim or because he believed or didn't believe in independence for the Annamites. He had to obey the orders he had been given.[37]

Indeed, with what I've learned about Gracey on the one hand, and the long-range, clearly stated British policies for postwar French Indochina on the other, the flexibility that Gracey's critics have demanded of him was never remotely possible.[38] In this context Moke told Barnett that in retrospect he felt that Gracey was:

> in a difficult position. He felt, as I did in a minor way, we felt ourselves as caretakers. As there were no French troops to deal with the situation. That's why we were so damned glad to see the general arriving on 5 October on the *Richelieu* with some troops.

Indeed, before he left French Indochina in 1946 Gracey spoke of his mission in similar terms, talking to the American journalist Harold Isaacs: "We have done our best by the French," the general said. "They are our Allies and we have discharged our obligation to them. Now it's up to them to carry on."[39]

---

[37] See Ellen J. Hammer, *The Struggle for Indochina, 1940–1955* (Stanford, Calif: Stanford University Press, 1966); Barbara W. Tuchman, *The March of Folly: From Troy to Vietnam*, 1st edn (London: Michael Joseph, 1984); See also John Springhall, "'Kicking out the Vietminh': How Britain Allowed France to Reoccupy South Indochina, 1945–46", *Journal of Contemporary History* 40, no. 1 (2005): 115–30.

[38] On British policy, see Lawrence, "Forging the Combination"; See also John Saville, *The Politics of Continuity: British Foreign Policy and the Labour Government, 1945–46* (New York: Verso, 1993), esp. 99–102.

[39] Harold R. Isaacs, *No Peace for Asia* (New York: Macmillan Co., 1947), 162. Isaacs' interview for the WGBH Vietnam series in July 1981 refers to Gracey's "unbelievably myopic" efforts in Saigon. To be fair, Isaacs is much harsher about the French.

The French "carried on", of course, into what soon became a full-scale war even while the country was still under Gracey's watch. It was fought mainly in the North and only ended nine years later after the defeat of the French Far East Expeditionary Corps at the hands of Viet Minh forces at Dien Bien Phu. In the closing months of 1945, a war of those dimensions was not in sight, and several months later General Leclerc told Mountbatten: "Your General Gracey has saved Indochina"—surely a more grandiose accomplishment than Gracey had ever had in mind and perhaps the ultimate irony given what would play out next.[40] Throughout his time in Saigon Gracey was fully supported by his military superior in Singapore, General Slim, who eased some of the tensions that developed between his old friend and Mountbatten, who was sensitive to negative views of Gracey's mission that circulated among recently elected British Labour Party politicians, most Western journalists and Indian leaders gearing up for India's independence.

Ten years later in *Defeat into Victory* Slim wrote that Gracey "was faced with a most difficult politico-military situation in Allied territory, which he handled in a firm, cool, and altogether admirable manner."[41] With hindsight Slim's verdict seems too gentle, given what we know now of Gracey's consistently abrupt and often bellicose behaviour, but Slim was obviously unwilling, in the closing pages of his triumphal memoir, to second-guess the conduct of his close friend, fellow Gurkha, and comrade in arms. It's impossible to say whether a smoother, more mannerly general than Gracey, given the same orders, would have done

---

40 Louis M. Mountbatten and Philip Ziegler, *Personal Diary of Admiral the Lord Louis Mountbatten, Supreme Allied Commander, South-East Asia, 1943–1946* (London: Collins, 1988). Cambodia is not mentioned in this book.
41 William Joseph Slim, *Defeat into Victory* (London: Cassell & Company, 1956), 532.

things differently or if the outcomes would have been different. There is no evidence that the Provisional Committee or the French would have watered down their respective positions, or that someone other than Gracey could have engineered a peaceful outcome to the volatile situation.

On 18 September Slim paid a flying visit to Saigon where at an improvised news conference he tried to reassure hostile Western journalists about the nature of General Gracey's mission. In his words, "We are not here to get involved in a situation that is as complicated as the one we have encountered in Burma. English troops are here only to insure the disarmament of the Japanese."[42]

In the same speech, reported by a different source Slim insisted, "We have no political aims whatsoever except for dealing with the danger rising."[43] On the following day Brigadier Maunsell, Gracey's chief of staff, met with DRV authorities and shortly afterwards, Gracey issued a wide-ranging decree that closed all newspapers, banned public meetings, demonstrations and processions, and enforced a night curfew. The decree amounted to declaring martial law. It ignited a massive anti-British demonstration and a paralysing general strike. With hindsight the decree seems too far reaching and premature, but Gracey stung by his reception in Saigon, was eager to get on with the task assigned to him. He didn't get a political adviser from Singapore for another ten days. Had the advisor arrived earlier—as Gracey would probably have preferred—it's likely that some of the general's brusque behaviour could have been muted or papered over.

By 21 September, in any case, Saigon seemed to be spinning out of Gracey's control. Writing to Mountbatten, Gracey

---

[42] Jean-Michel Hertrich, *Doc-Lap !: l'indépendance ou la mort* (Paris: Jean Vigneau, 1946), 63; Dunn, *The First Vietnam War*, 157, which asserts that Slim "immediately recognized the impossibility of Gracey's task".

[43] *New York Times*, 20 September 1945.

somewhat disingenuously justified his wide-ranging decree:

> I would stress that though it may appear that I have interfered in the politics of the country, I have done so only in the interest of the maintenance of law and order and after close collaboration with some senior French representatives.[44]

Two days earlier, as conditions worsened Gracey had radioed Moke in Burma and summoned him to come to Saigon as soon as he could assemble a skeleton staff and a platoon of Gurkhas.[45] Moke was not told why he had been chosen or what he would be expected to do. When he enquired about the rationale for his Saigon posting, "all I heard was that there seemed to be a spot of bother in Saigon".

---

44 TNA, WO 203/5562 Gracey to Mountbatten, 21 September 1945. Gracey issued the proclamation under pressure from de Gaulle's representative in Saigon. The text appears in Dunn, *The First Vietnam War*, 169–70.

45 In 1981, Moke could not pinpoint the date of his arrival in Saigon. Barnett concluded that it was late at night on 24–25 September. We know that Lt Col. E. Mullaly assumed command of 4/10 GR on 19 September, so with weather-induced delays considered, Barnett's guess is plausible. Moreover, on 25 September, Gracey began to use Japanese troops for the first time and authorised Moke to use them to maintain order in Saigon.

EIGHT

Moke in Saigon

MANY YEARS AFTER HIS POSTING IN SAIGON, WHEN ANTHONY Barnett asked Moke why Gracey had singled him out to assist with the situation in Vietnam, Moke replied, 'I'd been in his division a long time, from Imphal. I knew him well. Perhaps he thought, Do we have all the chaps that can be called in? What about old Moke? Something like that, I hope.'[1]

To accompany him to Saigon, Moke assembled what he later described as "a mere four officers and a few other ranks, British and Gurkha". Owing to the monsoon his contingent's flight was delayed and was reduced from three planeloads to one. As he recalled:

> Anyway, we all got into only one Dakota. There was only one spare. The Royal Air Force was scattered all over the place: Java, Sumatra, Malaya, God knows where. They were very short. So, we had to leave various things behind, like our escort, equipment. We just had a wireless detachment and my staff officers. That would have been myself, my brigade-major,

---

[1] Moke's policing experiences in the Assam Rifles, if Gracey had been aware of them, would also have worked in his favour.

David Wenham[2], John Arnold, my liaison, a signals officer and about half a dozen men—my driver, my orderly and so on. Nearly all Gurkhas, yes, oh I forgot there was one marvellous chap, Pakistani, who became my intelligence officer. He had his own Pakistani orderly.[3]

Moke and his companions arrived at Saigon in the early hours of 26 September and by then his mission had changed dramatically. Gracey had authorised Moke to use Japanese troops the day before the latter's arrival but they had yet to be used before that.

In his book *The First Vietnam War*, Peter Dunn cites a 20th Division operational order dated 23 September 1945 "that dealt with the proposed establishment of headquarters in Phnom Penh and Camranh Bay, to be commanded respectively by Brigadier Hirst Royal Artillery and Lieutenant Colonel Murray of 4/10GR, representing the 100th Brigade".[4] Moke's posting to Camranh Bay never went into effect and his mission to Cambodia was postponed, because immediately after he landed in Saigon on 25 September, Gracey set him to work commanding Indian and Japanese troops against insurgent local forces as the First Indochina War had effectively broken out on the night of 22–23 September. The decision to keep the Japanese under arms and use them to supplement Allied forces was brought on by the deteriorating situation in Saigon as well as the continued limitations

---

2   Moke's second-in-command, Major (later Lt Colonel) David Wenham had earned a Military Cross in Burma, where he had served in the same Brigade as Moke. He retired from the Army after the Partition of India, and rarely talked about his time in Cambodia. I'm grateful to his son Tony Wenham (email 10 December 2017) for this information.
3   Of course, the term "Pakistani" was not in use in 1945.
4   Dunn, *The First Indochina War*, 199. The book contains a good deal of valuable interview material.

in the number of British and Indian troops available to Gracey.[5]

The general had also made an audacious gamble—which backfired—when he chose to release and arm the imprisoned French troops of 9ᵉ *régiment d'infanterie de marine* [9th Marine Infantry Regiment] on 23 September 1945 who assisted in executing the French *coup d'etat* proposed by Cedile. They used the unruly, recently imprisoned French troops from the 9ᵉ RIC to remove Viet Minh officials from their remaining offices in Saigon. Although the *coup* itself was almost bloodless, Gracey was dismayed by the indiscipline and aggressive behaviour of the French soldiers, as they rampaged through the city harassing and beating local people. Gracey ordered them back to barracks until French officers arrived with reinforcements in early October. It was too late.

Most of the French soldiers had been imprisoned since March. They were restless, unkempt and poorly led. After the *coup*, when Gracey had confined them to barracks, the French population of Saigon, feeling safer, expressed collective rage at the Vietnamese in general and harassed local people on the streets. At this point, the Committee probably decided that Gracey and his soldiers were impossible to deal with and should be driven out of Saigon by force. The French indiscretions had unleashed Vietnamese furore against their former colonial masters, culminating in what has come to be known as the Cité Herault massacre on 24–25 September 1945.[6] On the night before Murray arrived, a mob of armed Vietnamese had attacked a residential section of the city known as the Cité Heraud that was inhabited by impecunious French and Eurasian families.

---

5   McHale, *The First Vietnam War*, 54.
6   Christopher Goscha, 'Herault Massacre', *Guerre d'Indochine*, https://indochine.uqam.ca/en/historical-dictionary/583-herault-massacre.html, accessed 7 July 2023.

In the ensuing fracas perhaps as many as 134 residents, including women and children, were killed or disappeared, and many more were seriously injured. No one claimed responsibility for the attack and the committee was slow to express regret but British and French authorities were quick to blame the Viet Minh. The Heraud Massacre, as it came to be called, hardened the Allied attitude towards the committee, whose animosity towards the British had intensified after by the misbehaviour of French soldiers earlier in the week. More than anything else, I would argue, the massacre made wider conflict inevitable and forestalled meaningful discussions between the British authorities and the Viet Minh.[7]

Moke and his companions landed in Saigon in pouring rain soon after the massacre. There was no one to meet them, but an RAF driver and a pick-up truck were eventually rounded up. Moke told Barnett that the driver said, "I can't understand why you're here, sir. We know nothing about you. You can't get into Saigon. It's besieged and surrounded." As Murray later quipped, "I felt someone in Burma might have warned us about 'the siege'. So this was the 'spot of bother'".[8] Talking to Barnett he recalled:

> Anyway, we eventually persuaded him to have a go. So off we went, tremendously wet, with the RAF chap and his mates in the cabin and us outside. Down the road there was a bridge over a river and I remember seeing some stupid French guard. They did a sort of "Halt" whatever, feebly. I thought at the time that they were pretty useless. We passed them, we went around and round Saigon looking for headquarters in the

---

[7] See Geoffrey Gunn, "The Heraud (Saigon) Massacre October 24–25 1945", in Chandler, Cribb and Narangoa (eds), *End of Empire*, 205–6; Dunn, *The First Vietnam War*, 203 quotes a French intelligence officer who suggested that the Trotskyites might have been involved.

[8] Murray, "Some Notes to Amuse Myself".

pouring rain. We passed the town hall, whatever you call it in French, and every time we passed it the chap said, "To arms! To arms!" We must have passed it half a dozen times. On one occasion we turned down a side road and right across it was a roadblock. Bren gun, or *mitrailleuse*, opened up on us.

AB: Directly or into the air?

Well, it didn't hit us! I had a pistol (*laughs*) but we said that's not the way to Headquarters! We'd come across lots of roadblocks in Burma, so we turned around and went the other way. Unfortunately, just as he got right across the road, as he was turning, the RAF chap stalled his engine, which is marvellous. Anyway, we got away, but that was our introduction to Saigon! I can see the road now: it was tree-lined. I remember the damned thing across it, and then they just opened up.

Eventually, we came across a British soldier leaning against a lamppost. I said, "Where's British headquarters?" He looked at me and said, "Ere, Sir". He thought I was a bloody stupid officer (*laughs*). We went in, absolutely soaked. It was late. It was dark. I found a staff officer who said, "Here you are at last, where have you been?" I said, "I don't know. What am I to do?" He said, "Well, you'd better go and have a kip." He told me to go around to the 1st Gurkhas headquarters. The 1st Gurkhas were my great friends, as any Gurkha is. God they were kind. We were sent through. They gave us lots of rum and looked after us splendidly. At about four in the morning I was sound asleep and a chap pulled back my mosquito net and said, "the general wants to see you for breakfast".[9]

In "Some Notes", Murray provided a slightly different account:

---

9   Moke Murray, interviewed by Anthony Barnett, 1981.

I passed through low grade ("Hullo sir, you *are* wet')—to the middle ("Good Lord sir, what are you doing here?")—to the high: "I don't know why you're here, you'd better see the General." I was ushered into the presence and this was better. [Gracey said:] "So you are here at last. I've got a job for you and your party. Stop the night with the [1GR] Gurkhas round the corner. I'll give you a guide." (Oh, blessed General).[10]

After a couple of hours' sleep, Moke changed into a dry uniform and reported for breakfast with Gracey and the general's staff. In 1981 he recalled:

I went around and had breakfast, there were extraordinary people around and eventually we had what was called Morning Prayers, intelligence reports. We all gathered round, I listened. I didn't take in very much because I didn't know what was going on, except that there was something going on. At the end of it, [Gracey] said, "Now, Moke, you're taking over Saigon. You've got the First Gurkhas, you've got part of the Hyderabad Regiment and you've got 2 Japanese battalions. Clear the area, I want the whole of Saigon cleared. I said "What of?" Or words to that effect and he said, "You'll find out". Which I did, being a good soldier.[11]

Originally, General Gracey had not planned to use armed Japanese troops to maintain order in and around Saigon. He had, after all, been sent to Saigon to *disarm* them. After 23 September, however, his hand was forced by the increasing violence of Viet Minh–dominated forces, the shortage of British and Indian troops

---

10   Murray, "Some Notes to Amuse Myself".
11   In his comments on this chapter (email 17 September 2017) Christopher Goscha suggested that for Gracey 'establishing order would include calming the volatile French populations as well as containing the Viet Minh'.

available to control them and by the unruly, racist behaviour of French soldiers and civilians towards not just the Vietnamese population but also Indian and Gurkha soldiers as well as coopted Japanese troops following the French *coup de force*.[12]

On the morning of 25 September, therefore, almost certainly the day Moke arrived, Gracey found himself forced to inaugurate a new, coordinated strategy, cleared with Slim, that involved using Japanese troops to protect the city of Saigon with force if necessary. When Brigadier Doidge Estcourt Taunton, commanding the 80th Brigade in Saigon, was interviewed in 1982, and was asked about the decision to use armed Japanese troops, rather than French, to maintain order, he recalled:

> Everything got out of hand and the only thing to do was to rearm the Japanese, who were highly skilled, they had surrendered, and at that time they were very reliable. It was a bit odd to do, I must admit, but it worked.[13]

Until he was dispatched to Cambodia on 9 October Moke was fully occupied in the northern parts of Saigon, commanding the troops that Gracey had mentioned as well as two companies of French Marines that had arrived in Saigon with Gracey. Moke was generally contemptuous of French military personnel but he admired these Marines, who joined him in Cambodia later on. "They were very good indeed,' he recalled. As for the Japanese, Barnett asked him, 'Did they distinguish between you the British, and the French?'

---

12   Marston, *The Indian Army and the End of the Raj*, 172.
13   Interviewed on 14 July 1982 for the WGBH series *Vietnam: A Television History*. Elsewhere in the interview, Estcourt called the French soldiery "overexcited and trigger happy" while noting that Gurkhas had extensive experience in policing and performed their tasks "almost instinctively". Until February 1946, when the last Japanese troops were repatriated from French Indochina, the Japanese continued to work with British and Indian troops. They refused to take orders from the French who had not, after all, defeated them.

> Yes, very much so. Well, it did shatter me. (Pause). One took things in quickly, you know. It did surprise me, but not all that much. I wasn't aghast at it. One took it in. Anyway, there we were. The two Japanese battalion commanders came and reported to me in my headquarters. One was Sato Butai—Sato's battalion—the other was Imugishi Butai. They were marvellous. One was a major, I think, and one a captain. Imugishi I put in for an MC (Military Cross) for some his actions. He didn't get it, naturally. Whatever I said, they did.

Happily, Moke didn't harbour any preconceptions that he might have had about the Japanese, seeking and obtaining their cooperation. In fact, I've not found any evidence that he disliked the Japanese as people. In Saigon, he'd been told to seek their help and he had always admired their military abilities.

Moke's mission was to secure the city's electric power station and water facilities and to restore order to the northern sector of the city, which included the airport, five kilometres from the centre. His memories of this period are vivid and mostly verifiable. One particular episode was unreported in other sources:

> I remember one extraordinary incident. I was sitting in my headquarters when Sato [the Japanese Battalion commander] came in, they were very good, intelligence wise, naturally, and he said, bowing and scraping … "I have information that a thousand Annamites are going to cross the bridge tomorrow morning at 4 o'clock in the morning and attack Saigon", or words to that effect. I said, "What are you going to do about it?" There was more breathing. I said, "Look, I have been fighting you for the last so many years and I know how good you are. I'll leave it to you." That was all I could do, in fact, because I didn't have anybody. I had one battalion in reserve that were scattered, and two Japanese. I thought, "Oh, God". I really did.

> In the morning I went down to the bridge and there wasn't a sign of anybody. Nobody. From the bridge I could see a lot of these chaps massing, Annamites, and I thought, My God, we really have had it. I didn't know what to do. I had a couple of chaps with me. [The Annamites] all started to cross the bridge like that, and half way across every window and doorway in this side opened up with Japanese. They caught them right at the bridge in an ambush. They were killed. That, incidentally, saved Saigon, I reckon, from a bloody massacre.[14]

When Barnett asked him if the incident had been reported, Moke replied, "Oh, hadn't got the time to report it", adding, "Everybody thinks that everything is written down as you go along." On what must have been the morning of 26 September Lt Colonel Peter Dewey, the commander of the OSS detachment in Saigon, visited Moke's office. As Moke recalled:

> I was in Saigon, in my office, sitting behind my table, when somebody came in and said, "There is an American Colonel to see you". I suppose I knew that there were Americans in one sense, but I had no idea that they had infiltrated into French Indochina. This figure appeared … stop, I'm not certain if this driver of his did not accompany him. Anyway, Dewey came in and said, "I am going to cross the bridge". Why he said it just like that, I don't know. He didn't tell me why. I think it was just informing me, he was on the way. I said, "you can't, you mustn't do that because things are happening on the other side". He said, "We are going anyway, in my Jeep". I said, "Well, don't". I said, "You mustn't", and then I said, "I can't order you because you're not under my command, but if you go over that

---

14   Moke Murray, interviewed by Anthony Barnett, 1981.

bridge you will be killed." I remember it distinctly. The next thing I heard, he had been killed.[15]

When Dewey was heading back to his headquarters from the airport where he had learned that his flight to Colombo was delayed, Viet Minh guerrillas ambushed his jeep and a machine-gun bullet hit him in the back of the head. He died instantly. There is no evidence that the killing was centrally planned or that Dewey's killers had any idea who he was.[16] He was the first American casualty in Indochina. He was also the son of a former US Congressman and a distant cousin of the governor of New York.[17] His death quickly attracted considerable international attention. Ho Chi Minh, still quixotically hoping for an alliance with the United States, wrote a letter to US President Harry Truman regretting the ambush.[18]

In the closing days of September, the politico-military situation in Saigon from Gracey's point of view continued to deteriorate. The city was without electric power for at least two days and the population was running short of food.[19] With hindsight we can speculate that had the Viet Minh–dominated committee been able or willing to maintain order in the city while Gracey disarmed the Japanese, he might have been happier to work with them and might have left Saigon sooner, but such a

---

15 Moke Murray, interviewed by Anthony Barnett, 1981.
16 Herbert Bleuchel, interview on WGBH *Vietnam: a Television History*. See also Dunn, *The First Vietnam War*, 214–23.
17 I'm grateful to Justin Corfield for the information that Peter Dewey and Thomas Dewey, who was the governor of New York in 1945, were sixth cousins.
18 On Dewey's death and its aftermath see Patti, *Why Viet Nam?*, 296–323; for a more balanced account than Patti's see Neville, *Britain in Vietnam*, 90–92.
19 For a vivid account of conditions in Saigon see Hertrich, *Doc-Lap !*, 72 ff. Major Philip Malins MC (1919–2012) was responsible for provisioning the British and Indian troops, Allied prisoners of war, and to a lesser extent the Japanese. See his detailed testimony (which includes some warm praise for Gracey) in his interview in WGBH, *Vietnam: a Television History*.

détente was clearly impossible after the *coup de force* and the Cité Heraut massacre. In any case, maintaining order may never have been within the capacities (or the interests) of the harassed and faction-ridden committee that had been in office for less than a month. Similarly, had Gracey taken a more open-minded view of Viet Minh aspirations instead of referring to them, as "puppets" and calling their followers "hoodlum elements", the Viet Minh might have been more comfortable dealing with him. At the time, however, these decelerating options did not present themselves with any intensity to either side.

The Allies and the Vietnamese opposing them worked uneasily, and under enormous pressure, within the framework of often contradictory orders and suggestions emanating from Paris, London, Singapore and Hanoi.

Gracey had no authority from Mountbatten, Slim or London to negotiate with the Viet Minh, and the French refused to negotiate with the committee on any issues of substance. These issues, of course, were the only ones that the Viet Minh wanted to consider. Moreover, the Viet Minh leaders were unable (and perhaps unwilling) to rein in their ragtag forces. Their superiors in Hanoi repeatedly urged them to do just that while Ho Chi Minh tried to negotiate a non-violent settlement with the French.

On 1 October, four days before substantial numbers of French troops came ashore in Saigon, Gracey met formally for the first time with members of the committee. He was under pressure from Singapore and London, as well as from Mountbatten in New Delhi, to reach some sort of agreement that would enable him to complete his mission speedily and in peace. Unfortunately, Gracey was a brusque and impatient man, his hard-pressed troops were being shot at, and his opening remarks to the committee reflected his impatience:

This is NOT a discussion of policy. That is a matter for the French and Annamites; but my task here is to get the Japanese forces disarmed and shipped as quickly as possible out of this country. Apart from the unnecessary bloodshed being caused by armed action of Annamites, the disarmament and extradition of the Japanese forces is being delayed by the necessity of employing both British and Japanese forces to stop attacks on Allied nationals and to keep the life of Saigon-Cholon going. My whole division with tanks, guns and the finest infantry in the world will shortly be here and the sooner the Annamites return to normal peaceful conditions and behave themselves the sooner can my task be completed.[20]

Gracey was eager to wind up his mission. He had not come to Saigon intending to kill anyone, to negotiate with insurgents or to challenge imminent French authority. He was angry that men from his division, after years of strenuous warfare, were being killed and wounded. After his baleful and condescending opening statement Gracey left the room, and his deputy made a set of sweeping, unviable proposals to the committee, whose administrative structures the French had forcibly dismantled with his encouragement a week before. He demanded that the committee act like a well-staffed governing body that could efficiently order "all armed bands to cease activity at once", remove road blocks, retrieve Dewey's body and "stop molesting Allied nationals". If and when these palpably unworkable requests were satisfied, in other words, Gracey could finish his job and leave the country. "Policy", which he considered to be none of his business, could at that point be discussed between the undermanned and unarmed Vietnamese Committee and spokesmen from the heavily armed

---

20   TNA, WO 203/5444, South East Asia Command: Military Headquarters Papers.

French expeditionary force, which was about to come ashore. In Gracey's unstated view, this outcome would amount to the rapid conclusion of his mission.

The committee's delegates replied to Gracey that "they had welcomed the British on their arrival as they thought they had come to liberate their country from the Japanese and from French domination". As a condition for further negotiations they demanded that the DRV administration be "reinstated with all its former power", knowing perhaps that Gracey would never agree.

A fragile cease-fire that lasted barely a week was all that emerged from this exploratory meeting. The cease-fire allowed both sides to consolidate their forces, to wait for French troops to arrive and to plan their next steps. Barnett asked Moke about subsequent meetings, which took place on 6 and 8 October, he said that he had not attended them, as he recalled:

> All these conferences and truces. I knew they were going on, but I didn't participate. I was well out of that. My impression was that they were trying to negotiate to settle things. Don't forget, we were not there to settle things for the French, although some people think we were, we were not. At least, I'm damned certain I wasn't. And I don't think Gracey was. All he wanted to do was to get on with his damned job.

Gracey never deviated from his "damned job" in Cochin China and neither did Moke, whose view of his responsibilities, with hindsight, was similarly straightforward:

> I was fighting Annamites. Um, I knew exactly what I was doing. We had to sort things out. In Saigon, these, whoever they were, let's call them Annamites, were being a damned nuisance and very dangerous to the French population and to us, and they were endangering the power station and the post

office and this, that and other things, we had to be guarded against whoever they were. Before we can get on with our primary job, we had to quieten things down and settle … and get rid of these people. So, my task was to clear the area, my area, of these whoever they were, anti-government or anti-establishment.[21]

The committee's goal, on the other hand, was simpler than Gracey's or Moke's and more incandescent. It was a *national* policy, laid down by Hanoi, to maintain and consolidate the total independence, under Viet Minh leadership of the single nation whose independence Ho Chi Minh had proclaimed in Hanoi on 2 September. Talking to Barnett, Moke seemed to realise that quashing the Vietnamese passion for independence was not an appropriate or feasible mission for the British to undertake in the wake of World War II, but he never went so far as to say so. In Moke's jaundiced view the French soldiery and the French civilians whom he encountered in Saigon were almost as obstructive and troublesome as the "Annamites". When Barnett asked him, "Did you feel the French were in your way?" he replied:

> Oh yes, very much so. They were frustrating. The extraordinary attitude they seemed to have was that they'd won the war. It infuriated us! It's quite true, in Cambodia also. They seemed to think they'd won the war —of course, they were French. Don't forget it was French Indochina. Really, we were helping them. Rightly or wrongly, I don't know. What we had to do was to help the French to get the Japanese out.[22]

In "Some Notes to Amuse Myself", compiled for the most part in the 1970s, Moke made a similar point: "Some of [the

---

21 Moke Murray, interviewed by Anthony Barnett, 1981.
22 Moke Murray, interviewed by Anthony Barnett, 1981.

French] were inclined to be obstructive and stubborn, and gave the impression that they had caused the collapse of Japan with whom they were not even at war."[23] When asked on the other hand whether he liked the Vietnamese, Moke said:

> Oh, yes, very much. We were *popular* with them. We liked them and they seemed to like us. There was a question of clearing the area of these Annamite types, making it peaceful. The thing that one has to remember, I think about our occur … occupation is not the right word—our going into the country, is that our main object which we never lost sight of, from General Gracey downwards, was to get the Japanese surrendered and out of the country. Whatever else happened, got in our way? This business of Annamites was a nuisance to our prime object. We had to deal with them to get the Japanese out.

This passage marks a unique moment in his interview with Barnett as Murray strayed on to large-scale political issues. His widely held views are not particularly cynical and probably more tolerant than those of many of his peers.

Returning to the action in Saigon, on 5 October, amid the cease-fire, elements of the 9th Colonial Infantry Division of the French Army came ashore in the Vietnamese capital. They paraded through the city in the pouring rain, cheered on by semi-hysterical French civilians and observed by a few silent Vietnamese. General Leclerc, who was to command the division, arrived by air two days later. The American journalist Harold Isaacs watched the French troops arrive. He recalled later that they "looked like GIs: with US uniforms and US weapons".[24] Paul

---

23   Murray, "Some Notes to Amuse Myself".
24   Conversation with author, 10 April 2012.

Mus (1902–1969), a noted Indianist who had been brought up in Hanoi, accompanied the troops as Leclerc's political adviser. In 1946, looking back on the event, Mus wrote: 'Our return in the shadow of the English was never regarded by local people as the return of France but rather like the arrival of a sporting team or a handful of adventurers."[25]

For the French and their Vietnamese opponents in Cochin China, just as what was later referred to as the First Indochina War was gathering momentum, full-scale warfare broke out in the North a year later and quickly spread to the rest of Indochina, and lasted for eight more years. On the other hand, most of the men of 20th Indian Division—including Moke—had been engaged in a war since 1942 that was well and truly over. Once their mission in Cochin China had been accomplished they expected to go home, briefly or for good. The Vietnamese, of course, were at home already and for them, their descendants and the French, American and locally raised armies that opposed them, almost thirty years of relentless warfare lay ahead.

In March 1946 after she had spent six months in Indochina, Germaine Krull wrote insightfully that "The Annamites will have their independence no matter what because they fight for their liberty. We will be obliged to talk to them one day. Why kill, when we can talk?" But almost no one on either side, unfortunately, was listening to ideas like this.

---

[25] David Chandler and Christopher E Goscha, *L'espace d'un regard, l'Asie de Paul Mus, 1902–1969* (Paris: Indes savantes, 2006), 32 Mus was an early and passionate opponent of most French post-1945 policies in Indo-China; See also Agathe Larcher-Goscha, "Ambushed by History: Paul Mus and Colonial France's Forced Re-Entry into Vietnam (1945—1954)", *Journal of Vietnamese Studies* 4, no. 1 (2009): 206–39.

NINE

Becoming Cambodia's Uncrowned King

On 8 October 1945, two days before General Gracey declared that the French had officially returned to power in Cochin China,[1] Moke was ordered to Phnom Penh where he was to serve as Supreme Commander of Allied Land Forces there until December. Moke travelled with the same Indian Army officers who had accompanied him to Saigon from Burma a month before, augmented by what he later called a "Pakistani" intelligence officer, some signals personnel, his interpreter Maurice Besson, and a platoon of Gurkhas from Company "A" of 4/10GR. The contingent was transported to Phnom Penh in a Japanese plane, landing at 1.00 pm on 9 October. The pilot of the plane, apparently, had trained as a Kamikaze: 'I saw his head thing," Moke told Barnett, referring to the headband that Kamikaze pilots wore. He added, "I was a little uneasy."

---

1   On the day that Moke arrived in Cambodia a Civil Affairs Agreement was signed in London that passed the responsibility of administering Indochina below the 16th parallel to France. See Scott L Bills, Empire and Cold War: The Roots of US-Third World Antagonism, 1945–47 (London: Palgrave Macmillan, 1990), 126.

The Allied decision to send someone to Cambodia had been made ten days before, when Generals Slim and Gracey met with Mountbatten at his recently established headquarters in Singapore. The three men agreed that it was important to stabilize what they felt was an uncertain situation in Cambodia. By then, as we have seen, open warfare had broken out in Saigon, which depended for much of its food, especially rice, on Cambodian imports. The Allied commanders feared that the flow of these essential supplies might be disrupted and that the unrest in Cochin China might spread to Cambodia, involving its sizeable Vietnamese population. Moreover, the scrappy information about Cambodia that was available to Gracey accurately suggested that the Cambodian Prime Minister Son Ngoc Thanh (1907–1976?), renowned for being anti-French, was also pro-Annamite and pro-Japanese.

Regarding the decision, Woodburn Kirby, the official British historian of the war against Japan and its aftermath has written:

> It was … decided to send a small force to take charge of Cambodia, and a British officer with a small personal escort, was sent from Saigon to Phnom Penh (the capital) on 9 October to take command of Allied and Japanese troops in the city, maintain law and order and ensure the stability of the Cambodian government.[2]

The British, including Moke, knew almost nothing about Cambodia. A report dated 25 September 1945 in the British National Archives sums up available intelligence. It had clearly been spoon-fed to them by the French:

---

[2] S. Woodburn Kirby, *The War Against Japan*, vol. 5 (London: Her Majesty's Stationery Office, 1969), 303. A footnote names "Lt Col E.D. Murray" as the officer concerned.

> [Cambodia] is the quietest region of the country (*sic*), the great mass of the population is reported to be pro-French as it always has been but there is small independence party created by the Japanese (*sic*) and the Prime Minister Sam Ngoc Khan (*sic*) who is described as a very dangerous character.[3]

The decision to send Moke to Phnom Penh was probably made a few days later. In "Some Notes", Moke expressed his *ex post facto* bafflement about the orders he had been given:

> Every time I read Mountbatten's *Report*, I am more and more astounded at the orders that were given to me. Tall orders indeed, there were the 55th [Japanese] Infantry Division and the 5th [Japanese] Air Division, both under the command of lieutenant generals. To deal with them there were only four of us. In the end, thanks to the cooperation of the Japanese, all, and more, was accomplished.[4]

After a few days in the country, Moke discovered that Cambodian Francophilia was not widespread and that Cambodia's political situation was more fluid, nuanced, and unpredictable than the paternalistic, scrappy, and high-handed reports that were made available to him by the French had suggested. Thinking on the run with many other issues on his mind, Gracey had originally favoured negotiating directly with the Prime Minister, Son Ngoc Thanh, comparing him from a distance with the Burmese patriot Aung San. But by the time Moke was ordered to Phnom Penh attitudes toward Thanh had hardened as Moke and Gracey had become convinced that the mission would probably involve

---

[3] TNA, WO252/604, 'Southern Indo-China, West Part: Report on Ports from Siamese Frontier to Saigon, inclusive, including Phnom Penh', 25 September 1945.

[4] "Some Notes to Amuse Myself".

removing Son from office.[5] Cambodia, unlike Burma, was a protectorate whose popular ruling monarch, crowned by the French, was already alienated from Thanh. With hindsight, it is fortunate that Murray was never asked to co-operate openly with Son Ngoc Thanh.[6] Ample evidence from the Cambodian National Archives and elsewhere suggests that by early October 1945 the prime minister, fearing the worst, had become extremely unstable.

Moke told Barnett emphatically that he never met Son Ngoc Thanh prior to the Prime Minister's arrest on 15 October 1945. His official diary, however, records that he had two meetings with Thanh.[7] After reviewing the transcript of his initial interview with Barnett, Moke admitted that he had indeed met Son Ngoc Thanh on one occasion. He did not expatiate. This is one of two places where I have found that Moke's official diary diverges significantly from what he told Barnett in 1981, or from his papers in the Imperial War Museum. It's hard to explain the slip-up or evasion, especially since so many of his memories of 1945 are vivid and verifiable. Possibly elements of a retroactive guilty conscience, reminders of his own behaviour when he gave false assurances to Thanh, especially during the second meeting, influenced the account he gave thirty-six years later.

The other contradiction between the official record and Moke's recollections is his statement to Barnett that he had an audience with the King on the day he arrived. The audience is

---

5 On Gracey's first view, see TNA, WO 203/5654, Supreme Allied Commander 31st Miscellaneous Meeting Minutes, 28 September 1945. T. O. Smith, *Vietnam and the Unravelling of Empire: General Gracey in Asia, 1942–1951* (Houndmills, Basingstoke, Hampshire: Palgrave Macmillan, 2014), 93. calls Gracey's view "far-sighted" while in fact Aung San and Son Ngoc Thanh had almost nothing in common.
6 Fortunately for Moke, there was no OSS contingent in Cambodia at the time.
7 TNA, WO 172/7009, Secret War Diary Headquarters Allied Land Forces Phnom Penh, 13 October 1945.

not recorded in the diary and Moke seems to be confusing it with his meeting with Sihanouk on the 17th, two days after Son Ngoc Thanh had been removed from office.

In Phnom Penh Moke was charged, as Gracey had been in Saigon, with freeing Allied prisoners of war, maintaining order and accepting the Japanese surrender. His orders were also to "ensure the stability of the Cambodian government", an injunction missing from Gracey's remit. In other words, Moke, unlike Gracey, was authorized to meet and negotiate with local officials. The phrase explains, in large part, the successes that he managed quite rapidly to achieve.

In 1981 Barnett asked him, "Did you drive around the city? What was your initial impression?". Moke replied, "God yes, quiet, marvelous. Everybody friendly. The only thing was the threat of something happening, but nothing in fact had happened."[8]

Moke knew from the start that his mission differed sharply from General Gracey's. For one thing, he faced no military challenges. As he recalled:

> The trouble was political really. That's why I said earlier that it was military in Saigon. In Cambodia, my military side was really nil. There were threats from the Annamites to come into Phnom Penh. One section of the city was French, another Chinese, Viet Minh. Not many Viet Minh living there, but there were threats from outside. So, one of the first things I did, again, was to post the Japanese on the roads to segregate the French. I also put the Japanese around the Palace, as there were threats on the King. But there wasn't anything militarily really, once I had to keep the peace and be friendly with everybody.

---

8 "Some Notes to Amuse Myself".

In Cambodia where almost nobody spoke English, Moke survived linguistically on the basis of resuscitated schoolboy French, but for official business he called on a French captain, Maurice Besson, who had worked as his interpreter in Saigon and accompanied him to Phnom Penh. The first ten days of his mission were the busiest and the most important. They culminated on the 15th with the arrest of Son Ngoc Thanh, but Moke's arrangements before this and on the succeeding days enabled him smoothly to assume military control of Phnom Penh and the surrounding countryside far more quickly than Gracey was able to do in Saigon.

The official diary's initial entry reads: "Assumed command of all Allied and Japanese forces in Cambodia".[9] That afternoon, October 9th, several Japanese officers suspected of war crimes were flown to Saigon for interrogation. One of them, Lt Col Saito Hiroo, the Chief of Staff of the 55th Division, had encountered Moke in Burma in July 1945. He returned unscathed to Phnom Penh later in the month and was of great assistance to Moke from then on.[10] On the same afternoon two Japanese generals called on Moke at the Hotel Royale and pledged their co-operation.

At 9:30 AM on the 10th, Moke called on Khim Tit, the Cambodian Minister of Defense, who had returned to Phnom Penh the night before from a brief visit to Saigon, not mentioned in Moke's diary, where he had pleaded with Allied officials for the Prime Minister, Thanh, to be removed from office. A Japanese officer told Moke afterwards that Khim Tit had travelled to Saigon with Major Gallois. His visit had the King's approval but was kept from Son Ngoc Thanh, according to Nhiek Tioulong,

---

9 TNA, WO172/7009, Secret War Diary, 20th Indian Division Headquarters Allied Land Forces Phnom Penh, 9 October 1945.
10 Most of the 55th Division had been transferred *en masse* from Burma to Phnom Penh in July and August 1945.

who was a member of the Council of Ministers at the time. Later, Khim Tit claimed that he had told Allied authorities in Saigon that several members of the Council of Ministers and the King were ready to welcome the return of French protection.[11]

This rivalry between the two leading politicians had almost resulted in a *coup* in late September. Lt Col Saito had dissuaded the Defense Minister from continuing with the plan, but Khim Tit was so deeply angered that he then accused Saito, baselessly, of being a war criminal.[12] The failed plot was known to General Sakuma, commander of the 55th Division, who informed Moke of it a few days later.

Later on the 10th Moke and his staff moved from what he called "tacky" rooms in the Hotel Royale to the impressive Art Deco building half a mile away that had been occupied until 9 March by the French *Résident Supérieur* and his staff and had since served as a Cambodian government guest house. Moke recalled the move with relish:

> Every modern convenience, marvelous bedroom. The first thing I did was to put on a show. I put two Gurkha sentries at the entrance that did nothing but walk up and down and stamp their feet. As you went through the great door, there was a *long* corridor at the bottom of which there was this enormous, beautifully polished table where I had this splendid Pakistani [Intelligence Officer]. My office was around the corner and every time anyone arrived, they had to go down this tremendously long corridor, getting smaller and smaller (laughs) and

---

11   It seems likely that Moke had known about Khim Tit's mission to Saigon but because it took place beforehand there was no need to mention it in his official diary. See Khim Tit, *"Un épisode de l'Histoire contemporain du Cambodge" Réalités cambodgiennes 2*, 6, 8 and 16 June 1967, a self-serving account that fails to mention either Huard or Moke.
12   Nhiek Tioulong. *Chroniques khmers* (Unpublished manuscript).

they eventually got to this splendid chap who said, "I'll see if his Excellency will see you". So, I made my presence felt!¹³

Soon afterwards, or in any case, long before the Japanese had surrendered, a photograph had been taken at Moke's new headquarters that showed his staff and other military associates. The photograph appears as the cover for this book. At the feet of Moke's entourage, the three Japanese officers are seated carrying their swords. That evening Moke and his staff attended a dinner at a restaurant in Phnom Penh in honour of China's National Day. This would have given them a chance to meet several Cambodian Ministers but the official diary fails to mention any contacts.¹⁴

In "Some Notes" Moke describes an incident, which he failed to mention to Barnett, that occurred in Phnom Penh on either the 11th or the 12th. The passage reads:

> Throughout our stay there was another reliable and accurate source of information. This was an [unnamed] Franco-English artist who lived in the "native quarter" of Phnom Penh who had an ear to Cambodian, French, Japanese and Annamese goings on. Soon after my arrival, he invited me and my officers to a Cambodian supper. The fact that it was in a high-class brothel made no matter. We were British and knew how to behave, dammit. Then and after [the artist] gave me all the information that I required; and the news finally made up my mind to fly to Saigon to see my General.¹⁵

---

13 Moke Murray, interviewed by Anthony Barnett, 1981.
14 A document prepared by the Cambodian police entitled "Situation politique en Kampuchea, 10–10–45" makes no mention of Moke's presence. Subsequent reports also fail to mention Moke, although a police report from 15 October notes that "two Hindu soldiers, British subjects", (i.e. Gurkhas) had been involved the night before in a confrontation with a Cambodian policeman who had refused them entry into an officially sanctioned brothel located some 200 meters from Moke's headquarters.
15 "Some Notes to Amuse Myself".

This amusing anecdote reveals another helpful source of local information, but it's likely that Moke was already planning to confer with Gracey in Saigon and to see to the deposition of the Prime Minister in one way or another.

On 12 October 1945 Khim Tit published an article in *Cambodge* (while Thanh was still Prime Minister) which declared, mendaciously, that Thanh had only requested that the French pressure the Japanese to rearm the Cambodian National Guard.[16] Khim Tit had been a sergeant in the French army in the Great War, and impressed Moke, who described him in "Some Notes": "[Khim Tit] was very pro-King, and a moderate over independence. He disliked and mistrusted the Prime Minister. We became fast friends."[17] On the same day, 12 October, according to the diary, Moke met with Son Ngoc Thanh in the Prime Minister's office. His translator Captain Besson and his second in command, David Wenham, accompanied him. At this meeting Moke took pains "to set out the parameters of his mission."[18] Thanh promised his full co-operation, specifically agreeing to order the disarmament of potentially unreliable "Annamite" members of the Cambodian police.[19] Before Moke left, Son Ngoc Thanh arranged to meet him at his headquarters on the following day.

---

16 This issue of *Cambodge* has disappeared from the Cambodian National Archives.
17 "Some Notes to Amuse Myself".
18 TNA, WO 172/7009, Secret War Diary, 20th Indian Division Headquarters Allied Land Forces Phnom Penh, 12 October 1945.
19 See NAC, 'Comments sur la commaunite annamite', 21 October 1945. A police document reports that several Vietnamese members of the Cambodian police who had defected to the Viet Minh had been executed for "high treason", news that "caused a certain inquietude" among Vietnamese policemen who remained on duty in Phnom Penh. A similarly titled tract dated 23 September, written by Police chief Lon Nol, asserted that the Annamites in Cambodia were "frightened of the prospect that they would be massacred by the French assisted by the Cambodian" and that they "burningly want to return to their own country" – an example of wishful thinking on the policeman's part.

That afternoon a French Lieutenant Colonel named Paul Huard (1903–1994) arrived in Phnom Penh by plane with a five-man military body guard and the company of French Marines that Moke had commanded briefly in Saigon. These welcome troops came under Moke's command. Huard had reached Saigon from China barely a week before. He proceeded to Phnom Penh as General Leclerc's personal representative, a powerless position in a city where Leclerc, unlike Moke, had no recognized authority. In "Some Notes" Moke referred to Huard as a "pleasant French full colonel" without mentioning his name, and he never mentioned Huard to Barnett. Moke's secret diary for 12 October 1945, however, notes that he "gave [Huard] a summary of events, explained the political situation and discussed tasks and future plans".[20]

Paul Huard, who eventually became a major general, was a career military officer. While on active duty in the 1930s he had done ethnographic work among the hill tribes of central Vietnam.[21] Aside from his acquaintance Paul Mus, Huard is the only Westerner in these pages (apart from those residing in the region) who had any first-hand experience of French Indochina, although his experience was almost ten years old. To an undefined extent, Moke deferred to Huard's local knowledge *and* the two men worked comfortably together, although Huard, writing

---

20   TNA, WO 172/7009, Secret War Diary, 20th Indian Division Headquarters Allied Land Forces Phnom Penh, 12 October 1945.
21   See Paul (Général C.R.) Huard, "La Rentrée Politique de La France Au Cambodge (Octobre 1945—Janvier 1946)," in *Les Chemins de La Décolonisation de l'empire Colonial Français, 1936–1956: Colloque Organisé Par l'IHTP Les 4 et 5 Octobre 1984*, ed. Charles-Robert Ageron (Paris: CNRS Éditions, 2013), 215–30, http://books.openedition.org/editionscnrs/480. I am grateful to Geoffrey Gunn for providing this reference.

in 1987, wrote demeaningly of Moke.[22]

Some sources, including General Gracey at the time and T.O. Smith in recent years have written that Leclerc and Gracey expected Huard to arrest Son Ngoc Thanh soon after he arrived, using the Marines who had accompanied him to Cambodia. Under Leclerc's orders, which Huard called "maximalist" in 1986, the French colonel was expected, very speedily, to achieve an agreement with the King and the restoration of royal authority and the Cambodian administration. As Huard noted, "The orders postulated an accord that didn't exist between the King and France and ignored the vigor with which the sentiment and the fact of independence had penetrated a population that was extremely hierarchical and loyal [to the King]".[23]

With hindsight again Huard seems to have read the ambiguous Cambodian political landscape more accurately than either Gracey or Leclerc. Using French Marines to arrest Son Ngoc Thanh without the King's knowledge or permission seemed to Huard a perilous step, and he refused to take it. The French had not yet arrived in Cambodia in force and Sihanouk, sensing no decisive shift in the balance of power, rebuffed Huard's initial request for an audience as soon as he arrived. Without official recognition from the King, Huard felt that he lacked authority to take action against Son Ngoc Thanh or anyone else. Moke,

---

22 Huard, 120 notes that "My influence on Murray, which played an important role, was based on my successive postings to headquarters, Force 136 and the connection between the 3rd RIC to the 20th Indian Division. On the local plane which was for [Murray] totally unknown and in which he was extremely isolated, … he deferred to my rank, my experience and my status without to mention our mutual sympathy." The passage fails to note Murray's close rapport with Gracey, his combat experience, or the fact that Murray, although only an acting lieutenant colonel, was technically Huard's commander.
23 Smith, *Vietnam and the Unravelling of Empire*, 70 calls Huard's hesitancy to arrest Thanh "a spectacular failure". The phrasing seems overwrought and Smith seems to have been unaware of Huard's nuanced account.

Gracey and Leclerc, unaware of the King's profound importance in Cambodian politics had no such qualms. As a result of Huard's inaction, which was later deplored by Gracey, Thanh remained in office for three more days. Indeed, on 16 October, after Thanh had been removed, Gracey produced a garbled summary of what had happened, writing to his superiors in Singapore that Huard:

> was appointed "Resident General" (*sic*) of Cambodia with orders to clear up the political situation, arrest the Prime Minister, and assist Col Murray in keeping law and order. Huard funked arrest of Prime Minister so Leclerc flew to Phnom Penh on 14 October (*sic*) and arrested him personally without any fuss.[24]

Unaware that a net was closing around him, on the 13th Son Ngoc Thanh visited Moke, as previously arranged, at his headquarters. This is the meeting that Moke later appeared to forget. According to the official diary Thanh told him at this time that he had arranged for Moke to meet the King on the 18th, when Sihanouk would have returned with his parents from a pilgrimage to a royally sponsored Buddhist *wat* a few hours' distance from Phnom Penh. The diary adds that the Prime Minister asked Moke about the precise meaning of the clause, "ensures the stability of the Cambodian government," in the orders that Moke had shared with him the day before. Moke replied that as far as it affected his task the clause meant assuring that the "government of Cambodia

---

24 TNA, WO 203/5563, Telegram from General Douglas Gracey to Admiral Louis Mountbatten, 16 October 1945. Huard was named Commissioner not Resident General, and Leclerc arrested Son Ngoc Thanh on 15 October and not the 14th. Leclerc's orders to Huard, which Gracey may not have seen, were less precise and more sweeping than Gracey suggests. The orders made no reference to Moke.

was not interfered with by any subversive influence or force".[25]

In the phrase "subversive influence" Moke was probably referring obliquely to Thanh's pro-Japanese credentials, his pro-Viet Minh diplomatic moves, his anti-French record, and to information about Thanh's erratic behavior as Prime Minister that Moke had picked up from Khim Tit and perhaps from the British artist. Thanh probably had no idea what Moke's deft but opaque phrasing meant and he left the meeting, it seems, feeling secure in his position. The Japanese who were still aligned with Son Ngoc Thanh posed another set of obstacles to Murray's mission, as did the "Annamite" population of Phnom Penh and the French. As Moke recalled:

> You are on the ground, you just get on with it. At least that's what I've always thought. We were told that there was the situation. It was political, starting off with the Japanese attitude to the locals. The Japanese attitude was a suspect one to start with, before we went in. We told them, "We'll stop this". Because they were collaborating, not with the French but with our friend the Prime Minister, no question of that. The French were so troublesome. The domineering attitudes. They would not let [the Cambodians] alone: The King, nice boy, happy, that sort of thing. Lovely country, lovely people, really delightful, why should the bloody French stick their nose in? That's the attitude we got. I was sent in to sort that out, to coordinate down because with Vietnam also coming in from the south, reports came that somebody would go in there—French, Japanese, the Cambodians and the oncoming Annamites".[26]

---

25 TNA, WO 172/7009, Secret War Diary, 20th Indian Division Headquarters Allied Land Forces Phnom Penh, 13 October 1945.
26 Moke Murray, interviewed by Anthony Barnett, 1981.

King Sihanouk and his parents left Phnom Penh as planned on the morning of the 13th, the same day that Thanh met for a second time with Murray. The pilgrimage had been arranged as recently as the 11th, perhaps because that was when Khim Tit or someone else informed the King and his parents that a *coup* of some kind was scheduled to take place when they were away. Sihanouk and his parents, naturally enough, failed to pass this information along to Son Ngoc Thanh.

Events moved swiftly on the 14th. In the morning Gracey's intelligence officer Colonel Cass flew into Phnom Penh to be briefed and to accompany Moke back to Saigon. Moke's diary notes that at this stage plans "were to be made to dispose of the Cambodian Prime Minister". In Saigon that afternoon Moke met with Gracey and Leclerc. He laid out his view (which was the same as theirs) that Son Ngoc Thanh needed to be removed from office urgently. As Moke remembered the event in "Some Thoughts":

Leclerc said "*Bon*! Arrest him!" And I replied, "Sir, I cannot do that, much as I would like to; he is a citizen of a French colony, and I am a British officer."[27] Talking to Barnett, Moke was more expansive:

> I felt that for the good of the country he should go. I suppose, perhaps, that was the wrong thing, but I did. General Leclerc had arrived in Saigon by that time, thank God, so I signalled to say I was flying in—by Japanese plane! – to meet the general. Everything was done by signal, there were no telephones. I went and we had a meeting. There were General Gracey and Leclerc, just the three of us. Leclerc said to Gracey about me, "Splendid officer" (*laughs*) and Gracey replied, "all my officers are splendid" (*laughs*). I said, "I think this chap should go".

---

27 Murray, "Some Notes to Amuse Myself".

I put the pros and cons and said, "I think he ought to go". Leclerc said. "Well, arrest him". I said to Gracey, "I can't do that sir. The British can't do that." Gracey agreed with me. So, Leclerc said, "I'll do it. Fix it".

The responsibility for what amounted to a *coup d'état* in Cambodia thus fell to Leclerc, the highest-ranking French official in the region. When Moke returned to Cambodia on the afternoon of the 14th he told Huard that "the affair was moving forward" and he arranged for Thanh to visit his headquarters on the following morning ostensibly to meet with Japanese officials.

In what is probably the most appealing and most memorable passage in his conversations with Barnett, Moke recalled what happened on the following day:

> The Prime Minister came, all smiley. Most friendly. I felt terrible afterwards … [He came] on his own. I invited him into my office. We had cups of coffee or something.
>
> What impression did he make on you?
>
> Oh, useless. A silly little man I thought, quite honestly. Sort of smiley. Anyway, I said, "I'm terribly sorry but I've got another duty. But Colonel Wenham will entertain you". They talked about hunting and I think they agreed to go on a tiger[28] shoot. Meanwhile I went off in my DeSoto flying the Union Jack (Japanese made) and halfway to the airport it broke down. I thought, What the hell do I do now to collect the general? Fortunately, along came a Japanese water truck. I stopped it dead and ordered them to take me to the airport. So, I arrived

---

28   Wenham, a keen shot, had hunted tigers in India. On 29 October 1945, Charles Dumas, a French official in Phnom Penh gave him a copy of his book *La faune sauvage au Cambodge, moeurs de chasse*, Phnom Penh 1944, with a polite inscription. I'm grateful to Wenham's son Tony for this information.

to meet Leclerc in a Japanese water tanker! Fortunately, there was a French car already there, very small. We all got in. Driving back, I'll never forget. I had this marvellous driver. He was standing there by my car saluting and he had remembered to furl the flag because I was no longer in it.

We arrived at my headquarters and went into my office. It was like a comic opera. There was the Prime Minister with my associate David Wenham chitter chattering about elephant shoots, and General Leclerc strode in, pushing me aside, with his ... He had a gunman[29], who had a gun in a shoulder holster up under his shoulder. The gunman put his hand up on the holster. And Leclerc just looked straight at the corner of the [very large] room. Poor little Prime Minister thought Leclerc was welcoming him and got up sort of to say "How lovely!" He was seized by the scruff of the neck by this gunman, hustled into the car and off they took him. I never saw him again. Or General Leclerc.

Did Leclerc say, 'I arrest you?'

Nobody said anything. Nobody said anything. It really was quite extraordinary. Leclerc and the gunman pushed me aside; in my own office, damn it, walked in. Leclerc had a stick, he looked at the top corner of the room, and the poor little man was down there. The gunman was walking with his hand [on his holster]. It really was ... David and I felt terrible about it afterwards. It was so unnecessary. We would have done it much better; I think. It could have been done much better.[30]

---

29   Huard, "La Rentrée Politique de La France Au Cambodge (Octobre 1945—Janvier 1946)," 221 identifies Leclerc's "gunman" as a Lieutenant Daveau.
30   Moke Murray, interviewed by Anthony Barnett, 1981.

TEN

Cambodia: Closing Phases

Huard claimed in 1986 that he was present with Leclerc at Thanh's arrest.[1] It's unlikely that he made this up, and more probable that Moke, who had undoubtedly told this story with relish many times, simply whited Huard's presence out of his narration. In fact, the "French car" mentioned by Moke had [probably] been commandeered by Huard to meet Leclerc. While it's unlikely that Moke invented the story of his cock-a-hoop trip to the airport, his failure to mention Huard suggests that Huard, as Leclerc's representative in Cambodia, went to the airport on his own and was the person whom Leclerc expected to meet. Probably Moke had been informed from Saigon about Leclerc's flight and had in turn informed Huard.

To confuse the story further, Moke's official diary notes only that Huard was "informed" about Thanh's arrest two hours after it had taken place.[2] Huard, on the other hand, claims in his 1986 account that only Leclerc, his assistant, and Huard knew what

---

1 Huard, "La Rentrée Politique de La France Au Cambodge (Octobre 1945—Janvier 1946)," 220.
2 TNA, WO172/7009, Secret War Diary, 20th Indian Division Headquarters Allied Land Forces Phnom Penh, 15 October 1945.

had happened—as if Moke was not on the scene. It's difficult to believe that Moke made up his eyewitness story out of whole cloth. His lightly edited recollection of this bizarre, undignified occasion belongs beside the fact that in his two unremembered meetings with Son Ngoc Thanh Moke had been disingenuous or dishonest, since for obvious reasons he had concealed the evolving Franco-British plans to remove the Prime Minister from office. Nonetheless the *brusquerie* of Leclerc's behavior and Moke's complicity in it seem to have left a lingering, unpleasant taste in Moke's mind that might explain, psychologically, why, in talking with Barnett, he whited out his two previous meetings with Thanh before sketchily recalling the first one.[3]

At 12:20 PM, in any case, Thanh was *en route* to prison in Saigon. Soon afterwards Huard named himself Acting Commissioner to Cambodia, a title that he had been authorized to use by General Leclerc, with an office in Moke's headquarters.[4] The French Marines who had accompanied him to Phnom Penh remained under Moke's command. On the 16th Moke decreed that a French flag be raised alongside the Union Jack outside his headquarters.

At 5:30 PM, according to the official diary, Khim Tit and the Minister of Justice, Chan Nak, visited Moke's headquarters. Khim Tit had certainly been forewarned of Thanh's arrest but, according to the diary, the Minister of Justice, "asked the reason

---

[3] This perhaps inadvertent "slip-up" makes it important to treat some of Murray's well-burnished recollections with caution. Thanh was tried in Saigon and sentenced to life imprisonment, but the sentence was later reduced to house arrest in France where he obtained a law degree. He returned to Cambodia in 1952, but soon went into the maquis. In the mid-1950s he began working with Thai and South Vietnamese authorities to undermine Sihanouk's popular regime. Thanh returned to Phnom Penh under the Khmer Republic, served briefly as its Minister and died in Vietnam in 1976.

[4] TNA, WO172/7009, Secret War Diary, 20th Indian Division Headquarters Allied Land Forces Phnom Penh, 15 October 1945.

for the sudden disappearance of the Prime Minister and was informed that the arrest had been made by General Leclerc, who should know his own reasons best."[5]

During the afternoon, warned by Thanh's chauffeur, Thanh's wife and several of his colleagues went into hiding in preparation for leaving the country.[6]

The Cambodian Minister of Education at the time, Nhiek Tioulong has written in his unpublished memoir that he visited Moke "toward the end of the afternoon" with the Minister of the Interior, Sum Hieng. When Moke told them what had happened Sum Hieng dispatched some Cambodian soldiers to the *wat* where Sihanouk and his parents were on pilgrimage to inform them of events. Earlier in the afternoon Moke issued orders to the Japanese forces in Phnom Penh to strengthen roadblocks along the Cambodian-Vietnamese border.

Moke reported to his superiors that Prince Monireth visited his headquarters at 6:20 PM presumably at Moke's invitation "to discuss the latest political developments". The Prince asked Moke to authorize the arrest of the "Annamite" members of the police, a body that came under Moke's orders. According to Huard's recollections, which seem persuasive, Monireth had spent much of the afternoon conferring with him and Gallois. He had accepted their suggestion that he replace Thanh as Prime Minister until other arrangements could be made. He also accepted the honorary rank of brigadier general in the French Army, proffered by Huard on Leclerc's authority. The gesture suggests that he expected and approved of Cambodia's return to French protection. By 7:30

---

[5] TNA, WO 172/7009, Secret War Diary, 20th Indian Division Headquarters Allied Land Forces Phnom Penh, 15 October 1945.

[6] Porée Maspéro journal, entry for 26 October 1945. Ten days earlier she reported a rumor circulating in Phnom Penh that Thanh had been "kidnapped by Gurkhas".

PM a new Council of Ministers had been set in place. Prince Monireth, the outgoing Council's Supreme Advisor, presided over the newly assembled group.[7] A decree issued on 17 October noted that Monireth would "have the same attributions and prerogatives" as the Prime Minister had enjoyed in the past but in fact he never formally adopted the title.

That same evening Gracey reported to Singapore that it was "altogether a very satisfactory *coup d'etat* by the French with a strong flavour [of] Ruritania" – a reference to the faintly comic eastern European kingdom described in Anthony Hope's popular 1894 novel *The Prisoner of Zenda*.[8] On the 15th and 16th Sihanouk and his parents were still absent from Phnom Penh. On the 16th as a precaution Prince Monireth, with Huard and Moke's approval, dispatched French troops to the *wat* to accompany the royal party back to Phnom Penh. The King and his parents arrived as scheduled in the afternoon of the 17th. They were met at the Palace by his uncle at the head of the newly formed Council of Ministers and also by Moke, Huard and a platoon of French soldiers who presented arms to him, an act that as Huard later observed symbolically reintroduced French "protection" of the kingdom.[9]

On the same day, Moke and his staff met with the head of the national police, Lon Nol (1915–1984), who was later to play a major role in Cambodian politics, and with Kouth Bouth, the head of the national guard. Moke told the two men that all armed

---

[7] Richard J Aldrich, *Intelligence and the War against Japan: Britain, America and the Politics of Secret Service* (Cambridge: Cambridge University Press, 2008), 352.

[8] See Anthony Powell's 1968 review of a re-edition of the novel in his collection *Under Review* (London, 1991), 247–48, where he compares the regime in Zenda to "a laxly run country house".

[9] Huard, "*La Rentrée Politique de La France Au Cambodge* (Octobre 1945—Janvier 1946)," 222.

forces in Cambodia still fell under his command and added that the "Annamite" members of the police force had already been dismissed. Lon Nol, foreshadowing his anti-Vietnamese stance in the 1970s, said that he was "worried by Annamites all over Cambodia performing subversive activities and sabotage."[10]

Sihanouk received Moke in audience on the following day. This was the meeting that Son Ngoc Thanh had scheduled when he met Moke on the 12th. At that time Thanh knew of the King's upcoming pilgrimage but did not foresee that Moke, Khim Tit, and Leclerc would use the King's absence to stage a *coup d'etat*.

In his audience on 17 October Moke told Sihanouk what had happened to Son Ngoc Thanh and urged the King to compose a proclamation about the event that could be distributed throughout the Kingdom. There is no evidence that Sihanouk acceded to this request, but the semi-official newspaper, *Cambodge*, soon published a text composed by Moke, which stated that Thanh had been removed from office "because of his activities contrary to the security of Allied troops and to the detriment of Cambodia."[11] With Gracey's permission, on the 18th Moke promoted himself to rank of (acting) brigadier so that he could outrank Lt. Colonel Huard, who claims in his memoir that Moke was "slightly confused" and didn't know what a brigadier's insignia looked like. It's likely that Moke was pulling Huard's leg, as he was to do with Harry Seaman in the 1980s when he claimed he was related to a Scottish Duke. I suspect that Moke, who loved

---

10   TNA, WO 172/7009, Appendix No. J.10, Minutes of a Conference at HQ ALF PP at 1700 hrs', 17 October 1945.

11   *Cambodge*, 18 October 1945 quoted in Michael Vickery, *Kampuchea: Politics, Economics, and Society* (London: Pinter, 1986), 9. In the 1960s, Vickery examined *Cambodge* files from the 1940s located in the National Library in Phnom Penh. The files of *Cambodge* for this period have since disappeared.

a prank, was playing the part of what the French call a *faux naïf*.¹²

On the same day a royal edict eliminated the position of Minister of Foreign Affairs. The Ministry of Defence disappeared soon afterwards. These crucial, nation-defining ministries did not resurface until the early 1950s, when a semi-independent Cambodia, with French encouragement, began to form a national army and started to post diplomats abroad.¹³ This was clearly an imposition made by the returning French authorities in order to bring Cambodia back into the Indochinese Federation they sought to create in late 1945.

The historian John Tully, citing a French archival document that I haven't seen, writes that Moke met with senior French officers, including Huard, on 20 October. At the time Moke raised concerns about French plans for the future of the kingdom. Moke said that it was necessary for the maintenance of public tranquillity to inform the population as quickly as possible whether Cambodia was to enjoy independence or revert to its status as a dependency of France.¹⁴ Huard brushed aside Moke's concerns and assured him that the French would soon return to power.

He was right. In his conversations with Barnett Moke said, "The French started to move out of Saigon, and arrived in Phnom Penh without so much as a by-your-leave". It's unimaginable, of course, for the French to have considered asking Moke's permission to return to power.

On Sihanouk's birthday, the 22nd, Moke orchestrated a

---

12   Huard, "La Rentrée Politique de La France Au Cambodge (Octobre 1945—Janvier 1946)," 223.
13   In what seems with hindsight a clueless gesture, on 30 September 1945 the Council of Ministers tabled an agenda item that called for establishing a Cambodian diplomatic corps.
14   John Tully, *France on the Mekong: A History of the Protectorate in Cambodia, 1863–1953* (Lanham: University Press of America, 2002), 401.

parade past the Palace using the French, Cambodian and Gurkha troops and the local police units in the city that fell under his command. The parade began at 7:30 AM. As he recalled:

> There was [Sihanouk's] birthday, it was just after the war and he decided to have a hell of a party and a parade. My advice was sought, being British and all that. I set up the Royal procession. It was passed to me, whether the British liked it done this way or that way. That happened in [1956 in] the coronation in Nepal,[15] they all came and asked me (*chuckles*). My life's been bloody funny. Anyway, going back to the King, he had a procession and I put my Gurkhas into part of it. And some damn French girl next to me said, "Ah, *les petits soldats*. Do they fight well?" I could have struck her. Having fought our way a thousand miles!

On the next day in a poignant example of what Paul Mus has aptly called the "monologue of colonialism".[16] Sihanouk officially welcomed the restoration of French protection, reading aloud from a message composed for the occasion by Huard and Jean de Lens, the reinstated French *Résident Maire* who was an old colonial hand.[17] The King's remarks (or more accurately those of his French mentors) charted a Franco-Cambodian future that pointedly failed to use the word "independence". Instead, a key passage reads, "In its relations with Our Kingdom, we have the assurance that France will follow a policy of generosity; liberalism and progress…Cambodia will enjoy a level of liberty *fully appropriate to its degree of evolution and its capacities* (Emphasis added)."

---

15 Moke was a member of a five-man British delegation to the coronation of King Mahendra of Nepal in 1956. See below, 162.
16 Paul Mus, *Le Destin de l'Union Francaise de l'Indochine a l'Afrique.* (Paris: Editions du Seuil, 1954), 5.
17 On de Lens' the authorship see Porée – Maspéro Journal, entry for 28 October 1945.

A day before, Huard had offered the King, on de Gaulle's behalf, the honorary rank of general in the French army, a rank higher than the one Huard had offered to Monireth earlier, without publicity. At first, Huard reported later, Sihanouk acted hesitant and overwhelmed, but as soon as he accepted the offer Huard knew that the Protectorate was back on track since the French had got their colonial king back. Sihanouk fails to mention the occasion in his memoirs. Cambodia's "degree of evolution" and its "capacities", of course, would to be determined by the French at a time to be announced.[18]

As soon as Sihanouk had spoken the words he had been given to say, a brief, lively and significant chapter of Cambodian history came politely to a close. On the same day a decree issued by the Minister of the Interior to "the populations of Cambodia prohibited any gatherings in the streets, any reunion in private residences, any fireworks as well as all demonstrations". Instead, the population of Phnom Penh was invited to "observe the most absolute calm". Despite the fearful tone of the decree, anti-French demonstrations, which would also at this point have also been demonstrations against the King, were never on the cards and never took place.

Over the next seven years, however, the memory of independence on Sihanouk's part and among the Cambodian people gradually evolved into a widespread longing, engineered in part by the King, to regain it. In 1952, when Sihanouk noticed that France was beginning to lose the First Indochina War, he dissolved parliament and took personal command of the struggle for independence. His effort soon came to be called a Royal Crusade and Cambodia gained its independence toward the end

---

18   Huard, "La Rentrée Politique de La France Au Cambodge (Octobre 1945—Janvier 1946)".

of 1953.[19] As I have written elsewhere, the so-called "Crusade" involved crushing existing political parties and ending the possibility of independent elected representatives to the Cambodian Assembly. No free and fair elections were held in Cambodia between 1952 and 1993.

In October 1945, of course, Moke had no long-term appointment in Cambodia and no stake in Cambodia's future. Nonetheless he was pleased to see how smoothly the transfer of power to the French had been accomplished. A week earlier he had written pensively to Gracey:

> The French are trying to do things much too fast. I am convinced that had a British headquarters not been sent here, the French would have rushed in with flags flying and trumpets blaring and French troops would have been all over Phnom Penh and that *would* have been trouble. The point being that Colonel Huard and presumably General Leclerc, believe that the new PM's (sic) and the Defence Minister's pro-French attitude is that of the Cambodians as a whole, but that is not so.[20]

Moke's intuition about the population's views is confirmed by several documents in the Cambodian National Archives. It's clear that most Khmer had welcomed the news of independence in March especially once they learned that it had

---

[19] On this period of Cambodian history, see David P. Chandler, *The Tragedy of Cambodian History: Politics, War, and Revolution since 1945* (Chiang Mai: Silkworm Books, 1994), 63–72; Tully, *France on the Mekong: A History of the Protectorate in Cambodia, 1863–1953*, 399 ff; Geoffrey C. Gunn, *Monarchical Manipulation in Cambodia: France, Japan, and the Sihanouk Crusade for Independence*, Nordic Institute of Asian Studies Monograph Series, no. 141 (Copenhagen, Denmark: NIAS Press, 2018), 377–98. In 1953 Sihanouk signed the royal proclamation that designated him as a national hero.

[20] TNA, WO 172/7009, Appendix No. J.7, Report of Lieutenant Colonel Murray's Conversation with General Sakuma, 18 October 1945.

the King's approval. In any case, despite French rhetoric to the contrary (one writer referred to the idea of Cambodian independence as a "virus") independence, once gained, was not something that the perennially powerless Cambodians were eager to give back.

The French for their part were glad to regain what they assumed was their rightful role in "protecting" Cambodia and continuing their *mission civilisatrice* in French Indochina. Very few French people in the region at the time (Paul Mus and Germaine Krull were notable exceptions, Huard perhaps another) noticed that a sea change had occurred in the thinking of local people in the months that had followed the Japanese *coup de force*. Interestingly, however, a French official named Paul Tramoni who had been interned on 9 March wrote later, in a novel, that Cambodia's *ambiance* had altered as the year 1945 came to an end:

> Everything had clanged. The Cambodians held the reins themselves and we found ourselves at the margin, without knowing what this would involve. We sensed the irreversibility of the situation, all the more when our Cambodian friends didn't come to see us as they had done in the past. Oh, when we met, they were friendly enough to be sure. But a certain reticence, something vague, a sort of mist was floating between them and us…did they cherish their independence, which had fallen out of the sky? In effect, the past had evaporated forever.[21]

At some point in late October Moke used some of the Japanese troops still under his command in Phnom Penh to

---

21 Paul Tramoni, *Camille* … (Blainville-sur-Mer: L'Amiti?? par le livre, 1966), 226. I am grateful to Ben Kiernan for drawing my attention to this passage.

Cambodia: Closing Phases

thwart a Viet Minh military incursion coming from the south, ostensibly to attack the city. As he recalled,

Mid-

Give me a date! (Laughter)

Anyway, I said, "We can't have that." So, I said to my old friend, Lt Colonel Saito, "Lay on an operation". I said I couldn't use my chaps, as I only had forty, so we had to use his. We had to do it very carefully because intelligence travelled bloody quickly. There was a Chinese café just about here (*Moke points to a spot by the river bank*). [I said] "David Wenham and myself will be there having a glass of something. Bring a boat up secretly. Don't let there be any Gurkhas aboard, because [the Cambodians] will twig if they see them, it must be completely Japanese". That's also why, if you went on board officially, they would know something was on. The boat came and drew in near the café and David Wenham and I jumped aboard. We went down the river, right the way down, until *(laughs)* we stuck on a sandbank. Absolutely typical of Cambodia. Everything gets stuck in the sandbank or something like that. So, the Japanese and I waded ashore and we stopped them.

Was there a fight, how many invaded?

It was a very small boat; there couldn't have been more than a hundred Japanese, David Wenham and myself. They were certainly surprised when we arrived. They were marching up by land. They had rifles, muskets.

You opened fire on them?

No, I think we just said, "Push off". There were some shots fired. But no engagement. What I'm trying to get at is that this was the only time there was a military event while I was there.[22]

Later in the week Moke was a guest of honor at the annual royally sponsored water festival:

> There were canoe races, fireworks, marvellous. It was happy. He had a floating palace; I was the chief guest and at dusk a boat came along with unlit candles. The King first lit one, then I did, and then we all did. Then it floated down, and then came back. That was the whole point of it. It came back along the Mekong as the river reversed, very interesting. It was marvellous. We all drank champagne out of silver which I don't like doing (*laughs*).[23]

In a formal ceremony on 25 November Moke presided over the surrender of a symbolic portion—some 800 officers and men—of the 55th Japanese Division, which had been one of the most-feared fighting forces in the Pacific. The division, formed in 1940, drew its soldiers from the countryside around the city of Osaka. It had invaded Burma from Thailand on 11 December 1941, and until 1945 it had often confronted Gracey's division before transferring to Phnom Penh shortly before the Japanese surrender.

By late October the division had been reduced in size because after Thanh's arrest over a thousand of its soldiers had been sent

---

22 Smith, *Vietnam and the Unravelling of Empire*, 72n. Smith asserts that "On 20 November [*sic*] Lt Col Wenham, a British officer, and 300 Japanese troops successfully pushed Vietnamese forces out of Ha Tien on the Vietnamese-Cambodian Border". The sentence is unsourced, and a more convincing date for the affair would be 20 October, because by late November the Japanese in Cambodia had all disarmed and because, in Moke's conversations with Barnett, his discussion of the water festival in late October follows immediately after his account of this brush with the Viet Minh.
23 Moke Murray, interviewed by Anthony Barnett, 1981.

to Saigon to assist Gracey and Leclerc's forces confronting the Viet Minh.[24] The precision of the surrender ceremony on the 24th as reported in *Cambodge* suggests that it had been carefully rehearsed:

> At 11.45 a.m. the ceremonial disarming of the Japanese took place on a stretch of grass inside the headquarters of the [55th] Japanese division. Brigadier General Murray presided over the ceremony.
>
> Eight hundred Japanese soldiers were formed into a square, with their officers and their commanding general at their head. They faced Brigadier General Murray, who was accompanied by ten Gurkhas. Murray was seated at a table covered with the British flag. The solemn silence was broken only by the sharp click of the officers' heels as they saluted Brigadier General Murray and the sound of their sabres being drawn out and disposed.
>
> One by one each Japanese officer and non-commissioned officer broke ranks, approached, saluted the Brigadier General and then turned to salute the non-commissioned Gurkha officers. At that point [the Japanese] lifted their sabres in both hands horizontally to the level of their faces before turning them over to a Gurkha, who placed each sword on the table. This was followed by a new salute to the Brigadier General and the Japanese officer returned to his place. The silence, the immobility, and the impassivity of leaders on both sides gave the ceremony a particular majesty.[25]

---

24   William Joseph Slim, *Defeat into Victory* (London: Cassell & Company, 1956), 537 notes that in post-war Southeast Asia he "required senior [Japanese] officers to surrender their swords to appropriate British commanders in front of parades of their own troops."

25   *Cambodge*, 24 October 1945. See also TNA, WO 172/7009, Headquarters ALF Phnom Penh, ALF/PP/23/G, 1–30 November Report, 3 December 1945.

Moke held onto a copy of this issue of *Cambodge*. In 1981 he *gave* it to Barnett, who passed it along, in turn, to Colin Murray in 2017. Talking to Barnett, Moke recalled:

> Some [Japanese} were allowed to keep their arms until the last. The officers were allowed to keep their swords, for instance, some of them because they were on duty; it was a sign of their leadership. But most of their arms were surrendered. In fact, they laid them down in a military parade; you can read about it in that copy of *Cambodge*. Eight hundred of them. Not to me. They bowed to me but they surrendered to a Gurkha officer. I was determined that should happen. They all handed their sword to a Gurkha, not to me.

> Why were you determined on that?

> Because the Gurkhas had beat them. I sat at a table, which the Union Jack was on, as we haven't any flagpole. I sat behind it. They came and stooped and bowed to me and handed their sword to my Gurkha officer, that's whom the Japanese surrendered to in Cambodia. The French were looking on.[26]

At no other point in writing this book did I feel myself transported to such an irrecoverable moment in the past. Wars in the twenty-first century are seldom declared and never seem to end. There's no longer such a thing as an honourable surrender, and former enemies, by and large, remain hostile to each other after they stop fighting. In arranging the Japanese surrender in this way Moke made two psychological points, namely that Asians had defeated Asians, and that a defeated general should surrender to a much lower-ranking officer, because it had been troops not senior officers who had defeated the general and the rest of the Japanese.

---

26   Moke Murray, interviewed by Anthony Barnett, 1981.

Above: Surrender ceremony, Phnom Penh, October 1945. Moke is hatless, right.

At the ceremony the prolonged, violent and yet in some ways honourable confrontation between the Japanese 55th Division and Gracey's 20th Indian Division that had begun in the spring of 1944 came to a peaceful, dignified end. A few days later Moke reported to Gracey that only 5,381 Japanese soldiers remained in Cambodia. By that time his fellow officers had presided over a series of additional small-scale surrenders. Following Moke's lead, the surrenders were accepted by ethnic Gurkhas. For the remainder of 1945 he had little to do and his official diary records no politically significant actions. General Gracey visited Phnom Penh on 14–15 November to pay his respects to Sihanouk. He gave the King a samurai sword. In his memoirs Sihanouk recalled that Gracey spoke a "picturesque form of Franglais".[27]

At the time Gracey, Moke and the officers in his staff were awarded Cambodian decorations. As Moke recalled:

---

27   Norodom Sihanouk, *Souvenirs Doux et Amers* (Paris: Hachette, 1981), 138.

I was presented with a medal. General Gracey got class one and I got class two of the Royal Order of Cambodia.[28] There was a tremendous party. We gave the King lunch. David Wenham and John Arnold got something like the order of the dancing girls. I was too senior for that, a pity. He was a tiny little chap, the King, and I'm six foot one. When he presented me my medal, he tried to kiss me! I stood strictly to attention; he kept jumping up (*hilarity*).

You didn't stoop?

No, I didn't.

In retrospect Moke's response to Barnett and his refusal in 1945 to accommodate the Cambodian King are jarring. They make it clear, like much of his light-hearted commentary about Cambodia and Vietnam, that Moke, unlike Huard, was never wiling to show respect to the King or to take Cambodia, that "somewhat Ruritanian" place, seriously as an ancient kingdom or as a potential modern state. By remaining erect, Moke literally looked down on Cambodia's impressionable young King. Unsurprisingly Sihanouk failed to mention Moke (or Huard) in his memoir of the period written forty-odd years later.

At this point Moke's mission to Cambodia was finished and on 1 December 1945 he was officially relieved. At the time, however, he had one more bridge to cross when the French Major General Marcel Jean Marie Alessandri (1895–1968) arrived in Phnom Penh to act as Commander of French troops in Cambodia. Alessandri outranked the British "Brigadier" but technically, for the time being at least, he came under Moke's command. As Moke recalled:

---

28 In his military records prepared in 1947, transferring him into the British Army, Moke lists the decoration he received as "Royal Order of Cambodia, First Class".

[Allessandri] suddenly arrived. A nice enough chap except that you would keep on shaking hands at breakfast! I put a stop to that. He was a bit troublesome. He was a Major General in charge of French forces. I thought, "My God, I can't give orders to a Major General", although I was the commander. So, I signalled Gracey asking if I could promote myself. Back came the signal from Gracey, I've got it somewhere, saying, "Agreed to your proposal, must not promote yourself above full general, planeload of insignia follows tomorrow." So, I first promoted myself to Brigadier then to Major General and I also promoted David Wenham to Colonel and John Arnold to Major. It was great fun!

In mid-December 1945 the uncrowned king of Cambodia (Moke's jocular description of himself, talking to Barnett) was replaced by acting French Commissioner Huard, who held the position well into 1946, and also by a British liaison mission. In a letter dated 2 December 1945 that Moke kept among his papers, Prince Monireth, the Prime Minister *pro tem*, thanked him for his efforts, "Our gratitude for the order and security, which thanks to your energy and your decisive spirit you, knew how to maintain in spite of the gravity of the hour."[29]

On the evening of 12 December Moke and his staff were honored with a dance party at the Cercle Sportif in the French section of the city, which has now become the site of the US Embassy. He was also offered a French military decoration, he recalled, but British regulations forbade him to accept it because the war was over. At this time Moke drove to Siem Reap with his staff to see the Angkorian ruins. He found them "breath-taking" and added, "The King sent the Royal Ballet to dance there for my own special edification. At night, with flaming torches. Wonderful!"

---

29 Letter from Prince Sisowath Monireth to Moke Murray, 2 December 1945.

The curator of the ruins, Maurice Glaize (1886–1964) told Moke and his colleagues that they were the first Europeans to visit Angkor since the Japanese troops had arrived in Cambodia in 1941. Glaize's guide-book to the ruins is still valuable for twenty-first century tourists and in 1981 Barnett noticed a copy of the book sitting in Moke's bookcase in Worthing.[30]

Early in 1946 Moke and his staff flew off to Saigon. Aboard the plane in what Moke later called a "convivial ceremony of demotion", the acting, unpaid Major General alongside his companions divested themselves of their temporary ranks and reverted to their pre-Cambodian status.

In the same month a *modus vivendi* was signed in Phnom Penh between the French authorities and a Cambodian delegation led by Prince Monireth. The document retained some of the positive reforms enacted by the Vichy regime and formally re-established a state that strongly resembled the French Protectorate, but Monireth and his Cambodian colleagues were rewarded for their co-operation and good faith. Sihanouk also signed off enthusiastically. In the agreement France granted Cambodians some unprecedented autonomy and freedom of manoeuver, including the right to have a constitution, form political parties and to hold elections—the first in Cambodia's history—for a national assembly. Yet, Cambodia also had to join the French Indochinese Federation with Laos and eventually Vietnam following the French attack on the DRV. The Kingdom of Cambodia's slow march toward complete independence had begun, unbeknownst to the French, most of whom probably wanted to restore something that restored most if not all of the non-negotiable, pre-1940 status quo.[31]

---

30 Maurice Glaize, *Les Monuments du Groupe d'Angkor* (Saigon: Albert Portail, 1948).
31 See NAC 55571, *"Accord fixant le modus vivendi provisoire"*.

In late January 1946, shortly before he left Indochina for good, Moke flew from Saigon to Angkor to accompany a flamboyant American travel writer named Hassoldt Davis. A Japanese soldier, still to be repatriated, piloted the plane. Like the man who had brought Moke to Phnom Penh three months before, the pilot had trained as a *kamikaze*. It's possible, in fact, that the pilot was the same man, neatly book-ending Moke's Cambodian adventure.[32]

---

32   *Montreal Gazette,* 16 March 1946.

ELEVEN

Back with the Gurkhas

On 12 February 1946, the British troopship *Riana* sailed from Saigon for Bombay, arriving on 18 February with elements of the 20th Indian Division, including Moke, on board. The Division was disbanded soon afterwards but several units attached to it, like Moke's 4/10GR, were occupied in the last fourteen months of its existence with peacekeeping missions in what were soon to become the independent states of India and Pakistan during the twilight months of the Raj.

In July 1947, less than a month before sovereignty over Pakistan changed hands, the 10th Gurkha Rifles—along with the 2nd, 6th, and 7th GR—was selected to be amalgamated into the British Army in arrangements reached after prolonged negotiations among officials in Great Britain, India, and Nepal. The four regiments, all severely undermanned at the time, became known collectively as the Gurkha Rifle Brigade.[1] The remaining six Gurkha Regiments transferred to the soon-to-be independent

---

1 According to Lionel Caplan, *Warrior Gentlemen: "Gurkhas" in the Western Imagination* (Providence: Berghahn Books, 1995) many British officers were nonplussed by the large number of Gurkhas who chose to abandon British patronage and opted instead to serve in the Indian Army.

Indian Army.[2]

In January 1947, well before the 4/10GR dissolved, Murray was posted to the Indian Army's Staff College at Quetta, as part of the last British–Indian Army intake. While he was there, he earned the reputation of being a heavy, but rarely inebriated, drinker. According to Colonel John Cross, who served with Murray in Malaya:

> At the Staff College at Quetta, none of the Directing Staff was allowed more than one drink with him as he seemed to have hollow legs and could drink all night and carry on the following morning as though nothing had happened whilst the staff were suffering from alcoholic remorse.

Poignantly, Murray was himself a student at Quetta when Tim sued him for divorce in 1947. As we shall see later, severe bouts of alcoholism dogged Murray throughout his second marriage (1957–68) and again in the closing decade of his life.

On 10 March 1947, barely five days before what would have been the battalion's sixth birthday, 4/10GR was officially dissolved in a three-day ceremony presided over by its wartime divisional commander, Douglas Gracey, recently knighted for his service in Burma.[3] Several former commanders of the battalion, including Murray were in attendance. Murray saved the program among his papers. Its first page reads: "Lieutenant General D.D. Gracey, accompanied by Brigadier C.H.B. Rodham, commander 100th Indian Infantry Brigade, and previous commanding officers of the Battalion inspected the battalion to the Slow March 'Will

---

2   See Raffi Gregorian, *The British Army, the Gurkhas, and Cold War Strategy in the Far East, 1947–1954* (New York: Palgrave, 2002) for a discussion of the complexities that surrounded the absorption of Gurkha units into the British Army.

3   It is not clear where the 4/10GR had served in 1946 and early 1947, after the 20th Division had been disbanded.

Ye No Come Back Again.'" The end of the program states that: "The battalion marches off on parade for the last time to the slow marches 'Happy We've Been Together' and 'Auld Lang Syne.'" There is no indication in the program of speeches that must have been delivered to the serving and former members of the battalion. Instead two days of strenuous games and celebrations (including a "Ladies' Night") left the most saddening part of the occasion, the final march past, to the end.

For most of 4/10GR's and the 20th Division's brief existence, its officers and men had been fighting Japanese troops in Assam and Burma as well as the Viet Minh-supported forces arrayed against them in Saigon and its outskirts in 1945. Since leaving French Indochina in early 1946 the 4/10GR had been helping to maintain order in British India as it moved tumultuously toward independence. Murray remained in command of the Battalion until he was assigned to Quetta.

In World War II, the battalion's officers and men had suffered heavy casualties but had also been highly decorated for their actions in the field.[4] Battle deaths in the Burma campaign also included hundreds of thousands of Japanese alongside tens of thousands of British, Indian, and Commonwealth troops, and uncounted thousands of civilians. Fighting was often face-to-face. For the victors like Moke, the casualties that the winning units suffered were part of a campaign that many of them were proud to have been part of. The campaign, as General Slim titled his memoir, transformed the humiliating defeat of 1942 into the sweeping victory of 1944–1945, fought to a large extent by Indian Army forces over much of the same terrain.[5]

---

4   Brian Reginald Mullaly, *Bugle and Kukri: The Story of the 10th Princess Mary's Own Gurkha Rifles*. (Edinburgh: W. Blackwood, 1957), 403.
5   It is worth noting, however, that neither Moke, the 4/10 GR, nor the 20th Indian Division had been involved in the 1942 retreat.

For the Japanese officers and men of the Burma campaign, Burma was for the most part a shaming horror even if—right up to the end—they had fought with extraordinary bravery and fervor. They sustained horrendous losses. Over 65 per cent of the 300,000 Japanese who fought in Burma died in combat, from suicide, or from illness. Only toward the closing months of the war were many of them willing to be taken prisoner.[6] For Murray and the Gurkhas of 4/10GR, on the other hand, what was probably memorable about their victorious campaign was not the casualties that they inflicted and sustained but that the "non-stop Gurkhas" had been judged by Gracey to be the best in the 20th Division, which in turn was thought by some to have been the best Division in the 14th Army.[7]

To cloud this triumphal picture, we will never know how many of these Englishmen and Gurkhas walked off the parade ground in 1947 afflicted with untreated mental and physical traumas caused by the horrors they had seen, inflicted, and endured. Much recent literature about the Burma campaign—the British Empire's last large-scale military success—masks the sheer butchery of the war as well as what were undoubtedly decades of often undiagnosed (and unrecorded) mental and physical suffering for the thousands of men who had taken part in it.

In April 1947, however, World War II was over and 4/10GR was breaking up, along with the rest of the British-officered Indian Army, which—except for four of its Gurkha battalions—was

---

[6] See Kazuo Tamayama and John Nunneley, *Tales by Japanese Soldiers of the Burma Campaign 1942–1945* (London: Cassell, 2000), an absorbing account. These figures are probably on the low side, as thousands of Japanese deaths would not have been accurately recorded at the time. Fifteenth Army losses, on the other hand, came to roughly 15 percent of the Army's strength. See also Louis Allen, *Burma: The Longest War 1941–45* (London: Dent, 1984), 637–45.

[7] For these assessments see Peter M. Dunn, *The First Vietnam War* (London: C. Hurst, 1985), 162 ff.

about to devolve to India and Pakistan. In miniature, the dissolution of the battalion signified the dissolution of the Raj. For its officers and men, especially those like Moke who had a sense of history, the closing ceremonies must have been both a proud, emotional, and bittersweet occasion, as well as a distinctly imperial moment: "Happy We've Been Together" and "Auld Lang Syne", indeed.

Talking to Anthony Barnett thirty-seven years later, Murray said that he felt that the end of the British Empire, symbolized by the break-up of the Gurkha regiments, was saddening but inevitable:

> I think that we British knew that independence [for India and Burma] was coming for a long, long time and we prepared for it. That's why it came smoothly. We admitted that it was going to be. Not everybody, not the cranks, but even I thought it was going to happen. I thought it was a pity, but I knew it was coming. Everyone knew it. Some very much against it like the blimps and some were very sad about it. I was very sad. Having admitted the fact that it was going to come we did our best to pave the way.[8]

Moke went on, perhaps defensively, to disparage the methods that the French employed in their reconquest of Indochina. When Barnett asked him, "Did you feel uneasy about the relationship between the French and the local population?" Moke replied:

> Yes, I did. I suppose it's putting my neck out a bit, after all we were colonising people, but we were good with our people, you know, I think. In India, we were good colonisers. The French weren't. The French were like *that (presses thumb against his palm)* "Don't forget, Annamites, we are the boss, we are the

---

8   Moke Murray, interviewed by Anthony Barnett, 1981.

French." This is a sort of thing I got, unlike the British who are always friendly. I think we were good. In fact, I'm certain we were, but the French were bad.[9]

By and large, Moke liked what he had seen of the British Empire in India, Assam and Burma. From 1937 onwards, he had been a happy, competent warrior, fighting on the empire's behalf. At the same time, he didn't see very much. On 20 March 1983, Moke wrote to Ursula Betts: "Are you watching *The Jewel in the Crown*? I must say that I have become bored with it and cannot abide the caricatures and the running down of the Raj".[10]

On 20 November 1947, as he finished his stint at Quetta, Murray asked to stay on as a British officer with one of the four Gurkha units that had shifted in the meantime to the British Army and was formally gazetted into the British Army in February 1948. Soon afterwards he took extended leave in England, where he visited his widowed mother and his sister Eileen who were living together in the village of Wrecclesham, Surrey, close to the market town of Farnham. Despite having returned to the same country in which they were also living, Moke made no attempt to contact estranged wife Tim nor his son Colin, who was twelve years old at the time.

Many British Gurkha officers and some of Murray's colleagues in the Indian Army like David Wenham retired at this point. Others, like John Masters, transferred—in his case briefly—into purely British units. Murray does not seem to have

---

[9] For nuanced and accessible critiques of the British Empire, see John Darwin, *The Empire Project: The Rise and Fall of the British World-System, 1830–1970* (Cambridge: Cambridge University Press, 2009); Bernard Porter, *The Lion's Share: A Short History of British Imperialism 1850–1970* (London, 1975); See also David Cannadine, *Ornamentalism: How the British Saw Their Empire* (London: Oxford University Press, 2001).

[10] In this context, see Margaret Macmillan's insightful essay "Elegy for an Empire: Paul Scott's Raj Quartet", *Spectator*, 11 December 2007.

considered either option and he remained affiliated with the Gurkhas for the remainder of his military career. Murray was assigned to command the 2/7GR, stationed in Kuala Lumpur in what was then the British colony of Malaya. He stayed with this battalion as its commander until the end of 1952.

In the aftermath of World War II, the British had given independence to the countries that would become independent India, Pakistan, and Burma, but it had no intention of abandoning the important entrepôt of Singapore and the patchwork of possessions in Malaya.[11] The latter's rich natural resources, particularly rubber and tin, which was in high demand for post-war reconstruction efforts across the world. Indeed, Whitehall had never promised independence to the multicultural communities that resided in British Malaya at any point before World War II nor during the conflict itself. Moreover, Malaya differed from Vietnam, India, and Burma in that no substantial mass nationalist movement had taken root there in the 1920s and 1930s, partially because the British favoured the Malays over other, more contentious ethnic groups, notably the ethnic Chinese communities that formed a substantial proportion of the Malayan population. While there was indeed discourse surrounding the making of an ethnically Malay nation, these ideas remained largely within intellectual circles and did not translate into a mass movement like it did in Indonesia during the interwar period.[12]

Hostility towards British rule in Malaya in the aftermath

---

[11] British Malaya, prior to 1946, had consisted of the directly-controlled Straits Settlements of Malacca, Penang, and Singapore; the Federated Malay States of Selangor, Perak, Negeri Sembilan, and Pahang which were administered centrally by the British in Kuala Lumpur; and the unfederated Malay States of Johor, Kedah, Kelantan, Perlis, Terengganu which were nominally independent and sovereign states indirectly-ruled by the British as protectorates of the empire.

[12] See William R. Roff, *The Origins of Malay Nationalism* (New Haven: Yale University Press, 1967).

of World War II was divided along sectarian and political lines. While Malay political leaders were able to temporarily forge a mass movement against the administrative structure of the Malayan Union, this unity was ultimately short-lived following their success in forcing the British to back down and replace the Union with the Federation of Malaya, which effectively reset the governance of the Malay Peninsula to the status quo antebellum.[13] Violent reactions to the re-establishment of British rule meanwhile was largely confined to the radicalized portions of the large, mostly working-class Chinese minority. This state of affairs differs significantly from the widespread, almost universal hostility to the French on display throughout the colonial era in Vietnam and more openly as we have seen following the Japanese *coup de force*. During the Pacific War, the British had backed ethnic Chinese anti-Japanese guerrillas in Malaya, many of whom were members of the clandestine Malayan Communist Party (MCP) while others were affiliated with the local Kuomintang chapter. This was driven by largely pragmatic reasons as prior to the invasion of Malaya, military and civilian officials on the ground believed that the Chinese would be more willing to put up a fight against the Japanese than the Malays, particularly in light of the violence wrought on mainland China by imperial Japanese forces since 1937.[14] Their gamble ultimately turned out to be correct but would also have unintended consequences following the defeat of the Japanese Empire. After 1948, a large

---

[13] The Malayan Union galvanised a response from Malay leaders particularly around the transfer of sovereignty away from the sultans of the Malay states to a centralised colonial administration based in Kuala Lumpur. For a detailed study of the short-lived Malayan Union experiment, see Albert Lau, *The Malayan Union Controversy, 1942–1948* (New York: Oxford University Press, 1991).

[14] For more on British policies of cooperation with the Malayan Communist Party, see F.S.V. Donnison, *British Military Administration in the Far East, 1943–1946* (London: Her Majesty's Stationery Office, 1956), 378–386.

number of the MCP-affiliated guerrilla fighters who had been trained and armed by the British would turn on their wartime allies in an attempt to overthrow the colonial government and establish a new, independent Malaya.

Soon after Murray arrived in Kuala Lumpur, he had a pleasing personal encounter that he recalled to Barnett:

> The Chief of the Imperial General Staff, Bill Slim or Burma Bill, visited the Battalion, which I had just joined; he was [honorary] colonel of the [7GR] regiment. When I was introduced he said, "Oh, you're the chap who commanded Japanese divisions in Indo-China". To which with simple modesty, I replied, "Only two, sir".[15]

Slim's visit to Malaya was not purely social. It involved consultations with British military officials regarding some unwelcome proposed reforms affecting the Gurkhas in general and 2/7GR in particular. The British had plans to transform Gurkha infantry battalions into artillery units, a decision, in Colonel Cross's view, would have meant the end of the Gurkhas as an effective military unit as Cross wrote to me in 2018. These reforms were rescinded and 2/7GR became an infantry battalion again after Moke took command of it. According to Cross, Moke was a popular commander, an assertion confirmed in Battalion newsletters from the period.[16]

Speaking about Malaya, Murray told Barnett about the peculiar hostility that existed soon after the war between the British civilians who had stayed behind and had been imprisoned and mistreated by the Japanese, on the one hand, and recently arrived Indian Army personnel such as Moke, on the other. The

---

15   Moke Murray, interviewed by Anthony Barnett, 1981.
16   Email to author from Col. J. Cross, 10 April 2018.

antipathy resembled the friction that Murray had noticed in French Indochina between newly arrived, idealistic Gaullists and those compatriots who had been in Indochina trying ineffectively to resist the Japanese. As he recalled:

> There was a curious element of the war. The Free French, the Gaullists, who got out to fight again, and the resistance who stayed behind to fight within their own country loathe each other's guts. The same thing happened in Malaya, curiously. There were those who decided to get out at all costs, away from the Japanese, to fight again. And those who decided to stay. They loathe each other, when we got back there. Those who stayed behind, whom we had fought to release, thought that they had won the war. They resented our not having been prisoners, interned with them. When we first went to Kuala Lumpur in 1948 anybody in uniform was practically booed out of the club by those who had stayed behind.[17]

The 7GR, formed in 1907, was the last Gurkha unit to be raised in the British Army. As a result, it lacked the nineteenth-century mess silver, battle honours, and anecdotal history of the older Gurkha battalions. Nonetheless, it appears to have one peculiar, endearing custom. Rather than wearing the white mess kit jackets as dictated by British Army convention, officers of the 7GR donned dark jackets. This was ostensibly because the orders to wear dark jackets in mourning for the death of Lord Kitchener, Secretary of State for War, on 5 June 1916 having never been rescinded for the regiment.

Soon after Moke arrived in Malaya, he was consulted on the Regimental War Memorial that was to be erected in London, but was not unveiled until 1997. He urged the organizing committee

---

[17] Moke Murray, interviewed by Anthony Barnett, 1981.

to make sure that the statue included in the memorial wore a proper, generic uniform and that its face had "Gurkha features".

British authorities in Malaya inaugurated the so-called Malayan Emergency on 18 June 1948, after the assassinations, just days before, of three British rubber planters by Communist insurgents. The subsequent "police action", as it was sometimes euphemistically called, lasted until 1960. At its height in 1952, some 40,000 British and Commonwealth troops, 7,000 police, and 240,000 Home Guard were pitted against some 7,200 insurgents in a battle over the hearts and minds of the Malayan people.[18] As recent scholarship has demonstrated, Commonwealth forces during the Emergency were far more violent and coercive to the Malayan Chinese population than has previously been acknowledged as colonial policymakers and counter-insurgents turned to oft-used tools including detention without trial, mass resettlement in what were effectively concentration camps, collective punishment, food control, property destruction, and banishment to break the back of the insurgency.[19] Many of these strategies and tactics were part of an extensive repertoire of violence that had been honed by British military and police officers since the Boer War. As the historian Caroline Elkins has shown in a sweeping study of its many conflicts, the British Empire thus left what she

---

18 Yao Souchou, *The Malayan Emergency: Essays on a Small, Distant War* (Copenhagen: NIAS Press, 2015) 42; The classic history of the Emergency, which Yao dismisses as a "victor's narrative" is Noel Barber, T*he War of the Running Dogs: The Malayan Emergency, 1948–1960*. (New York: Bantam, 1971); See also Robert Jackson, *The Malayan Emergency: The Commonwealth Wars 1948–1966* (London: Routledge, 1991); Richard L Clutterbuck, *The Long, Long War: The Emergency in Malaya, 1948–1960* (London: Cassell, 1967); Anthony Short, *The Communist Insurrection in Malaya, 1948–1960* (London: Frederick Muller Limited, 1975).

19 For an overview of the historiography of the Malayan Emergency, see Bernard Z. Keo, 'A Small, Distant War? Historiographical Reflections on the Malayan Emergency', *History Compass* 17, no. 3 (2019): 1–12.

has aptly described as a legacy of violence not just in its former colonies that have since achieved independence but at home as well.[20]

When he arrived in Malaya in 1948, Murray served for a time as a General Staff officer in Kuala Lumpur, attached to 2/7GR. At that stage, the British high command, as mentioned above, envisaged transforming the Gurkha battalions into artillery units, a move vigorously opposed by the Gurkha officers, including Murray. The situation was resolved when the Gurkhas were allowed to revert to their traditional status as infantrymen. Moke took command of the battalion for the calendar years 1950, 1951, and 1952. According to his fellow Gurkha, J.P. Cross, Murray's popularity with his troops was partly because he helped convince higher authorities to abandon the proposal to shift the Gurkhas into artillery units.[21] Moke's success in prosecuting the case for the Gurkhas to remain as an infantry unit was influenced partially by the shift in strategy entailed by the 'Briggs Plan', a comprehensive strategy developed by Director of Operations Lieutenant-General Sir Harold Briggs and executed by his successor General Gerald Templer. The broad thrust of the strategy relied on the mass resettlement of Malayan Chinese communities into so-called 'New Villages', which would be defended—and surveilled—by militia forces raised under the Home Guard and Village Guard schemes.[22]

The Briggs Plan suited Murray and his Gurkhas as it freed up units like 2/7GR to undertake military operations in the jungle. Under his command, the Gurkhas were active combatants,

---

20 Caroline Elkins, *Legacy of Violence: A History of the British Empire* (New York: Random House, 2022).
21 Email to author from Col. J. Cross, 10 April 2018.
22 Richard Clutterbuck, *The Long Long War: The Emergency in Malaya, 1948–1960* (London: Cassell, 1967).

tracking down and engaging units of the Malayan National Liberation Army (MNLA) under difficult conditions in which Moke's combat experiences in Assam and Burma were undoubtedly useful. Murray's old unit the 10GR (minus the disbanded 3rd and 4th battalions) was also involved in the Emergency. Its *Official History* briskly summarized its activities as follows: "The battalion achieved a record number of kills and won an exceptional tally of medals."[23]

British official literature rejected the MNLA's nationalist credentials, including its name, just as Gracey had done with the Viet Minh in 1945. Instead, the insurgents were variously referred to as "terrorists", "Communists", "Communist terrorists" (CT) and "bandits". Although complete victory for the MNLA was never in sight, its highly-motivated guerrilla forces posed a serious threat to stability in Malaya, and putting down the insurgency was a drawn-out and extremely costly exercise for Britain, its Commonwealth allies who contributed to the conflict, and the nascent Malayan government.

The insurgents, described by the official historian as "kills", were made to sound like grouse or vermin. A severe but undemanding "othering" was in effect, a process that ultimately led to a range of atrocities committed by government forces which continues to go unacknowledged even today.[24] Yet, at no point in Murray's recorded conversations or his private papers, on the other hand, did Moke ever demean or dehumanise any of his opponents in combat in this way.

Under Moke, 2/7GR took part in a series of combat operations throughout 1951 and Murray's performance in the field earned him a DSO in March 1952 for "gallant and distinguished

---

23 Email to author from Col. J. Cross, 4 April 2018.
24 Benjamin Grob-Fitzgibbon, *Imperial Endgame: Britain's Dirty Wars and the End of Empire* (New York: Palgrave Macmillan, 2011).

service." At some point before this. he had received a Mentioned in Despatches citation. The long-winded citation reads:

> Since the 1st August 1950 Lt Col E.D. MURRAY OBE has commanded his Battalion on operations first in PAHANG until April 1951 and later in Negri Sembilan. The area for which he was responsible for operations in PAHANG was one of the most disturbed in the state and as a result of bandit activities the morale of the civilian population was very low.
>
> Lt Col MURRAY rapidly appreciated the operational situation and from the start attacked the problem with most commendable energy and ability. His enthusiasm and his skilled leadership were an inspiration the officers and men of his Battalion, and his excellent arrangements and plans quickly achieved success. During the period that they remained in the area, his Battalion killed 30 bandits, captured 5 and wounded many more. This undoubted success achieved in very difficult country and in the face of many difficulties the chief of which was the loss of faith io the security forces on the part of the civilian population, completely disrupted the local bandit organisation and forced them to split into small parties.
>
> By the time they left the area, Lt Col MURRAY's personal reputation and that of his Battalion was very high amongst all classes of the population. The success achieved and the infectious optimism and fighting spirit of Lt Colonel MURRAY himself had restored, and more than restored, confidence. For his all round success Lt Col MURRAY is deserving of the highest praise.
>
> Since arriving in NEGRI SEMBILAN Lt Col Murray has been equally successful. His Battalion has achieved important successes against the bandits and as a result the number

of terrorist incidents in this area is very small. This satisfactory state of affairs in an area, which was at the time prolific of bandit incidents of a major kind, is a reflection of Lt Col MURRAY's outstanding services in the cause of law and order.

The confident, verbose phrasing of the award masks the persistent difficulties that local security forces and Commonwealth troops including the 2/7GR, were to encounter before the Emergency officially ended in 1960, seven years after Murray had left the region, and three years after Malaya had achieved its independence from the British Empire.

In his years with the Assam Rifles and V Force, Murray had often been a guerrilla soldier himself, and he had confronted irregular forces in Saigon and Waziristan. His views on the guerilla and counter-guerrilla aspects of the Malayan Emergency and successive wars in Indochina, drawing on his own experiences, would have been interesting to hear, but sadly they have gone unrecorded.

Murray spent part of 1952 inspecting Gurkha units elsewhere in Asia before relinquishing command of the battalion on the last day of the year. Soon afterwards, his professional life took a brief but glamorous turn that may have marked the pinnacle of his military career.

TWELVE

Queen Elizabeth's Coronation, Anthony Barnett

Undoubtedly, for us, the greatest moment of many great moments was when, passing under Admiralty Arch, we entered and moved up The Mall. There ahead of us was that broad red road, boarded by banks of tumultuously cheering crowds and lined by the Foot Guards in their scarlet and bearskins. And there, at the end, was Buckingham Palace, wither we were escorting Queen Elizabeth the Second. Under the arches we passed, those most dignified and splendid of all London's decorations, and, as the officers came to the carry, every man put a little extra into his marching and held his already proud head a little higher. We had done our small part in bringing the Queen home from her crowning.

Edward 'Moke' Murray, 1953

ON 20 JANUARY 1936, WHEN MOKE WAS TWENTY-SIX AND finding his feet in India, George V died aged seventy. He had been crowned in 1910, the year Moke was born, and had been celebrated as Emperor of India with a massive Durbar in Delhi in 1911. On his death his eldest son became Edward VIII

Above: Ghurkas on parade at coronation.

Queen Elizabeth's Coronation, Anthony Barnett

and his coronation was scheduled for May 1937, sixteen months after his father died. But in the meanwhile Edward declared that he would marry a twice-divorced American. The prospect of Britain's ermined establishment and assembled bishops being obliged to pay homage to her as their new Queen was a 'modernisation' too far. Edward had to abdicate in December 1936. His younger brother Arthur succeeded to the throne and took the regnal name of George to signal continuity with their father—and Elizabeth, his ten-year-old daughter, became heir to the throne. George replaced Edward VIII at the planned coronation on 12 May 1937.

A coronation has two parts. The ceremony itself takes place in Westminster Abbey, where monarchs are anointed and crowned. It is a profound ritual that transforms the person into the representative of God while bestowing the legitimacy of earthly power upon him or her. It has roots going back to Anglo-Saxon kingship and Byzantine imperial ceremonial. In addition there are the surrounding celebrations that take place after the monarch is topped out. These have been remade across the centuries. In one period there were huge, post-coronation feasts. Most important, the newly invested monarch parades in front of the people in a public display that confirms, celebrates and refreshes the system that binds ruler with the ruled as they cheer their new sovereign.

In Britain, since 1688, the 'absolute sovereignty' that accompanies monarchical power has been shared between the Crown and Parliament, and the latter has become the dominant, ruling element. But the monarch's role was never reduced to the simply decorative. It remains to this day a significant, even defining influence on Britain and its international character.

This strange duality has huge significance for the period of Moke's lifetime. The importance of the monarchy as a source of 'meaning' for the British grew, as it defined 'who we are' in the world, even while its administrative importance in the running of the country shrunk away. There is a picture taken in 1953 that captures part of this. The tall, upright bespectacled figure of Moke, chest out, standing firmly to attention, the strong, fit, ruthless jungle fighter who has just led his Gurkha contingent successfully through the endurance parade of the Coronation, and his young, short, relaxed Queen, reaching out to pin the coronation medal to his chest.

Disraeli once wrote, "Nobody is forgotten when it is convenient to remember them".[1] This was a moment designed to be remembered. Why, then, did it become inconvenient to recall it? Moke could hardly have imagined, as he "came to the carry" at the head of the Mall and, to massive cheers of the crowd, "put a little extra" into his marching as he helped bring the Queen "home from her crowning", that he was marching into insignificance.

The importance of understanding the Coronation chapter of Moke's life is that it highlights his "rise and fall". That he should be singled out to lead the most distinctive contingent of the British Army was thanks to the reality of his competence as a fighter and officer. Everything he fought for was validated by this celebration. Yet it took him nowhere. To understand why, we have to start with the nature of the celebration itself: the twentieth-century British coronation.

The first was that of Edward VIII. Sixty-nine years after the chaotic, unrehearsed crowning of the nineteen-year-old Queen Victoria, the Coronation of 1902 was a "carefully stage-managed imperial apotheosis" and its "cultivation of the imperial spectacle was completely new", to quote Roy Strong, a traditionally inclined historian of British coronations. In his words,

---

[1] Letter to Lord Stanhope (17 July 1870), cited in William Flavelle Monypenny and George Earle Buckle, *The Life of Benjamin Disraeli, Earl of Beaconsfield Volume 5* (London: Arkose Press, 2015), 123–25 (with thanks to John Naughton).

the Empire, created under Victoria with its old dominions and new colonies, "was a jumble", but "Coronations were deliberately transformed into occasions when representatives of this global domain could gather" in front the world. They were thus designed to make an international impact. The jumble of Empire was thus branded by the coronation with imperial unity and the unique power of Great Britain projected onto the rest of the world. Two coronations later, in his account of 1937, Strong quotes approvingly a contemporary observation that "the English Coronation was a pageant more splendid than any dictators can put on: beating Rome and Nuremberg hollow at their own bewildering best, and with no obvious side of compulsion or horror".[2]

It is true that in Britain there was little or no sense of compulsion to the public manifestations. In India, however, where Moke may well have looked forward to participating in the planned Durbar, by 1937 there would have been. The leaders of the nascent independence movement declared that George VI should stay in England. With the risk that any Durbar would turn into a showcase for opposition to the Raj, it was scrapped; an early sign that George VI was to be the last Emperor of India, a role that was abolished in 1947.

But while the Coronation was a domestic expression of authentic, popular loyalty not authoritarian regimentation, after 1902 the celebration became a massive show of force and a demonstration of worldwide influence. In 1937, the 27-year-old Moke would have known about Indian contingents sent to the procession for George VI. It was an immense affair that mobilised representative units from imperial forces around the world. Its route was the longest ever, six and a quarter miles (just over

---

2   Roy Strong, *Coronation: A History of the British Monarchy* (London: HarperCollins, 2005), 437–39.

ten kilometres). The procession itself was two miles (three kilometres) long and took forty minutes to pass any fixed point. It involved 32,000 soldiers and sailors from around the world with 6500 in support and 20,000 police officers to help line the route.[3]

Nor were the demonstrations of force limited to the roads of London, they were accompanied by naval reviews with foreign navies invited to participate as observers. In June 1910, when George V reviewed the Royal Navy at Spithead he was saluted from 167 warships, along with eighteen ships from foreign navies arranged in five lines, each six miles (ten kilometres) in length, "through which the royal party steamed in review, aboard the royal yacht, HMY *Victoria and Albert*". There were an estimated quarter of a million spectators on the shore.[4] The future George VI, who was participated in the royal party, was fifteen.

In 1937, just over 100 surface ships saluted George VI, including four aircraft carriers, and an additional twenty submarines. It was described as the last parade of the Royal Navy as "the world's greatest and most prodigious navy". A newsreel from the time shows the eleven-year-old Elizabeth watching from the royal yacht.[5]

Fifteen years later, in February 1952, the King, who had been a heavy smoker, died aged only fifty-six. His passing came a crucial moment for the United Kingdom, one that saw the end of the 1945 Labour government and the start of what would become a postwar Britain under the Tories. It would become a transition as momentous domestically as the passing of the Empire externally. One personified by the new Queen, who was twenty-five.

---

[3] Hansard, 16 March 1937, <http://hansard.millbanksystems.com/commons/1937/mar/16/the-coronation>.
[4] J. Hogarth Milne, *Great Britain in the Coronation Year* (London: W.H. Allen and Company, 1914).
[5] See <https://www.youtube.com/watch?v=dcgOXmo3Ajw>.

Another coronation had to be planned. The date chosen was 2 June 1953. The hope was that it would be a sunny day and it allowed for sixteen months to plan and organise. Britain would then enter what was declared to be the coming 'New Elizabethan Age'. The context would be all important for Moke. He became a victim of the country's two-faced desire. On the one hand it wanted real change—from the class-bound humiliations of appeasement and the 1930s and the bleak austerity of years of war—and at the same time, continuity—as a military society that was proud of itself and victorious.

Looking back, the latter remains obvious. The former, the enormous, popular desire for domestic, social improvement, is less evident. It was perhaps best symbolised by the 1951 Festival of Britain across twenty-seven acres of London's South Bank, nominally organised by liberal planners to mark the 100th anniversary of the Great Exhibition of 1851. It became a celebration of modern life: "No one had ever seen anything like it before … a brilliant microcosm in which every single object had been designed for its job". It was a "knockout" success. More than 8.5 million visited between May and September (some like myself, then a boy of nine, did so twice). At its centre was the Dome of Discovery, packed with magnificent technological exhibits and the newly built South Bank concert hall (the only structure that remains), while a futuristic tower of light known as the Skylon lit up the Thames.[6]

Churchill loathed it and had his minister of works order its destruction as soon as he returned as prime minister, when Labour was voted out in October 1951. He also opposed the televising of the Coronation but was overruled, apparently at the

---

6   Michael Frayn, 'Festival', in *Age of Austerity 1945–1951*, ed. Michael Sissons and Phillip French, First Edition (London: Penguin, 1964), 330–52.

instance of Elizabeth's husband, the Duke of Edinburgh. What followed was to fuse modernity and tradition in a media-political framework that became increasingly disabling.

Two days before the Coronation, Moke was familiarising his contingent with their role by making a final reconnaissance of the route they would be marching. When they got to Buckingham Palace he overheard a Gurkha's observation and later wrote, "It was very early in the morning ... We had just finished walking round the route for the Procession. The blinds of London were still drawn, and the street lamps were still alight. As we passed, almost tiptoed past, the sleeping Palace, one whispered, 'The queen has indeed become a goddess'."

Elizabeth became a twentieth-century goddess of the media spectacle. The presence of TV promoted television sets into British homes. There was only one television channel at the time, the BBC, which now issued 2.3 million domestic licences. It was estimated that an average of nine or ten people gathered around each set, more than 18 million of us. As a young boy I was taken across the road to neighbours to join one such group (and my family acquired its own TV set soon afterwards) and 1.5 million watched in pubs or cinemas.[7] It meant that 56 per cent of the adult population watched at least thirty minutes of the service, twice as many as listened on the ubiquitous radio. Across the country, "especially in working class areas", there were street parties.[8]

On mostly small screens, and in black and white, the country witnessed Elizabeth being transformed from a young woman into a robed and blazing emblem. The Imperial State Crown, which she wore on the long procession back to the palace, was placed on the Queen's head, with the 'Black Prince's Ruby', worn by Henry

---

7 Francis Wheen, *Television: A History* (London: Century, 1985), 226.
8 David Kynaston, *Family Britain, 1951–1957* (Bloomsbury Publishing, 2010), 298–308.

V at the Battle of Agincourt in 1415, embedded in it. Sitting on the Abbey's throne, as the new head of the Church of England, she held in her left hand the orb of Christ's dominion and in her right the sceptre of temporal power, embedded with the world's largest diamond, the First Star of Africa.

The BBC's film of the Coronation ceremony was transmitted to France and flown to Canada and the United States. Apparently 85 million watched across North America. "No other country has succeeded in turning its state occasions, whether royal or presidential, into such a marketable international commodity."[9] This process was to lead, in July 1981, to a claimed 750 million people in seventy-four countries watching the wedding of Prince Charles to Diana Spencer.

The combination of enjoyment and modernity reproduced the spirit of the Festival of Britain and demonstrated a powerful desire for change and improvement as well as solidarity and self-belief. But now they were embedded in a regressive media-political frame that sought to amplify and at the same time control the cheering. The rejuvenation of tradition that became an important aspect of the Coronation's domestic success and importance had an authentic component. Part of the delight in celebrating the Queen was that while young she had trained as a driver to help the war effort and she had experienced the Blitz. In her, the country celebrated a victorious continuity as well as an emergence from post-war austerity. But it also became a continuity reinforced by the hard determination of the authorities, political, religious, diplomatic, administrative, cultural and military, to retain Britain's role as a world power.

The procession part of the Coronation that Moke took part in represented the bipartisan 'Warfare State' created under

---

9   Wheen, *Television*, 229.

Labour after 1945.[10] About 30,000, almost all men, were mobilised for the procession. Their route was just over five miles (eight kilometres), somewhat shorter than George VI's. If anything the numbers involved were greater, as the procession took 45 minutes to pass any one spot. Contingent after contingent of armed figures marched in parade, representing every section of the army, navy and air force as well as most Commonwealth countries, but not India.[11]

At the time, nearly ten years after victory in 1945, the armed forces of Great Britain still numbered 868,000 servicemen and women.[12] Along with the active reserves they came close to 10 per cent of the active male population aged between fifteen and fifty of approximately 12 million.[13] This immense army was engaged in an ongoing war in Malaya; the Korean War was winding down into a ceasefire (more than 80,000 British troops had been sent there, more than 1000 were killed, 2500 wounded and more than 1000 were taken prisoner),[14] and there was armed opposition to imperial bases in Egypt and elsewhere. At the same time the British Army had become primarily a European force, with four armoured divisions in West Germany. Those serving were only

---

10 David Edgerton, *Warfare State: Britain, 1920–1970* (Cambridge University Press, 2005); David Edgerton, *The Rise and Fall of the British Nation: A Twentieth-Century History* (Penguin UK, 2018).
11 All the contingents, Colonial, Commonwealth, Air Force, Army, Navy and Marines, are listed in small print down seven columns in the *Approved Souvenir Programme* of the *Coronation of Her Majesty Queen Elizabeth II* but I have not been able to find an official account of the numbers involved, equivalent to the announcement made to the House of Commons in 1937 by Ramsay MacDonald, then the lord president of the Council.
12 See <https://www.statista.com/statistics/579773/number-of-personnel-in-uk-armed-forces/>.
13 See <https://www.populationpyramid.net/united-kingdom/1950/>.
14 See <https://lordslibrary.parliament.uk/korea-remembering-the-uks-contribution-70-years-after-the-outbreak-of-a-forgotten-war-how-was-the-uk-involved/>.

half the story; a huge scientific, technological, industrial and administrative effort was needed to deliver the tanks, aircraft carriers (five were deployed in Korea), jet bombers and nuclear weapons that ensured Great Britain was one of 'The Big Three'.

The large military component of the Coronation procession was just the first of a three-fold celebration of Britain's armed might. A week after her Coronation, it was Elizabeth's turn to review the fleet at Spithead as her father and grandfather had done after theirs. There was an even larger number than in 1936, 197 in all, although they no longer 'ruled the waves'.[15] There was also a naval flypast of 300 aircraft from the Fleet Air Arm and Commonwealth forces. Moke took his entire Gurkha contingent and they boarded the aircraft carrier *HMS Indomitable* and formed up on the flight deck to salute the Queen and the royal party as they sailed past.

In addition, not to be outdone, the Royal Air Force now mounted its own separate review. It deployed 300 aircraft on the ground for inspection by Her Majesty and the Duke of Edinburgh, and a flypast of 600 including "protypes of the three V-bombers".[16] Like the naval review it was a huge exercise in self-inflation.

The effort put into the Coronation procession can be garnered from Moke's account of the Gurkhas' contribution, a modest 160 soldiers out of the 30,000. He published it in 1954 after raising subscriptions to pay the costs. It is a 100-page, hardcover book, 70 pages of which are photographs, put together as a "souvenir"

---

15 Coronation Spithead Fleet Review 1953, <https://hmsgambia.org/Spithead.htm> and the 64-page Official Souvenir Programme, <https://hmsgambia.org/docs/Coronation-review-1953-3mb.pdf, which sets out the vessels deployment>.
16 Edgerton, *Rise and Fall of the British Nation*, 341.

of the Gurkhas and their Coronation adventure.[17]

The Gurkha contingent were brought together at Sungai Petani, near Penang on the west coast of what was then Malaya in February 1953. Officers and men were chosen from a selection of battalions. On their way some had been behind a train that was derailed by terrorists in the ongoing conflict. The contingent was made up of three groups: the "marchers", the "Pipe, Drums, and Bugles", whom Moke would later take to Scotland, and a small administrative staff. They were kitted out, vaccinated and began to be drilled as a unit—as jungle fighters they had lost familiarity with parades. On 19 March the contingent boarded the twin-tunnelled troopship *Empire Orwell* in Singapore, and sailed for Southampton on England's south coast.

From there they boarded a train to the Commonwealth Camp at Purbrite, south of London. From its windows the Gurkhas looked out at the green fields, huge horses and a lack of rice, an unfamiliar landscape for those who had never left Asia. After they arrived and began to prepare, two issues became a "constant problem". The first was the slow pace of the march, at 112, thirty-inch paces to the minute, when the Gurkhas' natural marching speed was 140 with a smaller step; the second was the need for them to carry rifles "at the trail for such a long time even with changing arms". For they did not hold their weapons sloped over their shoulder, but horizontally between fingers and thumbs. By the end of the procession many were in acute pain.

At Purbrite there were inspections, including one by the Duke of Edinburgh, who "arrived by helicopter, having taken off from the gardens of Buckingham Palace for the first time ever". It was a sign of the modernity that was "in the air". The contingent

---

[17] *The Brigade of Ghurkhas at the Coronation of Her Majesty the Queen Elizabeth II*, A supplement to the "Kukri", the *Journal of the Brigade of Ghurkhas*, 1954.

trained with others for more than two months, including full-scale practice marches and the procedures for how they would join the procession.

On the day itself they were camped at London's Kensington Gardens and it rained. They prepared in the morning and were inspected and set out for Parliament Square where they would be signalled into the procession. On the way, "many recognised us and there were encouraging cries of 'good old Johnny Gurkha' and one, at least, I heard cry, 'Ayo Gurkhali'". At 1.30 they broke for a sandwich lunch from the mobile canteens as loudspeakers carried the broadcast of the three-hour service at the Abbey.

An estimated crowd of three million were spread out along the route. As the Gurkhas took up their positions, "we were nearly overwhelmed by the noise, almost hesitating in our step as it hit us. We had expected cheering, but nothing like this." While they stood easy waiting for the Queen to leave the Abbey, "We could listen to the exuberant good humour and happiness of the crowd. They were wetter than we were, for they had been in the rain longer; but 'It ain't going to rain no more, no more' and 'Stormy Weather' were sung as loudly and joyfully as 'You are my sunshine!'—and the great moment arrived ... we were off again, this time as escort to the Queen."

Mollie Panter-Downes, a British novelist who wrote the *New Yorker*'s "Letter from London" (and did not realise that the Gurkhas were a British regiment), reported for her American readers:

> The return parade began in pouring, relentless rain, which turned khaki uniforms to greenish black as they clung to the soldiers' backs ... But the rain could not dampen the mad excitement of the crowds camping out on the sidewalks and watching the old glamorous, Kiplingesque trimmings of

Empire swing by—the dark faces and the white, the smart scarlet tarbooshes of the Africans, the turned-up Australian hats, the wild-looking men from Papua and Samoa, the small, neat Gurkhas, and the Pakistan pipers hung round with leopard skins. The British regiments were also quite a sight in their various bottle-green or scarlet frogged tunics, their plaids, their coloured pants and their fur caps, and with their standards decorated, by tradition, with bouquets of fresh white roses or laurel wreaths or sprigs of bay ... It was the first really remarkable show of men marching wonderfully in all their wonderful-looking prewar finery that London had seen since the war.[18]

Moke describes the "greatest moment", quoted at the head of the chapter, when his Gurkha contingent swung under Admiralty Arch and entered the Mall with the Palace in front of them, and "every man put a little extra into his marching and held his already proud head a little higher. We had done our small part in bringing the Queen home from her crowning."

After that, "as we left the processional route at the Palace we were suddenly conscious or being wet and tired, and our swords and rifles became unbearably heavy. But we maintained the proper bearing, and reached the camp ... we would gladly have done it all over again."

The next morning, as the rain continued, they marched to Buckingham Palace to receive their well-earned Coronation Medals. The Queen pinned Moke's to his chest and he then distributed their medals to his contingent.

Over the next three weeks Gurkhas were shown off at various events and the Queen asked to see the Truncheon, a long

---

18 Mollie Panter-Downes, 'The Coronation of Queen Elizabeth II', *New Yorker*, 13 June 1953.

Above: Moke receives Coronation Medal from Queen Elizabeth II, June 1953

baton "held in reverence by the 2nd Goorkhas" [NB this is the correct spelling], which had been carried in the Coronation procession. On 24 June the marching contingent returned to the conflict in Malaya, while Moke took the Pipes, Drums and Bugles to Scotland, where they spent two months, participated in the Tattoo and concluded with a demonstration of loyalty and remembrance at the Scottish National War Memorial on 17 September.[19] The train to Southampton followed, and they also sailed back to Malaya, from where Moke returned to England in 1954. In the epilogue to his account, Moke uses a Gurkha perspective to reveal his love for what Britain could be and his despondency at what he fears it is:

> As all who know the Gurkha remember, it is difficult to fathom his thoughts. He is impassive and shows little emotion. His reactions and impressions have to be drawn out of him by the question and answer. To those who, alas,

---

19   In Edinburgh, Moke met his former battalion commander, Major-General David Murray-Lyon, now retired and still active in Gurkha affairs.

live in the British Isles a life of pessimism and depression, and fear the imminent collapse of the British Empire and Commonwealth, it may come as a well-earned jolt to know what these shrewd and observant visitors from Nepal thought. On his return to Malaya, one senior Gurkha officer, with much service, addressed his officers and men unprompted, and here is what he said, *verbatim*, "I come from a tiny village in the hills of Lamjung. I had no schooling, and knew nothing of the outside world. But I had an old and wise mother. She told me of the world of Hell and of Heaven. The world I now know—I have lived long enough in it. Hell? Well, that is below man's dignity, and is somewhere down there. And having been to England and the Coronation, I have some idea where Heaven might be."

Three aspects of the way Moke saw his world are captured in this concluding reflection on what, in ceremonial terms, was the high point in his life. There is the "otherness" of the Gurkhas with whom he had lived and fought for much of his life up to that point and his respect for them. There is his desire to admire England and the Queen as they do, with uncynical clarity as a paradise on earth. At the same time he is resigned to the reality that his country is filled with gloom and depression, fearful of the imminent collapse of everything he was deployed to fight for, and already knowing, as he was to tell me thirty years later, that, even if it wasn't imminent, its disappearance was inevitable.

In a famous article on the Coronation published soon after it, the sociologists Michael Young and Edward Shils argued that "British society … has achieved a degree of moral unity equalled by no other large national state". Something that transformed its society "from one of the most unruly and violent into one of the most orderly and law-abiding". They saw this as "one of the great collective achievements of modern times". In their view its achievement came about thanks to "the unifying function of the monarchy", which connected all the civil associations "with the sacred properties, the charisma, of the Crown", making it "the central value system of the society". Not least, this was achieved through its relationship with the armed forces, "with their multiplicity of royal connection, by fleet, regiment and squadron". All of which meant that the Coronation became "a great act of national communion" thanks to its "intensive contact with the sacred".[20]

Moke certainly felt the royal connection and experienced the Coronation as an act of communion even if he would have scoffed at the pomposity of declaring it to be sacred. Also, he was indeed modern in his use of weaponry and embrace of photography. So why were Moke's loyalty, sacrifice, bravery and success not recognised? And not just him, but many others who were discarded as an uneasy embarrassment, even as the monarchy they served continued proud and rampant?

Shils and Young fundamentally misunderstood what was taking place in 1953 when they saw it as a "great collective modern achievement" of British society as a whole. Their claim updates a view, originally set out by Bagehot in 1867 in *The English Constitution*, that the country had developed a more efficient "republic" than the United States (which was then recovering from its Civil War) by draping it in royal decoration. By "republic" the Victorians meant government by men, with negotiation and reason, rather than the arbitrary commands of divine right. They enjoyed pomp and ceremony but were not taken in by it. This was the no-nonsense culture that Moke expressed in his prime and it fills the pages of his Coronation "souvenir".

---

20   Edward Shils and Michael Young, 'The Meaning of the Coronation', *The Sociological Review* 1, no. 2 (1953): 63–81.

From this perspective, the monarchy's popularity ensures rational and effective government by protecting it from the dangers of irrational populism. It was a self-congratulatory view succinctly expressed by Queen Victoria's poet Laureate Alfred Tennyson, in his poem "To the Queen", when he hailed "our slowly-grown and crowned Republic's crowning common-sense".[21]

But in 1953, the opposite process was underway. It was no longer a crowned republic like the Victorian machinery of government, in which the rulers were realistic and the populace untrustworthy; rather it became a monarchical democracy in which the rulers were increasingly delusional while the populace was grimly realistic. In terms of government, common sense was abandoned in favour of illusions of grandeur, while the British public was embracing progressive, reasonable change, as expressed in the popularity of the Festival of Britain. The economy, media, family life, travel, sexual mores and culture increasingly moved away from repressive religions and deference, especially in the 1960s. But this modern spirit was tied to a political system that was not republican enough. In terms of government, change was stifled, and democracy was encased within a "winner-takes-all" politics.[22]

Page three of the *News Chronicle* of Saturday, 30th May, three days before the Coronation, provides a vivid cameo of this process, naming Moke in a news story in the London press.[23] It illustrates the way an energetic spirit of post-war modernisation was captured by an exhilarating expression of monarchism. The *News Chronicle* was a middle-class daily broadsheet that was

---

21 "… our slowly-grow / And crowned Republic's crowning common-sense, / That saved her many times …": Alfred Tennyson, "To the Queen", 1859.
22 An argument developed from that set out by Tom Nairn, *The Enchanted Glass: Britain and Its Monarchy* (Verso Books, 2011), 123.
23 With thanks to Justin Corfield for locating this.

broadly liberal. My parents had it delivered. The bottom half of page three is a huge advert for Mars and Bounty bars, Maltesers and Spangles, spread on a Union Jack behind which families on modern clothes are watching TV or picnicking, across the middle the flag advert declares: **"Everybody's Happy! Everybody's Gay!"** And below: **"Buy your favourite sweet treats to crown a perfect day."**

The lead story on the top left announces that millions will "hear us" behind the Iron Curtain as the coronation would be broadcast to them in their own languages. Below this is a longer story announcing how maharajas and millionaires were packing the Savoy for the celebration as its chefs are "becoming accustomed to specialised cooking for visitors from the East". Below this, *News Chronicle* reporters revealed that the six maids of honour "gave away one of the closest Coronation secrets" as their dresses were revealed in the final full-dress Abbey rehearsal. A smaller story tells us that people in two blocks of council flats in London or considering setting up all night guards to prevent "spivs" stealing the Union Jacks after nearly 100 yards of red, white, and blue bunting was stripped from their balconies, such was the appetite for royal decoration.

The main story whose pictures dominate the page has nothing to do with the coronation but reveals the transformation a way of life that was underway. Jack and Kathleen Bryant had won a house in the *News Chronicle* competition. Having been married for seven years with two children, they had "never had a real home of their own" before. Their winning entry put a two-storey house as "The sort of home an average family would like", but noted that they might choose a bungalow "because Mrs Bryant does not like the idea of stairs". In choosing their house, they would concentrate on a first-class heating system with a central boiler, lots of cupboard space, large windows, and above all lots of hot water and "would prefer these amenities to a refrigerator, washing machine and ultra-modern labour saving devices". It is, they said, "Best Coronation year present we could have had".

Two small news items complete the coverage. Under a close up picture of a Gurkha, it reads:

> Next to his kukri fighting knife, the last thing a Gurkha piper will be parted from is his tin of treacle. Without it, the leather pipe bag would rot.
>
> Within an hour of marching into the armed camp known as Kensington Gardens yesterday, the tough brown-skinned five-footers of the Gurkha Coronation contingent were hard at it.
>
> The pipers were pouring their treacle, and tuning their pipes.
>
> But the commanding officer, Lieut.-Colonel E. D. Murray, is worried.
>
> With only four days to go. the Number One uniforms arrived yesterday. Now, as any soldier knows. Army uniforms are not made in Savile Row. So a tailor will be busy over the next three days making them fit.

Thus, a touch of native exotica was added to the mix of communist listeners, millionaires at Saville Row, spivs stealing bunting and maids of honour. Few readers would have registered Moke's anxiety at the last-minute arrival of his men's parade uniforms. But below it, in a one paragraph item of less than an inch headlined **Best-seller**, nearly "3,000,000 copies of the half-crown Coronation Souvenir Programme" had been sold and 3,700 Boy Scouts would be selling them along the route on the day.

Shils and Young saw all this showing how the role of the monarchy bound the country together in an exceptionally well-governed process of modernisation in which Elizabeth would now represent, "a crowned republic's crowning common sense". Instead, the deep irrationality of the royal "decorative" was to displace "republican" realism. An exoskeleton of ceremony and procedure, organised around the monarchy, proved to be as tough and lasting as the Black Prince's Ruby. But below its shell, the magnificent machine of rational British government, which had proved so effective in wartime, shrivelled away. Elizabeth II's Coronation, and especially her procession and the reviews of the Royal Navy and the Royal Air Force strengthened the outer encrustation, which was primarily concerned with the projection of force and thereby also repressed facing up to the inner reality, the genuine need to replace the mental legacies of empire. Instead of the imperial system being superseded in a positive fashion, its passing was associated, as Moke observes, with pessimism and depression as the country clung to its greatness.

Moke's personal story turned with the way Britain's military power was now expressed. The monarch remained as commander-in-chief but any attempt to keep the colonies was hopeless, let alone retain a world empire. To replace it an Americanisation was undertaken after 1945, so as to regenerate Britain's world role, a transformation neatly captured in the Powell and Pressburger movie of 1946, *A Matter of Life and Death*, as mentioned in this book's Introduction. For Moke himself, the war he was fighting in Malaya was a continuation of its long colonial occupation but was now rebranded as a defence against communism. He had lived through a similar shift when his role in the violent suppression of Indian emancipation turned into his heroism in the battle against Japanese fascism. But now he was a participant in a rear-guard action while the main emplacements of the country's considerable military were dedicated to NATO and West Germany.

The Suez debacle of 1956 brutally confirmed both the new

order and the inner irrationalism that now gripped the British state. Anthony Eden had succeeded Churchill as Tory premier, and decided to invade Egypt to gain direct control over the Suez Canal after Egyptian President Nassar nationalised it. President Eisenhower opposed the invasion, which the British secretly coordinated with the French and the Israelis. With the Russians supporting Nassar, the United States did not want its leadership of the West to be tainted by colonialism. It pulled the plug on Britain's currency; Sterling plunged and Eden was forced to withdraw.

Meanwhile, the British and the French attacked Port Said, at the head of the canal, by air, with parachutes and helicopters (used for the first time in warfare in this way) and by sea with forces based in Malta and Cyprus (where the army was also engaged in fighting a Greek-backed independence insurgency). It was a military feat to mount an invasion thousands of kilometres away at relatively short notice. Moke's son Colin was in one of the tanks that was landed and ordered to capture the airport at Port Said; he told us he was relieved that the Egyptians had fled from their Soviet tanks with superior fire-power.

A humiliating reversal, Suez confirmed that the only route to 'world influence' was via subordinate collaboration with the priorities of Washington. There would be no resiling from the glamour and greatness celebrated in 1953, but its colonial and overtly imperial forms were from now on to be discarded without a "fuss". Eden had blatantly lied to parliament when he denied that there was collusion with Israel in advance of the invasion. Yet neither he nor his Cabinet colleagues who knew this was the case were brought to political justice. Nor was the country confronted with the duplicity of its leaders. Instead, it was condemned to half-hearted self-deception alleviated by satire, as Eden was shuffled off to the House of Lords. Counter-insurgency campaigns continued in Kenya and Cyprus without enthusiasm until formal handovers took place. Neither purged nor celebrated, the colonial legacy was discarded as a thief in the night might relieve himself of his swag in case it incriminates him. The pomp, pride and military power celebrated in the twentieth-century Coronation processions and their naval reviews, in the last of which Moke participated with such pride, were expelled to the phantom zone along with him and those like him.

In 2023, the Coronation of Charles III sought to reproduce the media-celebration that plays a central role in injecting the British polity with its illusions of modernised continuity. Stories were planted and encouraged about the regalia and investiture in the Abbey and how "ordinary heroes" had been invited to attend the ceremony. But the huge imperial procession that accompanied the return of the crowned monarch throughout the twentieth century was abandoned, drawing a line between it and the four coronations that preceded it. The same golden coach that has been used in every Coronation since William IV in 1830 was wheeled out, to ensure a connection to eighteenth-century bling. But its journey was reduced to the minimum possible—a return straight to the Palace—short enough to ensure that 'the crowds' would not appear too thin on the ground.

The program for the 1953 Naval Review in which Moke and his Gurkha contingent participated from the deck of the aircraft carrier HMS *Indomitable* includes a short history of 'Some Naval Reviews of the Past'. It describes the rapid technological changes that marked every review after 1783 and concludes, "Plus ça change, plus c'est la même chose"—the more things change, the more they remain the same. That was the false hope and benighted determination of the country's rulers. Those like Lt Colonel Edward D. Murray really did not change. By remaining true to themselves they revealed that the country was not the same in that it was no longer Great Britain. But as this needed to be denied, remembering them and their contributions became inconvenient and they were forgotten.

THIRTEEN

Flotsam of Empire, 1954–2002

MOKE WAS POSTED TO LONDON IN 1954, TAKING UP DUTY in Britain (and outside of Asia) for the first time since his days in the Territorial Army. For the next four years, he commuted to London from the hamlet of Wrecclesham in Surrey where he lived with his widowed mother. Until his retirement in 1958, Moke worked under the Assistant Adjutant General in the War Office. He served simultaneously as the British Army's Gurkha Liaison Officer. In 1957, he finally reached the permanent rank of lieutenant colonel during a period when the War Office was treating Gurkhas shabbily. Gurkhas commissioned into the British Army from Sandhurst, for example, were paid less than their British counterparts, and even when equity in pay was achieved, this was balanced out by their pensions being paid out at a deliberately lower rate.[1]

In April 1956, five months before the Suez Crisis, Murray attended the coronation of the King of Nepal (1920–1972) as a member of a four-man British delegation. The visit brought back memories of the time he had spent in Kathmandu as a subaltern

---

[1] Tony Gould, *Imperial Warriors: Britain and the Gurkhas* (London: Granta, 2000), 339–40.

twenty-two years before. Newsreel footage of the ten-day-long event shows honoured guests, including Moke, arriving at the coronation riding elephants in palanquins and in groups of four. The other British delegates were the Earl of Scarborough (1896–1969) Viscount de L'isle, VC (1909–1991), and the Sanskritist Professor Sir Ralph Turner (1888–1983), Turner had also served as a Gurkha officer in World War I. Some lines by Professor Turner praising the Gurkhas appear on the base of the Gurkha Memorial in London.[2] The hundred-man Gurkha contingent that marched at Mahindra's coronation probably included many of the soldiers that had paraded past Queen Elizabeth under Murray's direction just three years before. In conversation with Anthony Barnett, Moke hinted that he had been helpful in making arrangements for at least one of the military parades associated with the Nepalese celebrations.

In October 1958, Murray retired from the Army after twenty-nine years of active service, with the permanent rank of lieutenant colonel. At forty-eight, he was a relatively young man, but he had few skills to offer the non-military world. Moke's decision to stay in the Gurkhas had limited his options and he would probably not have been made a brigadier had he shifted to the British Army. As such, he likely felt his career had reached a logical conclusion. Recently married for the second time, on this occasion to a wealthy woman, Moke was likely to have viewed the future with equanimity. However, he had forty-five years left to live, thirty-five of them alone, with very limited means.

In the late 1950s, Murray was leaving what the historian

---

2   See "Royal Occasion in the Himalayas: Coronation of King Mahindra of Nepal", *The Times*, 1 May 1956. Queen Elizabeth's gifts to the King included an honorary commission as a general in the British Army and an ornately decorated ceremonial sword. On Turner, see Gould, 41. Murray and the other members of the British delegation seems to have arrived at the ceremony on an elephant. After the ceremonies, Moke was awarded the Order of Nepal.

Alistair Horne has called "a half century that would leave its mark on world history as the nastiest, cruellest, and most brutal ever recorded".[3] After fighting in Waziristan, Assam, Burma, and Malaya, Moke's mind was now on other things, and it is doubtful if he looked back on his years of service with regret or dismay. If asked, he would have said that he had been given a succession of jobs to do and he had done them. That many of the jobs involved killing other people, often face to face, does not seem to have distressed him, at the time or later.

An anecdote from Moke's final years brings this point into focus. In April 2018, Moke's neighbour, friend and occasional carer, Liam Fox, told Barnett that Moke had told him: "On one occasion an elephant was causing havoc in local village so Moke did what he had to do. Funny thing, this was the only time he had wet eyes during our conversation. He bitterly regretted that shot. Men, no problem."[4]

In November 1957, toward the end of his London posting and his military career, Murray's life swerved again as it had in 1935 and his subsequent marriage to Tim Ellery, when he married Valerie Easton-Smith (*née* Gallaher, 1926-?) in a civil ceremony in Surrey. Easton-Smith had been her second husband, making Moke her third husband.

Valerie was sixteen years younger than he was and had been born in the Marylebone district of London. Her father, Major Alexander Gallaher DSO, MC (1887–1938) was a member of a prominent Belfast family as well as an Etonian and Sandhurst graduate. He was wounded five times, and decorated twice, as

---

[3] Alistair Horne, *Hubris: The Tragedy of War in the Twentieth Century* (London: Weidenfeld & Nicolson, 2016), 339.
[4] Liam Fox, interview with Anthony Barnett, April 2018.

a cavalryman and pioneer pilot in World War I.[5] He retired from the Army in 1924. A year later, he married Valerie Haine (1915–1960). Their only child, named after her mother, was born two years later.

On 4 January 1939, when his wife was away in Ireland, Major Gallaher committed suicide in a field in Stanmore, just outside London, six miles from his Regents Park home. A dairyman discovered the body as well as a three-page letter to Gallaher's wife. The letter was partially covered by a whisky flagon. According to *The Daily Mail*, it referred to Gallaher's wartime "head wounds" and begged his wife's forgiveness. Hearing news of his death, Gallaher's widow Valerie flew to London from Ireland, acted hysterically at the police station (according to *The Daily Mail*) where Gallaher's body had been taken and subsequently locked herself inside her flat where reporters had trailed her, seeking to report about her grief. A friend of Gallaher's told *The Daily Mail* that after 1918 "the remainder of [Gallaher's] life was a tragic aftermath to the war."[6] The major left his widow and daughter an estate of £121,000. A memorial service in his honor, reported in *The Times*, drew an array of high-ranking military figures.[7] We can safely assume that the Major's suicide had a traumatic effect on his young wife and their twelve-year-old daughter.

Unfortunately, no information is available about Valerie's schooling or what activities she took part in, if any, during the War. In 1945, her mother remarried a Czechoslovakian pilot with

---

5   As a young officer in the 4th Irish Dragoon Guards (whose pre-war colonel was Kaiser Wilhelm IV) Gallaher had qualified as a pilot on Salisbury Plain. In 1914 after the retreat from Mons, Gallaher was briefly a prisoner of war before escaping. See Richard Van Emden, *The Soldier's War: The Great War through Veterans' Eyes* (London: Bloomsbury Publishing, 2010), 77 citing a recorded, oral memory of Gallaher's.

6   The sub-head to *The Times* obituary of Gallaher read "Wounded 5 Times."

7   The lead story in the Daily *Mail* 5 January 1938 refers to Gallaher's "throat wounds" but fails to specify a weapon.

the surname Provoznik, sporting an eye patch, who had been attached to the RAF. In April 1949, at the age of twenty-four, Valerie Gallaher married Samuel T. Jackett (1908–1979) in what *The Times* referred to as "a quiet wedding" in London. At the time, she was living with her mother and Provoznik at 41 Wilton Place in the Knightsbridge district. Jackett, a journalist, had been a Reuters correspondent in India during the war.

The couple began their married life in a handsome building in Hollywood Road in Chelsea in 1950 but the marriage was short-lived. The grounds for their divorce are not known but in 1952, Valerie married Donald Easton-Smith (1910–1985), a stockbroker and Chelsea neighbour who had been an RAF officer in the War. Easton-Smith had interests in Argentina, which he had visited in 1949. Valerie was his first wife. The Easton-Smiths continued to live in the Chelsea district and their daughter, Penelope, was born there in 1953.

Two years later, when Moke was posted to London the Easton-Smiths had moved to Evershed House near Farnham, an architect-designed Georgian style residence, not far from the Moke's residence in Wrecclesham. According to a September 2018 interview conducted by Anthony Barnett with the godmother of Moke's daughter Louise, Moke and Valerie appear to have met in a local pub. At some point in 1957 in any case, Easton-Smith moved back to London with his daughter because Valerie had decided to divorce him and marry Moke.[8]

In his late forties, Murray must have been flattered to be found attractive by a young, rich and presumably glamorous woman.

---

8   Local telephone directories show that Valerie was living alone in Evesham House in 1957 (Moke returned to his mother's cottage) and that Moke joined her there in 1958. The early months of 1957 would have been taken up with arrangements for divorce that caused Easton Smith to move out. In the 1950s it was not yet socially acceptable, at least in Moke's and Valerie's "set" to establish a household together until divorce proceedings were complete.

Valerie, for her part, may have come to prefer the company of a man who had been decorated for bravery like her father, had lived among the Nagas, and had arrested Wingate to living indefinitely with a stockbroker who probably commuted five days a week (bowler hat, furled umbrella) to and from Waterloo Station and the City. Until Easton-Smith left Wrecclesham, he and Moke were probably commuting to and from Farnham on some of the same trains.

We have no access to the ensuing drama, if there was one, and we cannot determine whether Moke or Valerie made the first move. Nonetheless Moke's second marriage is in marked contrast to his first over twenty years earlier, when he and Tim Ellery had ambushed each other into an unwelcome relationship. Getting Easton-Smith out of the picture, marrying Valerie and obtaining what looked like financial security for life resembled a well-planned (if miniature) military operation. Moke must have known from the beginning that Valerie was connected to the Gallaher Tobacco Company, a hugely prosperous cigarette-manufacturing conglomerate whose original headquarters were in Belfast. Valerie's father was the great-nephew of the firm's founder.[9]

Moke and Valerie were married in the Kingston registry office on 1 November 1957.[10] According to the Surrey electoral rolls, Moke and Valerie stayed on in Evershed House (which was in Valerie's name).[11] Their daughter Louise Jane Murray was born

---

[9] Easton-Smith and Valerie's daughter Penelope died in London on her fourteenth birthday in 1967.

[10] Easton-Smith married again in 1973 and died in the Chelsea district of London twelve years later. Moke's and Valeries' marriage certificate listed Valerie's address as a house in nearby Surbiton owned by Harold Denn who was probably her lawyer. Denn acted as a witness at the wedding, which was Murray's second and Valerie's third.

[11] Supplement to *London Gazette*, 9 June 1965 p. 5529.

nearby in 1962. Moke and Valerie lingered in Wrecclesham until 1965 to be near Murray's aged mother and for Murray to complete his reserve obligations, which he did when he reached the official retirement age of fifty-five. Evershed House was sold at auction in October 1966, after the Murray's had relocated to the Channel Islands. During their years in Surrey, Moke and Valerie would have had opportunities to socialize with General Gracey who retired to Farnham and died in nearby Woking in 1964.

Toward the end of 1965, the Murray's moved with their daughter to Alderney in the Channel Islands.[12] Given Valerie's inherited wealth it is likely that the family's sojourn on Alderney reflected the fact that residents of the Channel Islands were not subject to British income taxes. Aurigny House, for its part, is a substantial five-bedroom residence with a garden, likely dating from the eighteenth century.[13]

Murray and Valerie were together on Alderney until 1968, it seems, when their marriage apparently broke down, buffeted by prolonged bouts of alcoholism and unresolved disagreements. Valerie departed—permanently, as things turned out—to Spain taking her daughter with her. There are no records to suggest that she and Murray ever divorced. It has not been possible to trace Valerie's whereabouts thereafter.

Murray's mother died in January 1968 aged ninety-five, foreshadowing the longevity of her three children. Her estate amounted a mere £238. It is not clear if Moke and Valerie were still together or when they parted but by March 1968 Moke was alone and living in Farnham again. Unlike Valerie's two previous husbands, Murray never remarried. Interestingly, neither

---

[12] Among Murray's papers at the Gurkha Museum is an undated letter to the couple, addressed to Alderney by an unidentified friend who thanks them for some recent hospitality.

[13] It sold in late 2015 for £590,000.

did Valerie. In any case, the separation altered Murray's lifestyle dramatically even though after 1957 he stopped supporting his son Colin, who left the Army with an honourable discharge and married at the British Consulate in Barcelona in 1967.

In any case, on 20 March 1969 writing once again from Farnham, Dymoke Murray as he styled himself addressed a letter to the *Telegraph* regarding a detail relevant to the uniform that Prince Charles was to wear for his upcoming investiture as Prince of Wales.[14] By then Moke was almost certainly living alone. In the following year he helped E.D. Smith for his book *Johnny Gurkha: Friends in the Hills*. E.D. "Birdie" Smith was a Gurkha officer who served in Malaya in the battalion that Moke commanded at the time.

Between January 1969 (if not earlier) and June 1973 (if not later), Murray was living in Morris Lodge, a residential hotel on the outskirts of Farnham. When I visited a family that lived there in the mid 1950s, it was a genteel, slightly threadbare semi-rural boarding house surrounded by cypresses on the outskirts of Farnham.[15] In those days, Morris Lodge was run by a retired but vigorous Gurkha lieutenant colonel named Crosse, his wife and her two sisters. Another retired Gurkha major named Harmon also lived in the Lodge and several other inhabitants who had spent much of their lives in India.

---

[14] *Daily Telegraph*, 20 March 1969. I am grateful to Justin Corfield for this reference. An unsigned letter addressed to Moke at Morris Lodge, dated January 1969, is the earliest date I have for Moke's return to England from the Channel Islands.

[15] In 1954 and 1955, I visited the Lodge when Moke was living nearby in Wrecclesham. Mike Rutherford, *The Living Years: The First Genesis Memoir* (London: Thomas Dunne Books, 2015). contains material on Morris Lodge at this time. The Lodge and some adjacent buildings were demolished in 2002. John Betjeman's poem "A Subaltern's Love Song" (1941) nimbly conveys the ambience of this highly militarized portion of southern England, still very marked in the 1950s.

Above: Lt Col E D Murray (about 1970)

One afternoon when I was visiting Morris Lodge, I watched an old lady sitting nearby as she woke from a nap. Looking out at the black cypresses that surrounded the hotel, she said, "Am I in India?" to no one in particular.

Murray had probably met some of the inhabitants of Morris Lodge when he lived nearby in Wrecclesham. In any case it is easy to imagine him in the early 1970s fitting snugly into a hospitable, curry-flavoured environment as he tried to negotiate a rough patch in his personal life. After his marriage to Valerie broke down, Moke's military pension was his sole source of income, and it lost a good deal of value in the recession that hit Great Britain in the 1970s. This meant that among other things, Moke lived the last thirty-five years of his life in a series of modest, leased accommodation. When he lived at Morris Lodge, his sister Eileen moved into a flat in the town of Farnham, taking with her what furniture she needed from the Wrecclesham cottage.

In his retirement, Murray took up several research projects, including an article about the British-Nepal Wars of 1814–16, which noted that "this was the heaviest fighting we ever experienced in India" as well as an unpublished, anecdotal memoir of his time in V Force, research on Japanese samurai swords, and a study of Gurkha regimental insignia.[16] Indeed, for the rest of his life Murray never held a paying job. He kept himself busy with occasional military research, but little of this seems to have been published. In 1959, however, he published an article in the *Army Quarterly and Defence Journal* on the 1879–80 battles of Kohima, which had been fought against, rather than alongside the Nagas. In this article, Moke drew on some research that he had begun "before the war, when I was in the Assam Rifles". In the 1970s, as we have seen, Moke assembled the typescript "Some Notes to Amuse Myself", now held in the Imperial War Museum.

At some point in the mid 1970s, if not before, Murray left Morris Lodge. He moved to the coastal town of Worthing, in Sussex. He stayed there for the remainder of his life. His sister Eileen, who left Farnham in 1974, preceded him to Worthing, and may have urged him to join her although they never pooled their resources and set up house together. Eileen died in Worthing in the 1990s.

Worthing has long been noted for its relatively mild climate and has attracted retired people for many years. With his literary turn of mind, Murray was certainly aware of Worthing's

---

[16] Among Murray's papers there are draft notes for some of these projects, but no offprints. This suggests that none of them was published.

moment of fame in Oscar Wilde's play *The Importance of Being Earnest*. In 1981, when Barnett met him, Moke was living in what Barnett had called a "nicely fitted, two room retirement flat" at 16 Wordsworth Road, a stone's throw from the seafront.[17]

A year later, Murray wrote to Barnett that he had moved to 27 Landsdowne Road, which is now (and may then have been) an attractive, modern-looking block of flats also close to the sea front. While he lived there, Moke carried on a friendly correspondence with Ursula Betts (*née* Bower), a colleague from his V Force days. In these years, encouraged by Ursula Betts, Moke seems to have toyed with the idea of writing a detailed memoir of his time in V Force and the Assam Rifles, although he admitted to Betts that he thought the word memoir "pretentious and ostentatious". He seems to have gotten no further on the project than to write "Some Notes to Amuse Myself". His letters from Betts indicate that the two of them discussed issues relating to the colonial history of Assam, the culture of the Nagas, and the war in Burma. The letters show that through the 1980s at least, Moke was actively interested in historical research.

In 1985, Moke served on the Gurkha Brigade's Honours Committee and a year later, he cooperated with Harry Seaman for Seaman's book *The Battle at Sangshak*.

Murray moved again in 1987, this time to 21 Shakespeare Court, an unprepossessing brick building presumably broken into flats. An invitation to the Gurkha Brigade dinner scheduled for November 1987 is among his papers. He may not have been well enough to attend. According to Liam Fox, Moke's neighbour in his closing years, Moke ran up substantial debts in Worthing that he was unable or unwilling to pay. I've discovered almost no

---

17 Number 16 is a charmless stucco-fronted terrace house on a street of roughly identical buildings. The building sold in December 2014 for £250,000.

published documentation from the last fifteen years of Murray's life. By late 1980s his recorded, semi-public existence seems to have come to an end.

Years before, as we have seen, Moke donated some of his papers to the Imperial War Museum in London. In 1981–82 he passed xerox copies of most of these along to Barnett, as well as a few other papers relating to Indochina that he had not given to the Museum. He probably used the papers he had bequeathed to the Museum, and especially "Some Notes to Amuse Myself", to refresh his memory before talking to Barnett.

An additional cache of Murray's papers came up for auction in 1992 at about the time he moved to Cedar Close, a semi-detached block of flats in a treeless *cul de sac* some distance from the sea, which would be his final residence. The papers were purchased by a prosperous acquaintance of Murray's named Jean-Luc Guitara, who promptly gifted them to the Gurkha Museum. The cache includes Murray's photograph albums from the Territorial Army, New Delhi, and Bakloh in the 1930s as well as several folders of miscellaneous, uncatalogued material, including seventeen amiable letters Betts wrote to him in the early 1980s.

There is a saddening edge to what we know about Moke's last years in Worthing. Talking to Liam Fox and his wife Monica about these years we sense that this convivial, decorated ex-soldier must often have been feeling restless, depleted, out of date, and lonely.

In Worthing, without knowing it, Murray joined a cohort of retired British and Indian Army officers scattered across Murray's native southern England, living often by themselves in cottages, small flats or with others of similarly limited means in residential hotels. These aging men were members of a vanishing breed, as veterans and occasionally heroes of one or both World Wars.

Many of them, like Moke, were flotsam and jetsam coming ashore from the wreckage of the British Empire.[18]

Moke's interior life in this period or any other is largely *terra incognita*. He never spoke or wrote about his life in an analytical way but some of his habits and certain aspects of his years in Worthing are possible to recreate. Until he slowed down drastically in his late eighties, Murray's activities would have likely included occasional trips to London for Gurkha-connected dinners, meetings and events, visits to a local library (there are five of these in Worthing nowadays), solving the *Telegraph* crossword, vigorous, head-clearing strolls in all weather along the sea-front (until he became crippled in the 1990s and walked with the assistance of two canes). Murray does not seem to have owned a car. The stories that he told to Barnett, including his arrest of Wingate and his aversion for drinking champagne from silver cups, were burnished occasionally while perhaps crucial details of other stories were whited out by the time he told them.

More pervasively, given the circumstances of the time Moke was likely to have had the feeling, seldom openly expressed by those in his class, that the world he had been born into, enjoyed, and served for the most part with skill and honour was drawing irrevocably to a close. The life that Murray, and so many people like him had led, and the ideology that had supported it, had passed their use-by dates, and he had become, in Mary des Chenes' evocative phrase (which she uses for the Gurkhas) yet another relic of empire.[19]

In 1994, Murray's sister Cicely, then eighty-eight years old, was living in Winchester in an elder care facility. Over the years, she visited Moke occasionally but never supported him financially.

---

18 Letter from Ursula Betts to Moke Murray, 10 July 1984.
19 Mary Des Chene, "Relics of Empire: A Cultural History of the Gurkhas, 1815–1987", PhD Dissertation (Stanford, Stanford University, 1991).

Liam Fox, who met her several times, called her a "tough old bird" whose relations with her brother were consistently cool and stormy from time to time, though she was proud of his distinguished military record. In July 1994, Cicely visited the Gurkha Museum to view her brother's papers. The correspondence about her visit, preserved at the Museum, fails to mention Murray's whereabouts at the time or the fact that he was alive.

At some point during the 1990s, his daughter Louise, who had settled in Seville, visited Moke in Worthing. Liam Fox remembers that Murray seemed awkward with her and had not found it easy to embrace his daughter. She would later only return to Worthing after her father's death and took away a silver bowl and Murray's campaign ribbons. By then, Moke had pawned off the campaign medals he had been awarded, leaving only the ribbons behind.

By the mid-1990s, in other words, the congenial, courageous and perceptive 71-year-old who lights up his private papers and his conversations with Barnett—as well as several moments of British imperial history and a crucial moment in Cambodia's recent past—disappears from the public record although he survives in the fond memories of his neighbours Liam Fox and Monica Millest. As for many people in their eighties, the musical term *diminuendo* best describes his final years.

In trying to come to terms with this period, I was drawn to a sentence in William Trevor's evocative short story "The General's Day", written in the early 1960s. The sentence seems to describe Moke at this stage of his life as well as Trevor's fictional character: "He was an elderly man with a violent past with neither wife nor means nor cellar to help him on his way".[20]

---

20   William Trevor, "The General's Day", *London Magazine*, January 1963. I am grateful to Ian Britain for drawing my attention to this story.

In January 1994, Moke's sister Eileen died in an aged-care facility in Worthing. She had never married. Moke's other sister Cicely died in November 2001, a couple of months earlier than Moke. Her profession on her death certificate was listed as "concert pianist, retired" but her career seems to have had no highlights as dramatic as those connected with her imperial tour with Dame Clara Butt and Kennerly Rumford in 1930–31.

Cicely bequeathed an estate of £1.24 million almost entirely to charity. Moke received £1,000. Cicely had amassed this fortune, it seems, largely in the 1960s through some astute purchases of real estate in Holland Park, soon to regain its status as a fashionable part of London. In the 1980s, she followed her sister Eileen (and Moke) to Worthing, where she and Eileen maintained a house together until the mid-1990s, when the sisters moved on to separate elder care facilities.

On 20 January 2002, Lieutenant Colonel Edward Dymoke Murray, DSO, OBE, once (albeit briefly) the self-styled uncrowned king of Cambodia, died at 25 Cedar Close in Worthing. Part of the building had been extended in the 1980s to form an additional apartment. Moke occupied the ground floor for the last seven years of his life. Liam Fox was present when Murray died, having acted informally as a part-time carer in Murray's final years.

Moke's death was diagnosed as due to pneumonia and heart failure, probably brought on by a combination of his advanced age and the English winter. There was a brief funeral ceremony attended by a representative sent to Worthing by the Gurkhas and Liam Fox and his wife but there is no indication of where his remains are located. His only asset seems to have been his military pension. There is no record that he left a will.

When he looked back on his career in 1981, Murray told Barnett that his life had been "bloody funny". It had taken him far from the prosperous safety of suburban Surrey and the camaraderie and public-school ethos—at first to his mother's cottage in Wrecclesham and the hospitable county of his youth. After a decade as the husband of a wealthy woman and several years in a congenial boarding house, Moke ended up alone in Worthing far from Bakloh, Nagaland, or Phnom Penh and a long way from the comforting permanence and pageantry of the Raj.

Although Moke's neighbours in Cedar Close were supportive and Moke was friendly to them in his final years, I suspect that by the 1990s, he was operating with diminished capacities. This meant among other things that the present had lost its importance for him as the past more or less systematically took over. For Murray in his eighties, as for the 76-year-old retired general in William Trevor's short story, "The past was his hunting ground, from which came his pleasure and a good deal of everything else."

APPENDIX

Murray's Promotion

WHAT FOLLOWS IS A QUASI-SERIOUS DISPATCH SENT BY Murray to General Gracey. The dispatch describes the binding but informal promotions and demotions granted by Gracey to Moke and his colleagues during their mission to Cambodia.

> Promotion cometh neither from the East, nor from the West, nor from the South. But God.
>
> —*Psalm XXV*

When I arrived in Phnom-Penh as, believe it or not, Allied Land Force Commander, I found that I had to deal directly with a French full colonel, two Japanese lieutenant-generals, a prime minister, a foreign minister, and sundry other important and influential personages of various nationalities – and a king. I very soon felt that a substantive captain, war substantive major, temporary lieutenant-colonel, acting captain, lacked a certain authority and presence. This was especially so because, as I learned later, preparations had been made, and practised, for flags to be flown and streets to be lined to welcome the Allied Force Commander of All French Indo-China. The very sudden and completely unexpected arrival of us few, by Japanese aircraft driven by a kamekazi pilot, took all by surprise, including us. So it seemed to me that steps up would be taken.

Except for the occasional Japanese road convoy there was no communication with Saigon other than by aircraft and by wireless telegraphy; both of these were Japanese because the British and Indian signals and air forces were overstretched in South East Asia from Burma to Papua. However I was able to send a strong, but prudent, recommendation to General Gracey by Japanese aircraft I received this signal:

> FROM ALFFIC TO HQALF PHNOM   161040 02267(.) RESTRICTED (.) for MURRAY (.) your DO of 12 OCT (.) agreed here that you and your staff should have rank and weight of metal appropriate to your exalted surroundings (.) such rank to be local unremunerated from our army funds (.) though you might press CAMBODIAN FINANCE MINISTER to make up balance NO announcement to be made in ALFSEA or any other orders we feel that the local ranks you suggest should be sufficient to start with (.) but suggest also that for any particularly ticklish interview public function or what not you should assume successively increasing badges of rank until you have achieved your object or browbeaten the opposition (.) the only stipulation is that you are not rpt not to promote yourself a local field marshall (,) full general is the limit (.) I am asking brig RODDY if he can supply a pair of immediate rpt immediate insignia for yourself (.) will see if ORD can fly you in an assorted plane load to carry you

Next day there appeared a brigadier, with the local title of 'Excellency', a lieutenant-colonel and a major. But, as French forces began to return to the Colony, there arrived one Major-General

Allesandri. Although he would eventually take charge on my leaving—not of Japanese affairs—he was then under my command. Here was a pretty how-de-doo. But my position was preserved by my taking advantage of that happily worded signal and my following its directions. A signal flashed to ALFFIC conveying a statement, not a request. Another promotion had taken place.

Bibliography

Ahmed, Akbar, and Harrison Akins. 'Waziristan: "The Most Dangerous Place in the World"'. Al Jazeera, 12 April 2013. https://www.aljazeera.com/opinions/2013/4/12/waziristan-the-most-dangerous-place-in-the-world.

Alan, Warren. *Burma 1942: The Road from Rangoon to Mandalay*. London: Continuum, 2011.

Aldrich, Richard J. *Intelligence and the War against Japan: Britain, America and the Politics of Secret Service*. Cambridge: Cambridge University Press, 2008.

Allen, Louis. *Burma: The Longest War 1941–45*. London: Dent, 1984.

Allport, Alan. *Browned Off and Bloody-Minded: The British Soldier Goes to War 1939–1945*. New Haven: Yale University Press, 2015.

Anonymous. 'The Story of V Force: The Phantom Army of Burma'. *Indian Army Review*, November 1946.

Banerjee, Dipankar. 'Working Class Movement in Assam Assam Oil Company Workers Strike of 1939'. PhD, Gauhati University, 2000. http://shodhganga.inflibnet.ac.in:8080/jspui/handle/10603/69783.

Barber, Noel. *The War of the Running Dogs: The Malayan Emergency: 1948–1960*. New York: Bantam, 1971.

Bartholomew-Feis, Dixee R. *The OSS and Ho Chi Minh: Unexpected Allies in the War against Japan*. Lawrence, Kansas: University Press of Kansas, 2006.

Barthorp, Michael. *The North-West Frontier: British India & Afghanistan, A Pictorial History 1839 – 1947*. Poole: Blandford, 1982.

Baruah, Ditee Moni. 'Polity and Petroleum Making of an Oil Industry in Assam, 1825–1980'. PhD, Indian Institute of Technology Guwahati, 2014. https://www.gyan.iitg.ac.in:8080/xmlui/handle/123456789/576.

Bayly, C.A, and Tim Harper. *Forgotten Wars: The End of Britain's Asian Empire.* London: Allen Lane, 2007.

Bills, Scott L. *Empire and Cold War: The Roots of US-Third World Antagonism, 1945–47.* London: Palgrave Macmillan, 1990.

Bower, Ursula Graham. *Naga path.* Murray, 1951.

Burchett, Wilfred. *Wingate Adventure.* Melbourne: Cheshire, 1944.

Burke, J. Bernard. *The Heraldic Register 1849–1850: With an Annotated Obituary.* London: Churton, 1850.

Burn, W. L. *The Age of Equipoise: A Study of the Mid-Victorian Generation.* New York: W. W. Norton, 1965.

Callahan, Raymond. 'Did Winston Matter? Churchill and the Indian Army, 1940–1945'. In *The Indian Army, 1939–47: Experience and Development*, edited by Patrick Rose and Alan Jeffreys. London: Routledge, 2017.

———. 'Were the Sepoy Generals Any Good? A Reappraisal of the British-Indian Army's Command in the Second World War'. In *War and Society in Colonial India: 1807–1945*, edited by Kaushik Roy, 305–29. New Dehli: Oxford University Press, 2010.

Cannadine, David. *Class in Britain.* New Haven: Yale University Press, 1998.

———. *Ornamentalism: How the British Saw Their Empire.* London: Oxford University Press, 2001.

Caplan, Lionel. *Warrior Gentlemen: 'Gurkhas' in the Western Imagination.* Providence: Berghahn Books, 1995.

Chandler, David, and Christopher E Goscha. *L'espace d'un regard, l'Asie de Paul Mus, 1902–1969.* Paris: Indes savantes, 2006.

Chandler, David P. *The Tragedy of Cambodian History: Politics, War, and Revolution since 1945.* Chiang Mai: Silkworm Books, 1994.

Chandler, David P., R. B. Cribb, and Li Narangoa, eds. *End of Empire: 100 Days in 1945 That Changed Asia and the World.* Asia Insights 8. Copenhagen, Denmark: Nias Press, 2016.

Cheesright, Paul. 'Queen Without a Throne: Ursula Graham Bower and the Burma Campaign'. *Asian Affairs* 45, no. 2 (2014): 289–99.

Bibliography

Clay, John. *John Masters: A Regimented Life*. London: Michael Joseph, 1992.

Clutterbuck, Richard L. *The Long, Long War: The Emergency in Malaya, 1948–1960*. London: Cassell, 1967.

Darwin, John. 'Orphans of Empire'. In *Settlers and Expatriates: Britons over the Seas*, edited by Robert A. Bickers, 329–46. Oxford: Oxford University Press, 2010.

———. *The Empire Project: The Rise and Fall of the British World-System, 1830–1970*. Cambridge: Cambridge University Press, 2009.

Decoux, J. *À La Barre de l'Indochine: Histoire de Mon Gouvernement Général 1940–1945*. Paris: Librairie Plon, 1949.

Des Chene, Mary Katherine. 'Relics of Empire: A Cultural History of the Gurkhas, 1815–1987'. PhD, Stanford University, 1991.

Devillers, Philippe. *Histoire du Vietnam de 1945 à 1952*. Paris: Éditions du Seuil, 1952.

———. *Paris Saigon Hanoi: Les Archives de La Guerre 1944–1947*. Paris: Gallimard/Julliard, 1988.

Donnison, F. S. V. *British Military Administration in the Far East, 1943–1946*. London: Her Majesty's Stationery Office, 1956.

Doulton, A.J.F. *The Fighting Cock, Being the History of the 23d Indian Division 1942–1947*. Aldershot: Gale and Polden, 1951.

Dower, John W. *War without Mercy: Race and Power in the Pacific War*. New York: Pantheon Books, 1993.

Dumas, Charles. *La Faune Sauvage Du Cambodge et Chasse*. Phnom Penh: Ed.Aymonier, 1944.

Dunn, Peter M. *The First Vietnam War*. London: C. Hurst, 1985.

Edgerton, David. *The Rise and Fall of the British Nation: A Twentieth-Century History*. Penguin UK, 2018.

———. *Warfare State: Britain, 1920–1970*. Cambridge University Press, 2005.

Edwards, Penny. *Cambodge: The Cultivation of a Nation, 1860–1945*. Honolulu: University of Hawaii Press, 2007.

Elkins, Caroline. *Legacy of Violence: A History of the British Empire*. New York: Random House, 2022.

Fergusson, Bernard. *Beyond the Chindwin*. London: Collins, 1955.

Fort, Adrian. *Archibald Wavell: The Life and Times of an Imperial Servant*. London: Jonathan Cape, 2009.

Fraser, George MacDonald. *Quartered Safe out There: A Recollection of the War in Burma*. London: HarperCollins, 1993.

Frayn, Michael. 'Festival'. In *Age of Austerity 1945–1951*, edited by Michael Sissons and Phillip French, First Edition., 330–52. London: Penguin, 1964.

Fussell, Paul. *The Great War and Modern Memory*. New York: Oxford University Press, 1975.

Gaudel, Andre. *L'Indochine Francaise En Face Du Japon*. Paris: J. Susse, 1947.

Gilmour, David. *The British in India: Three Centuries of Ambition and Experience*. London: Allen Lane, 2018.

Glaize, Maurice. *Les Monuments Du Groupe d'Angkor*. Saigon: Albert Portrail, 1948.

Gogoi, Bijoy. 'Organized Labour Movement in Assam: A Historical Study between the Period of Two World Wars'. *International Journal of Humanities & Social Science Studies*, May 2017, 450–58.

Goscha, Christopher. 'This Is the End? The French Settler Community in Saigon and the Fall of Indo China in 1945'. [unpublished], n.d.

Goscha, Christopher E. *The Penguin History of Modern Vietnam*. London: Penguin, 2017.

Gould, Tony. *Imperial Warriors: Britain and the Gurkhas*. London: Granta, 2000.

Graves, Robert. *Goodbye to All That*. London: Jonathan Cape, 1929.

Green, Henry. *Pack My Bag: A Self-Portrait*. London: THe Hogarth Press, 1939.

Gregorian, Raffi. *The British Army, the Gurkhas, and Cold War Strategy in the Far East, 1947–1954*. New York: Palgrave, 2002.

Grob-Fitzgibbon, Benjamin. *Imperial Endgame: Britain's Dirty Wars and the End of Empire*. New York: Palgrave Macmillan, 2011.

Bibliography

Gunn, Geoffrey. 'The Heraud (Saigon) Massacre October 24–25 1945'. In *End of Empire: 100 Days in 1945 That Changed Asia and the World*, edited by David P. Chandler, R. B. Cribb, and Li Narangoa. Asia Insights 8. Copenhagen, Denmark: Nias Press, 2016.

Gunn, Geoffrey C. *Monarchical Manipulation in Cambodia: France, Japan, and the Sihanouk Crusade for Independence*. Nordic Institute of Asian Studies Monograph Series, no. 141. Copenhagen, Denmark: NIAS Press, 2018.

———. *Rice Wars in Colonial Vietnam: The Great Famine and the Viet Minh Road to Power*. Lanham: Rowman & Littlefield, 2014.

Halley, David. *With Wingate in Burma*. W. Hodge & Co.: Glasgow, 1945.

Hammer, Ellen J. *The Struggle for Indochina, 1940–1955*. Stanford, Calif: Stanford University Press, 1966.

Hertrich, Jean-Michel. *Doc-Lap !: l'indépendance ou la mort*. Paris: Jean Vigneau, 1946.

Horne, Alistair. *Hubris: The Tragedy of War in the Twentieth Century*. London: Weidenfeld & Nicolson, 2016.

Huard, Paul (Général C.R.). 'La Rentrée Politique de La France Au Cambodge (Octobre 1945 – Janvier 1946)'. In *Les Chemins de La Décolonisation de l'empire Colonial Français, 1936–1956: Colloque Organisé Par l'IHTP Les 4 et 5 Octobre 1984*, edited by Charles-Robert Ageron, 215–30. Paris: CNRS Éditions, 2013. http://books.openedition.org/editionscnrs/480.

Hughes, Geraint. 'A "Post-War" War: The British Occupation of French-Indochina, September 1945–March 1946'. *Small Wars & Insurgencies* 17, no. 3 (2006): 263–86.

Ignatieff, Michael. *Isaiah Berlin: A Life*. New York: Metropolitan Books, 1998.

Isaacs, Harold R. *No Peace for Asia*. New York: Macmillan Co., 1947.

Isoart, Paul. *L'Indochine Francaise, 1940–1945*. Paris: Presses universitaires de France, 1982.

Jackson, Robert. *The Malayan Emergency: The Commonwealth Wars 1948–1966*. London: Routledge, 1991.

Jagel, Matthew. 'Son Ngoc Thanh, the United States, and the Transformation of Cambodia'. PhD Dissertation, Northern Illinois University, 2015.

James, H. D, and D. Sheil-Small. *The Gurkhas.* London: Macdonald, 1965.

James, Henry. *English Hours.* London: W. Heinemann, 1905.

Jennings, Eric T. *Vichy in the Tropics: Pétain's National Revolution in Madagascar, Guadeloupe, and Indochina, 1940–1944.* Stanford, California: Stanford University Press, 2001.

Keane, Fergal. *Road of Bones: The Epic Siege of Kohima.* London: HarperPress, 2010.

Keo, Bernard Z. 'A Small, Distant War? Historiographical Reflections on the Malayan Emergency'. *History Compass* 17, no. 3 (2019): 1–12.

Khim Tit. *Un Épisode de l'histoire Contemporaine Du Cambodge. Réalités Cambodgiennes,* 1967.

Kiernan, Ben. *How Pol Pot Came to Power: A History of Communism in Kampuchea, 1930–1975.* London: Verso, 1985.

Kirby, S Woodburn. *The War Against Japan.* Vol. 5. London: Her Majesty's Stationery Office, 1969.

Krull, Germaine. 'Diary of Saigon, Following the Allied Occupation in September 1945', [c1945]. Box Folder 7. Douglas Pike Collection and Vietnamese Archive, Texas Technical University.

Kynaston, David. *Family Britain, 1951–1957.* Bloomsbury Publishing, 2010.

Larcher-Goscha, Agathe. 'Ambushed by History: Paul Mus and Colonial France's Forced Re-Entry into Vietnam (1945—1954)'. *Journal of Vietnamese Studies* 4, no. 1 (2009): 206–39. https://doi.org/10.1525/vs.2009.4.1.206.

Lau, Albert. *The Malayan Union Controversy, 1942–1948.* New York: Oxford University Press, 1991.

Lawrence, Mark Andrew. 'Forging the Combination: Britain and the Indo-China Problem, 1945–1950'. In *The First Vietnam War: Colonial Conflict and Cold War Crisis,* edited by Mark Atwood Lawrence and Fredrik Logevall, 105–29. Cambridge, Ma: Harvard, 2007.

Le Bourgeois, Jacques. *Saigon sans La France: Des Japonais Au Viet-Minh (Souvenirs).* Paris: Plon, 1949.

Bibliography

Legrand, J. *L'Indochine a l'heure Japonaise: La Verite Sur Le Coup de Force, La Resistance En Nouvelle-Caledonie*. Cannes: Imprimerie AEgitna, 1963.

Logevall, Fredrik. *Embers of War: The Fall of an Empire and the Making of America's Vietnam*. New York: Random House, 2012.

Lunt, James. *A Hell of a Licking: The Retreat from Burma 1941–2*. London: Collins, 1986.

Lyman, Robert. *A War of Empires: Japan, India, Burma and Britain*. London: Bloomsbury, 2021.

———. *Japan's Last Bid for Victory: The Invasion of India, 1944*. Barnsley, South Yorkshire: Praetorian Press, 2011.

Macdonell, Ranald, and Marcus Macaulay. *A History of the 4th Prince of Wales's Own Gurkha Rifles, 1857–1937*. Vol. 1. Edinburgh: W. Blackwood, 1940.

Mackay, James Nobel. *A History of the 4th Prince of Wales's Own Gurkha Rifles 1938–1948*. Vol. 2. Edinburgh: Blackwood, 1952.

MacMillan, Margaret. *Women of the Raj: The Mothers, Wives, and Daughters of the British Empire in India*. Random House, 2007.

Marston, Daniel. 'The 20th Indian Division in French Indo-China, 1945–46'. In *The Indian Army, 1939–47: Experience and Development*, edited by Patrick Rose and Alan Jeffreys. London: Routledge, 2017.

———. *The Indian Army and the End of the Raj*. Cambridge: Cambridge University Press, 2014.

Mason, Philip. *The English Gentleman: The Rise and Fall of an Ideal*. London: André Deutsch, 1982.

Masterman, Charles F.G. *England after War: A Study*. London: Hodder & Stoughton, 1922.

Masters, John. *Bugles and a Tiger*. New York: The Viking Press, 1956.

McHale, Shawn F. *The First Vietnam War: Violence, Sovereignty, and the Fracture of the South, 1945–1956*. New York: Cambridge University Press, 2021.

McLynn, F. J. *Burma Campaign: Disaster into Triumph, 1942–45*. New Haven: Yale University Press, 2014.

Milne, J. Hogarth. *Great Britain in the Coronation Year*. London: W.H. Allen and Company, 1914.

Mol, Bounchan. *Kuk Niyobay*. Phnom Penh: Apsara Press, 1971.

Monypenny, William Flavelle, and George Earle Buckle. *The Life of Benjamin Disraeli, Earl of Beaconsfield Volume 5*. London: Arkose Press, 2015.

Moreman, T. R. "Small Wars' and "Imperial Policing": The British Army and the Theory and Practice of Colonial Warfare in the British Empire, 1919–1939'. *Journal of Strategic Studies* 19, no. 4 (1996): 105–31. https://doi.org/10.1080/01402399608437654.

Moreman, T. R. *The Army in India and the Development of Frontier Warfare, 1849–1947*. Basingstoke: Palgrave, 2001.

Moreman, T. R. *The Jungle, the Japanese and the British Commonwealth Armies at War, 1941–45: Fighting Methods, Doctrine and Training for Jungle Warfare*. London: Frank Cass, 2005.

Mortyris, Nina. 'When Rudyard Kipling's Son Went Missing'. *New Yorker*, 26 September 2015.

Mountbatten, Louis M, and Philip Ziegler. *Personal Diary of Admiral the Lord Louis Mountbatten, Supreme Allied Commander, South-East Asia, 1943–1946*. London: Collins, 1988.

Mullaly, Brian Reginald. *Bugle and Kukri: The Story of the 10th Princess Mary's Own Gurkha Rifles*. Edinburgh: W. Blackwood, 1957.

Murray, E. D., ed. *Brigade of Gurkhas at the Coronation of Her Majesty Queen of Elizabeth II*. London: Gale & Polden, 1954.

Mus, Paul. *Le Destin de l'Union Francaise de l'Indochine a l'Afrique*. Paris: Editions du Seuil, 1954.

Nairn, Tom. *The Enchanted Glass: Britain and Its Monarchy*. London: Verso Books, 2011.

Neville, Peter. *Britain in Vietnam: Prelude to Disaster, 1945–6*. Military History and Policy 27. London: Routledge, 2007.

Ngo, Van. *Revolutionaries They Could Not Break: The Fight for the Fourth International in Indochina 1930–1945*. London: Index Books, 1995.

Bibliography

Omissi, David. *The Sepoy and the Raj: The Indian Army, 1860–1940.* London: Palgrave Macmillan, 1994.

Orwell, George. *Coming up for Air.* London: Victor Gollancz, 1939.

———. 'Such, Such Were the Joys'. In *A Collection of Essays.* London: Harcourt, 1946.

———. 'The Spike'. In *Collected Essays,* 7–14. London: Penguin, 2000.

Otley, C.B. 'Militarism and Militarization in the Public Schools, 1900–1972'. *British Journal of Sociology* 29, no. 3 (1978): 321–39.

———. 'The Social Origins of British Army Officers'. *Sociological Review* 18, no. July (1970): 213–39.

Panter-Downs, Mollie. 'The Coronation of Queen Elizabeth II'. *New Yorker,* 13 June 1953.

Patti, Archimedes L. A. *Why Viet Nam? Prelude to America's Albatross.* Berkeley: University of California Press, 1980.

Pevsner, Nikolaus. *The Buildings of England: Surrey.* Harmondsworth, Middlesex: Penguin Books, 1962.

Pickford, Nigel. *Lost Treasure Ships of the Twentieth Century.* London: Pavillion, 1999.

Pilleul, Gilbert and Institut Charles de Gaulle, eds. *Le General de Gaulle et l'Indochine, 1940–1946: Colloque.* Paris: Plon, 1982.

Porter, Bernard. *The Lion's Share: A Short History of British Imperialism 1850–1970. Bernard Porter.* London, 1975.

Powell, Anthony. *The Kindly Ones.* London: Heinemann, 1962.

———. *Under Review: Further Writings in Writers 1946–1989.* London: Heimann, 1991.

Prasad, Bisheshwar. *Official History of the Indian Armed Forces in the Second World War: Reconquest of Burma.* Vol. II. Calcutta: Combined Inter-Services Historical Section (India & Pakistan), 1959.

Richards, Jeffrey. *Imperialism and Music: Britain, 1876–1953.* Manchester: Manchester University Press, 2001.

Roberts, Andrew. *Churchill: Walking with Destiny*. London: Penguin Books, 2018.

Roff, William R. *The origins of Malay nationalism*. New Haven: Yale University Press, 1967.

Rutherford, Jonathan. *Forever England: Reflections on Race, Masculinity and Empire*. London: Lawrence & Wishart, 1997.

Rutherford, Mike. *The Living Years: The First Genesis Memoir*. London: Thomas Dunne Books, 2015.

Sacks, Milton. 'Marxism in Vietnam'. In *Marxism in Southeast Asia: A Study of 4 Countries*, edited by Frank N Trager, 109–34. Stanford: Stanford University Press, 1965.

Sasge, Gerard. 'Review of Vietnam: A New History, by Christopher Goscha'. *H-France* 17, no. 19 (October 2017). https://www.h-france.net/vol17reviews/vol17no194sasges.pdf.

Saville, John. *The Politics of Continuity: British Foreign Policy and the Labour Government, 1945–46*. New York: Verso, 1993.

Seaman, Harry. *The Battle at Sangshak, Prelude to Kohima*. London: Leo Cooper, 1987.

Seldon, Anthony. 'The Real Eton Rifles: The Heroism of Public School Boys in the First World War'. *New Statesman*, 18 December 2013. https://www.newstatesman.com/uncategorized/2013/12/real-eton-rifles.

Seldon, Anthony, and David Walsh. *Public Schools and the Great War: The Generation Lost*. Barnsley, South Yorkshire: Pen & Sword Military, 2013.

Shils, Edward, and Michael Young. 'The Meaning of the Coronation'. *The Sociological Review* 1, no. 2 (1953): 63–81.

Short, Anthony. *The Communist Insurrection in Malaya, 1948–1960*. London: Frederick Muller Limited, 1975.

Sichel, Kim. *Germaine Krull: Photographer of Modernity*. Cambridge, Mass.: MIT Press, 1999.

Sihanouk, Norodom. *Action Royale Pour l'independantce Du Cambodge 1941–1955*. Phnom Penh: Penn Nouth, Doyen du haut Conseil du Roi, 1959.

———. *Souvenirs Doux et Amers*. Paris: Hachette, 1981.

Bibliography

Sihanouk, Norodom, and Jean Lacouture. *L'Indochine Vue de Pekin*. Paris: Editions du Seuil, 1972.

Slim, William. *Unofficial History*. London: Cassell, 1959.

Slim, William Joseph. *Defeat into Victory*. London: Cassell & Company, 1956.

Smeeton, Miles. *A Change of Jungles*. London: Hart-Davis, 1962.

Smith, E. D. *Britain's Brigade of Gurkhas*. Havertown: Pen & Sword, 1983.

———. *Valour: The History of the Gurkhas*. Stroud: The History Press, 2016.

Smith, T. O. 'A British Interlude: Allied Peace Enforcement, 1945–1947'. In *Cambodia and the West, 1500–2000*, 67–114. London: Palgrave Macmillan, 2018.

———. *Vietnam and the Unravelling of Empire: General Gracey in Asia, 1942–1951*. Houndmills, Basingstoke, Hampshire: Palgrave Macmillan, 2014.

Spector, Ronald H. *Advice and Support: The Early Years of the United States Army in Vietnam, 1941–1960*. New York : London: Free Press ; Collier Macmillan, 1985.

Springhall, John. '"Kicking out the Vietminh": How Britain Allowed France to Reoccupy South Indochina, 1945–46'. *Journal of Contemporary History* 40, no. 1 (2005): 115–30. https://doi.org/10.1177/0022009405049269.

Streets, Heather. *Martial Races: The Military, Race, and Masculinity in British Imperial Culture*. Manchester: Manchester University Press, 2004.

Strong, Roy. *Coronation: A History of the British Monarchy*. London: HarperCollins, 2005.

Tamayama, Kazuo, and John Nunneley. *Tales by Japanese Soldiers of the Burma Campaign 1942–1945*. London: Cassell, 2000.

Taylor, Philip. *The Khmer Lands of Vietnam: Environment, Cosmology, and Sovereignty*. Singapore: Asian Studies Association of Australia in association with NUS Press and NIAS Press, 2014.

Thompson, Julian. *Forgotten Voices of Burma: The Second World War's forgotten conflict*. London: Ebury Press, 2009.

Tinker, Hugh. 'A Forgotten Long March: The Indian Exodus from Burma, 1942'. *Journal of Southeast Asian Studies* 6, no. 1 (1975): 1–15.

Tønnesson, Stein. *Vietnam 1946: How the War Began.* Berkeley: University of California Press, 2010.

Tosh, John. *A Man's Place: Masculinity and the Middle-Class Home in Victorian England.* New Haven: Yale University Press, 1999.

Tramoni, Paul. *Camille ...* Blainville-sur-Mer: L'Amiti?? par le livre, 1966.

Travers, R.J. 'The Battle of Sangshak'. *The Kukri: The Journal of the Brigade of Gurkhas*, 2001.

Tuchman, Barbara W. *The March of Folly: From Troy to Vietnam.* 1st ed. London: Michael Joseph, 1984.

Tully, John. *France on the Mekong: A History of the Protectorate in Cambodia, 1863–1953.* Lanham: University Press of America, 2002.

Van Emden, Richard. *The Soldier's War: The Great War through Veterans' Eyes.* London: Bloomsbury Publishing, 2010.

Verney, Sébastien. *L'Indochine Sous Vichy: Entre Révolution Nationale, Collaboration et Identités Nationales, 1940–1945.* Paris: Riveneuve éditions, 2012.

Vickery, Michael. *Kampuchea: Politics, Economics, and Society.* London: Pinter, 1986.

Wagner, Kim A. *Amritsar 1919 an Empire of Fear & the Making of a Massacre.* New Haven: Yale University Press, 2019.

Ward, Yvonne M. '"Gosh! Man I've Got a Tune in My Head": Edward Elgar, A.C. Benson and the Creation of "Land of Hope and Glory"'. *The Court Historian* 7, no. 1 (2002): 17–39.

Wheen, Francis. *Television: A History.* London: Century, 1985.

Williams, Olivia. *Gin Glorious Gin: How Mother's Ruin Became the Spirit of London.* London: Headline Publishing, 2014.

Winter, J. M. *Remembering War: The Great War Between Memory and History in the Twentieth Century.* New Haven: Yale University Press, 2006.

Womersley, Julian. *The Surrey Union Hunt: Our History Unbuttoned.* Crawley: The Surrey Union Hunt, 2007.

Bibliography

Woolf, Leonard. *Sowing: An Autobiography of the Years 1880–1904*. London: Hogarth, 1960.

Yao, Souchou. *The Malayan Emergency: Essays on a Small, Distant War*. Copenhagen: NIAS Press, 2016.

Acknowledgments

This book began to be written in October 1981 when my friend Anthony Barnett conducted a two-hour interview with Lieutenant-Colonel E. D. Murray in the English seaside town of Worthing where Murray had been living for several years. When Anthony showed me the transcript in 1982, it piqued my interest but neither of us did much about it for a long time. In 2015 I got in touch with Anthony and asked if I could use the interview in a book of excerpts about World War II that was being assembled at the Nordic Institute of Asian Studies (NIAS) in Copenhagen. Anthony happily granted me permission to use passages from the interview. much of the interview appears verbatim between Chapters 7 and 10 of this biography. Soon afterwards, aided by helpful research from my friend Justin Corfield, I penetrated the internet and found lots of material relating to Murray's early life and his career. Justin provided a good deal of help as the project continued and made some last-minute suggestions that proved invaluable. I embarked on a biography in 2016 and completed it five years later. During this period, I was aided generously by Andrew Hassam, a free-lance scholar in the UK who uncovered masses of material about

Murray and even managed to locate Murray's son, Colin, who had been living on the south coast of England. Later, he located the couple who had been Moke's landlords in Worthing during the final years of his life. Anthony and I interviewed Colin in 2018 and his Worthing landlords in the following year. These helpful men and women provided much invaluable information.

From 2016 to 2019 I visited the UK on an annual basis and completed research at the National Archives, the Imperial War Museum, the National Army Museum, and the Liddell-Hart Centre in the University of London. More rewardingly, I spent three days working in the Gurkha Museum in Winchester which contained invaluable primary materials relating to Murray, the military units he served in, and his career. I'm very grateful to the director of the museum Gavan Edgerley Harris, his assistant Christine Bernath, collections officer Doug Henderson, and archivist Roy MacEwen for their support.

In 2018, when I visited Cambodia, I spent two days in the Cambodian National Archives in Phnom Penh and was able to retrieve several hundred pages of documentation relating to Cambodia in 1945. As my research progressed, I enjoyed several visits with Anthony and his partner, the historian Judith Herrin in their house in Oxford. Our discussions and their support were invaluable to my work. In 2019, Anthony agreed to write two chapters for the book. One was to discuss his interaction with Murray in 1981, and this chapter now serves as an introduction to this book. He also volunteered to write a chapter on the Coronation of Queen Elizabeth II in 1953, Chjapter 10 [chk. On this occasion, Murray led a contingent of Gurkhas in the parade and received a Coronation Medal from the Queen herself.

About 1945, the period when Murray was there to accept the Japanese surrender, I am grateful to the staff of the archives for their support and enthusiasm about the project.

Acknowledgments

During the years that I spent writing the book, I was buoyed up by comments from my colleagues in the Melbourne Life Writers Group and also by detailed comments from fellow historians including Joan Beaumont, Ian Britain, Graeme Davison and Sally Low. When the manuscript was completed, the historian Christopher Goscha provided many penetrating and constructive suggestions in relation to the Indochina chapters.

On the last few months I spent working on the project, I was greatly assisted by Dr Bernard Z. Keo, an historian of Southeast Asia, who helped me to shepherd the manuscript to publication as well as contributing to the pages dealing with the Malayan Emergency. For a short time, Dr Jodie Boyd also assisted with preparing the manuscript. Jodie's time was generously funded with support from the Australian National University's Strategic and Defence Studies Centre.

The text was ably copy-edited by Richard McGregor. And my publisher John Kerr and book designer Paul Taylder have been very supportive of the project.

In 2018 Anthony and I spent an invaluable afternoon and evening with Moke's son Colin and his wife Bernice. Sadly, Bernice died two years later. The book is dedicated to Colin, Bernice, and their children.

David Chandler
Melbourne, September 2023

DAVID CHANDLER IS EMERITUS PROFESSOR OF HISTORY AT Monash University. He has published five books about Cambodia, and a family memoir.

ANTHONY BARNETT IS A CO-FOUNDER OF THE LONDON-BASED openDemocracy and the author of six books on contemporary politics.